Everyday Politics

Everyday Politics

Reconnecting Citizens and Public Life

Harry C. Boyte

PENN

University of Pennsylvania Press
Philadelphia

10   9   8   7   6   5   4   3   2   1

Published by
University of Pennsylvania Press
Philadelphia, Pennsylvania 19104-4011

Library of Congress Cataloging-in-Publication Data

Boyte, Harry Chatten, 1945–
    Everyday politics : reconnecting citizens and public life / Harry C. Boyte.
       p.   cm.
    ISBN: 0-8122-3814-1 (cloth : alk. paper)
    Includes bibliographical references and index.
    1. Political participation—United States.   2. Political culture—United States.   3. Power
(Social sciences)—United States.   I. Title.
JK1764.B697   2004
306.2′0973—dc22   2004041297

To Elizabeth Tornquist, Dorothy Cotton, and Deborah Meier—three fine mentors, who taught me lasting lessons about politics

Contents

Preface: Developing a Theory and Practice of Everyday Politics

Everyday Politics began as a series of action research projects on civic engagement in higher education supported over several years by the Kettering Foundation. In 2002, the Center for Information and Research on Civic Learning and Engagement (CIRCLE) awarded a grant for this research as well, especially for study of the public engagement efforts at the University of Minnesota. As the research unfolded, it became clear that a broader study of democratic politics was important in order to situate higher education's civic engagement efforts in a larger context. Thus, *Everyday Politics* was conceived, drawing on work over the last sixteen years at the Humphrey Institute.

In 1987, at the urging of Harlan Cleveland, then dean of the new Humphrey Institute of Public Affairs at the University of Minnesota, I began a project aimed at finding workable remedies for democracy's troubles. The challenge was daunting, but resources for such an effort on democracy had been accumulating in the civic experiments of recent decades at the grassroots of society, resources which I believed had many lessons for theory about democracy and politics. This effort became the Center for Democracy and Citizenship (CDC).

The most effective civic efforts, especially broad-based citizen organizations in networks such as the Industrial Areas Foundation, the Gamaliel Foundation, and the Pacific Institute for Community Organization, had accumulated evidence in support of Thomas Jefferson's profession of faith in the people as the repository of the powers of the society. Though Americans' penchant for self-directed action to solve public problems in general seemed to be in decline, powerful countertrends had also developed. Citizens in communities across the country were successfully taking up tough problems, from crime to economic development or environmental restoration. It was clear from their experiences that an increasing number of challenges that cannot be solved by government action alone (even though government remains an essential resource) require skilled, savvy citizen action if there is to be resolution.

The emphasis Jefferson placed on education—especially civic education—was also vindicated by the most successful low income, working class, and middle class citizen groups. Organizations like those in the broad-based citizen organizing networks had come to include a wide range of political and religious viewpoints, racial and cultural groups, and income levels. One of the keys to their success was an intense emphasis on development of the political skills of leaders in dealing with difference, a process detailed in Chapter 3.

These organizations did not shy away from conflict. They had also become sophisticated in forming what they call "public relationships" with people in power. This aimed at building their own citizen power, but it also depended on highly developed capacities to understand the interests, backgrounds, and perspectives of establishment leaders whom many once saw simply as adversaries or targets for demands. Citizen organizations also stressed moving from "protest to governance," adding an emphasis on citizen responsibility to citizen empowerment. A story from the IAF affiliate BUILD in Baltimore helps illustrate. When BUILD leaders met for the first time with Paul Sarbanes, distinguished senior senator from Maryland, he welcomed them, took out his notepad, and asked, "What can I do for you?" "Nothing," was the answer. "We will be around for a long time, and you are likely to be as well. We want to develop a relationship. We need to understand your interests, why you went into politics, and what you are trying to achieve."[1]

On local and sometimes state levels, broadly based citizen groups like these have accumulated remarkable successes. For instance, the BUILD group pioneered living wage legislation for city workers, an initiative that has since spread across the country. The COPS group in San Antonio, pioneering many of the approaches later taken up by other organizations across the country, has won hundreds of millions of dollars in infrastructure improvement in the barrios of the West and South Side of the city. It has shifted development patterns, changed the make up of the city government, and led in the creation of a statewide network that has won significant victories on issues such as school funding and health care.

Such successes, I became convinced, depend not only on development of individuals' public skills but also on a fundamental change in the cultures of the religious congregations that are the main base of these citizen groups. Civic renewal especially involves a shift in the work of clergy. In broad-based citizen organizations, clergy change their practice from simply a pastoral role toward work with their congregations that is far more energizing and politically educating and empowering, a process described in Chapter 7. This work, using music, liturgy, biblical interpretations, homilies, and other means, involves congregations as a whole, not simply activists, in civic action. They demonstrate the importance of seeing civic engagement and the empowerment of citizens as a function of institutional cultures, not simply of individual proclivities.

Thus, from the outset, our approach differed from the studies that diagnose the "crisis of democracy" in terms of voting levels and participation rates. A focus on institutional cultures draws attention to other questions: "Why are people turned off?" and crucially, "What works to develop cultures that sustain powerful citizen action?"

Breaking the Tyranny of Technique

Finally, broad citizen organizations' successes seemed to me to depend crucially on a bold conceptual act: they *deprofessionalize* politics. This conceptual change goes against the grain of twentieth-century developments that have seen more and more authority and decision making vested in experts, who in turn view themselves as a class apart from a common civic life, what the labor economist Robert Reich describes as the secession of knowledge workers from the society. Conventional experts imagine their specialized knowledge to be the superior (or even singular and sufficient) resource in solving problems. The professionalizing impulse, justified by the ideology of meritocracy described in Chapters 1 and 2, is also accompanied by the domination of technical languages in professional systems, from law to education, dental hygiene to human relations. Studies, reports, techniques, procedures, methods, flow charts, and information updates—what can be summarized as a technical approach holding ends constant and focusing on efficiency of means or the "one best way"—are the idiom of such systems, the stuff of conferences, the material of continuing education.[2] "Politics," in an older meaning of the word, is absent.

In fact, formal politics itself reflects the same technical dynamic. Politics, from the Greek, *politikos*, meaning of the citizen, in its original meanings is the activity of amateurs, not specialists. As Aristotle argued in the *Politics*, politics involves the negotiations of a pluralist world, people of different views, interests, and backgrounds interacting in order to accomplish some task. Politics is the opposite of relations based on similarity; Aristotle used the examples of military alliance and families to make the contrast.[3] But in the expert dominated environments of our age, both in highly technological, wealthy nations such as the United States and also in new democracies of the developing world such as South Africa, politics has become largely controlled by specialists. Pollsters, think tank advisors, consultants, media and public relations specialists, and other experts dominate. Volunteers are active, sometimes in large numbers, but in tightly circumscribed roles, not expected to think or act independently. Expert domination of politics also prevails in citizen participation itself. For instance, advocacy and issue groups use a language of politics and citizen involvement. But the way such groups define the problem is largely predetermined by professional staff and participation activities are often highly scripted. Citizens are reduced to passive roles, manipulated by emotional appeals, and mobilized against some enemy.

In sharp contrast, broad-based groups like those in the IAF explicitly reclaim politics as the activity of ordinary citizens. Other organizations that the CDC has worked with also engage in a process of reconceptualizing public practices that puts citizens back at the center of the action. For instance, Project for Public Spaces (PPS), a remarkable resource based in New York, has worked with more than a thousand communities across the world on the revitalization of places, on projects ranging from local markets to high profile efforts like Rockefeller Plaza in New York. As part of its approach PPS trains professionals in a number of fields related to the built environment, such as traffic engineering and city planning. Yet the premise of their work is that citizens always need to guide the process of creating vital spaces. "When the issue is place, people are the experts," is the first of their principles, which include a variety of other commonsensical rules of thumb, such as start small ("begin with the flowers") and "money is no object."[4]

A distinctive feature of the broad citizen groups is to conceptualize the process of deprofessionalization in explicitly conceptual and political ways, drawing on theorists such as Bernard Crick and Hannah Arendt. This has far ranging effects. Thus, for example, leaders in such organizations, usually uncredentialed in conventional academic terms, become proficient in discussing the conceptual frameworks that guide their efforts. It is a striking experience to hear a group of low income African Americans in inner city Baltimore or Spanish-speaking parish members with no college education in the barrios of San Antonio analyze the meaning of self-interest in *The*

Federalist Papers or John Paul II's theory of human labor with sophistication and confidence.

Moreover, the issues such groups address and the ways issues are defined and developed are the product of extensive discussion and debate within their ranks. Citizen organizations do not deny the value of specialized knowledge or the importance of professionalism, rightly understood. Indeed, organizers themselves play key roles as professionals and their work is highly valued. Attention to the idea that organizing is a profession, needing adequate benefits, vacations, and time for recuperation and continuing learning and study, has become one of the defining features of the new broadly based organizing. The IAF gives organizers sabbaticals, for instance. But the meaning of professional is recast in ways analogous to the redefinition of the role of clergy: organizers are coaches and political educators while citizen leaders take center stage. Citizen ownership of the activity of politics is constantly stressed, and politics is based upon a deep and unromantic respect for the capacities of ordinary people. What is called the "iron rule" of such organizing, "never do for others what they can do for themselves," is constantly reiterated to contrast it with a service approach. Meanwhile, politicians are respected when they produce results and are accountable, but are not allowed to dominate meetings or to single-handedly define issues. Interestingly, as recent scholars such as Richard Wood, Carmen Sirianni, Lewis Friedland, and others have demonstrated, this process makes for better political leadership, as well as powerful citizen organizations. The pattern reframes the debate between "participatory" and "representative" democracy by highlighting the importance of the dynamic interaction between politicians and citizens.[5]

It struck me that the nonprofessional politics of citizen groups has large potential to break the tyranny of technique, not only in formal institutions of political life such as political parties and advocacy groups but also across the entire fabric of modern society. In Chapter 10, I argue that nonprofessional, everyday politics points toward the distinctive freedom of the twenty-first century that comes through democratizing the hierarchical structures of knowledge power in a technocratic age. Chapter 7 details several examples of democratizing professional practice in different fields.

To explore what a citizen-centered politics might look like outside of the organizations that I had studied, we developed the concept of citizen politics at the outset of our work at the Humphrey Institute.[6] We defined citizen politics as "ordinary people of different views and interests working together to define and to solve problems," and further articulated the framework with a set of other concepts constitutive of politics—power, self-interests, and public life, connected to but distinct from private life. We also began to use and further develop methods such as one on one interviews and training workshops, drawn from IAF organizing, and what we soon called "interest maps" and "power maps." These methods proved applicable in widely diverse settings. They are effective ways for people to learn and practice a citizen-centered politics. A group of institutional partners soon emerged who were interested in using this conceptual framework as a way to experiment with the revitalization of their own civic cultures.

Through our initiatives at the CDC we have focused on developing practice-based concepts and civic learning methods that are effective in engaging citizens in public life. In partnership with others we work to invigorate the civic cultures of what we call "mediating institutions," connecting people's daily lives to arenas of policy. Multiple action research projects have grown out of these initiatives.

Informed by the evident power of explicit attention to ideas in the most effective citizen organizing, we combined action research—seeking to understand in conceptual terms those processes in which we are also engaged—with social and political theory that included an emphasis on the nature, formation, and uses of political ideas.[7] We have also sponsored a variety of qualitative and quantitative evaluations.[8]

One result of our approach is that *Everyday Politics* has many different voices and modes of presentation. These include analysis of contemporary theory, historical treatments of ideas like politics and commonwealth, story telling, and interviews.

The work of the Center for Democracy and Citizenship has involved a constant testing of ideas in practice, especially in partnerships, building on the original framework of citizen politics. It has been based on the assumption that the interests, as well as the talents and insights, of people of all backgrounds and views—from young people to seniors, from Republicans to Greens, from Evangelical Christians to Unitarians—are important in public life.

We also integrated an ongoing process of collective self-evaluation into our work. In the early years these included semi-annual meetings of our partners—a freewheeling mix including teams from K-12 schools, Minnesota Extension Service, the College of St. Catherine, the Association for Retarded Citizens low income parents group, Central Medical Center, an African American hospital in St. Louis, Augustana Nursing Home, and the Metropolitan Council.

The conceptual work was also enriched by Washington seminars, beginning in 1991, on the theme of improving politics, which included leading civic practitioners, journalists, leaders in higher education, and policy and political innovators. We used the theme that government is best seen as a civic resource of citizens, neither "the problem" nor "the solution" to a growing number of problems that can't be solved without government but that government alone cannot solve. Bill Clinton had picked up this idea and used it from our Washington seminars during the 1992 campaign. After his election, building on the idea of citizen-government partnerships, we organized the nonpartisan New Citizenship, a confederation of civic groups, universities, and foundations. We worked with the White House to analyze the gap between citizens and government and to develop strategies to overcome it. The Walt Whitman Center at Rutgers, the Progressive Policy Institute, the Advocacy Institute, and the Kettering Foundation were key partners.

Since the mid-1990s, we have worked with and learned from St. Paul's West Side new immigrant communities in the Jane Addams School for Democracy, an interactive, intergenerational teaching and learning environment. The Jane Addams School draws on the learning and civic resources of diverse cultural traditions. Discussions and actions are influenced by concepts of public work. At the same time, we have worked throughout Minnesota, in other states beginning with Missouri, and in other countries, beginning with Northern Ireland and Turkey, on Public Achievement. Public Achievement is an expanding partnership that teaches young people politics and citizenship through real public work projects on issues of their choosing. It has proven a vital laboratory for the theory and practice of everyday nonprofessional politics, constantly demonstrating the latent political interests of young people in the United States and in other societies. We also have benefited from a three-year partnership with Minnesota Community Education that explored the role of community education in organizing and activating citizens; from the Families and Democracy partnerships organized by the Family Social Sciences Department at the University of Minnesota whose civic work is described in Chapter 7; and from our work in the higher education movement for more publicly engaged colleges and universities, described in Chapter 8. In higher education, we have learned especially from colleagues at the College of St. Catherine, the effort at the University of Minnesota to "renew the land grant mission" of the University, and our partnership with Minneapolis Community and Technical College.

In scholarly and intellectual terms, our work has been challenged and enriched by partnerships as well. Colleagues at the Kettering Foundation have supported our research for many years, as well as proving a vital public space for ongoing interaction. Several journals created regular forums for these ideas, including the *New Democrat, Dissent,* and *PEGS Journal: The Good Society.* Conversations and collaborations with conservative colleagues have also been important. Especially, the forum on "What is Populism?" undertaken with the Bradley Foundation in 1994, and the process Nan Kari and I undertook in 1997 of writing "The Commonwealth of Freedom" for *Policy Review,* the publication of the Heritage Foundation, produced insights about the way themes of public work and everyday politics bridge partisan divisions. We also learned something of what conservatives can contribute to commonwealth politics.

Campus Compact has provided outlets and settings for discussion about higher education and politics. The *Campus Compact Reader,* a lively major forum for debate and learning about the fledgling democracy movement in higher education, has provided a regular forum for the ideas of public work and everyday politics. Many Campus Compact events in which I have participated in the last several years have given opportunities for feedback and discussion. I have often felt in these meetings the energy and hopefulness of an emerging movement and also have learned about ways in which service learning efforts can be a seedbed for democratic change when they develop a political dimension.

The meetings of the senior advisors and commission members of the National Commission for Civic Renewal and more recently the CIRCLE board of advisors generated valuable intellectual conversations. So, too, have the conferences and board meetings of Imagining America, an exciting and growing movement to involve scholars in public humanities work. Recently, I have also benefited intellectually from participation on the advisory board of the American Democracy Project, organized by the American Association of State Colleges and Universities and the *New York Times.* And experiences over the last two years with colleagues in South Africa, described in more detail in Chapter 9, have aided enormously in gaining greater clarity about what a political approach, contrasted with a technical approach, looks like in the United States, as well as in emerging democracies. Work in other countries, I have found—especially a society as dynamic as South Africa—can generate a unique mirror in which better to see ourselves.

Taken as a whole, these research methods, partnerships, and forums have given a public cast to the Center for Democracy and Citizenship's work, a process of ongoing conversation, debate, and learning, though one not without its ironies and limits.[9]

Over time and out of this mix, we developed the concept of public work—work with public meanings, purposes, and aspects—as a resource for civic engagement.[10] The concept acquired richer meanings as we wrestled with the problem of culture change in highly professionalized settings, where "organized knowledge" keeps most people relatively powerless and locked into passive roles as clients or customers.

Public work has proven a useful way to name, in conceptual terms, the vernacular, work-centered traditions of citizenship in America. It is a valuable conceptual tool for civic change, a way to re-imagine professionals as part of the political and civic mix, not as outsider fixers, and a way to highlight the civic contributions of groups, from minority and low income communities to new immigrants and young people, often seen in terms of their needs or deficiencies not their talents and intelligence. Finally, public work is a way to illuminate the productive side of politics—to see politics not simply as a fight over scarce resources, who gets what, but as the way for people with diverse interests and views to build the common world.

Public work conveys the idea of the citizen as co-creator of democracy, understood as a way of life not simply periodic elections. In politics, it enriches the metaphor of Hannah Arendt's famous table around which people gather in public life, by paying attention to the process of creating the table itself.

Chapter 1
The Stirrings of a New Politics

The American political culture is rooted in two contrasting conceptions of the American political order, both of which can be traced back to the earliest settlement of the country. In the first, the political order is conceived as a marketplace. . . . In the second, the political order is conceived to be a commonwealth. . . . These two conceptions have exercised an influence on government and politics throughout American history, sometimes in conflict and sometimes by complementing one another . . . with marketplace notions contributing to shaping the vision of commonwealth and commonwealth ideals being given a preferred position in the marketplace.
—Daniel Elazar

The late Senator Daniel Patrick Moynihan once argued, "The central conservative truth is that it is culture, not politics, that determines the success of a society."[1] Today, politics, as conventionally understood, illustrates the unspoken dangers in Moynihan's observation. Current politics reflects broad cultural trends that point not toward success but toward social failure.

Elections are the only way in which whole societies can decide about the future. Yet increasingly over the last generation, electoral debates have become polarized and the outcomes less productive. Today's problems— whether corporate scandals or global warming—often quickly become yesterday's forgotten headlines.

This unproductive politics contrasts with older, richer senses of what politics can mean. Politics, when engaged in by the broad citizenry, is the way a society as a whole negotiates, argues about, and understands its past and creates its present and its future. Such expansive politics depends on a feeling of ownership by citizens. And it requires citizens to have many settings for interaction and engagement with each other across lines of difference, beyond elections alone. Today, the "red" and "blue" electoral map of

America marks an electorate bitterly divided by cultural patterns and life styles as well as by partisanship. The nation urgently needs a politics that engages citizens across these lines, just as politics has largely become a spectator sport run by professionals with disdain for ordinary people.

Joan Didion details this pattern in her book, *Political Fictions*, based on her *New York Review of Books* essays on American political campaigns from 1988 to 2000. Among most Democratic candidates and their staffs, she found a palpable assumption of superiority. "I recall pink-cheeked young aides on the Dukakis campaign referring to themselves, innocent of irony and so of history, as 'the best and the brightest,'" she writes. Conservative pundits and politicians were as arrogant.[2]

"Given their obstinate lack of interest in the subject, asking a group of average Americans about politics is like asking a group of stevedores to solve a problem in astrophysics," wrote Andrew Ferguson, a senior editor of the *Weekly Standard* in 1996. "Before long they're explaining not merely that the moon is made of cheese, but what kind of cheese it is." The impeachment controversy of the late 1990s, according to Didion's account, illustrated how widespread the political establishment's sense of superiority and detachment from most Americans has become.[3]

A 1998 *New York Times* editorial by Senator Alan Simpson argued that Republicans' failure to win impeachment would have little consequence, since "the attention span of Americans is 'which movie is coming out next month?'" But the impeachment debate revealed a wider pattern. "What remains novel, and unexplained, was the increasingly histrionic insistence of the political establishment that it stood apart from, and indeed above, the country that had until recently been considered its validation," argued Didion. "Under the lights at CNN and MSNBC and the Sunday shows, it became routine to declare oneself remote from 'them,' or 'out there.'"[4]

Politicians' rhetoric illustrates the erosion of the role of citizens in public life. President Bush invoked citizenship often, but he defined the idea in private ways, as individual acts of kindness. America's greatness, he argued in his convention speech in 2000, is to be found "in small, unnumbered acts of caring and courage and self-denial."[5] Yet after the attacks of September 11, 2001, his call for "all of us [to] become a September 11 volunteer, by making a commitment to service in our communities" turned citizenship into a sentimental footnote to the undertakings—the war on terrorism, the war in Iraq—through which his administration sought to reshape the Middle East and the world.[6] In less turbulent times, former

President Clinton put citizens on the therapy couch. "I feel your pain," was his mantra.

Politicians express cultural dynamics as well as shape them, and political language is no exception. Broad trends feed the problems with politics and the loss of a public life. Public spaces like community centers and lodges (or, in Robert Putnam's famous example, bowling leagues) that used to bring people together across lines of difference have eroded. We are, increasingly, a society of gated communities, not only of neighborhoods but also of imaginations. Interests, ideologies, races, and classes separate us from each other. Housing designs reflect the pattern: front porches used to connect homes to the public world. Today, they have been replaced by recreation rooms in the basement, or decks in the back yard.

At the same time, in the last generation, weekend therapy sessions and television talk shows, the total quality management movement and the language of self-esteem have mingled with varieties of New Age phenomena. All this has generated a personalized culture of encounter among strangers. Today's public stage is often a fantasy world of instantly shared vulnerabilities. Quick fixes take the place of substantial engagement with others unlike ourselves.

The terms of the marketplace, giving a price tag to everything, have spread to the crevices of our society. "Some things money can't buy. For everything else there's Mastercard," the television ad declares. The number of things money cannot buy seems constantly to shrink.

Superficial sloganeering, domination by marketplace modes of thought, and bitter sectarian divisions, all larger cultural patterns reflected in election campaigns, made being political an accusation of choice in the 2002 elections, even while political professionals thought themselves a breed apart. Yet it is worth recalling that Moynihan also offered a redemptive alternative: "The central liberal truth," he said, "is that politics can change a culture and save it from itself."[7]

Everyday Politics rests on the conviction that politics, in the longer term, beyond the elections of 2004, holds resources to reverse the negative directions of our society and to renew democracy. The question is what a redemptive politics might look like.

For all the travails of what passes as politics, the United States in the last generation has also been a laboratory for creative civic experiments, with parallels in other societies. These have generated an everyday politics of negotiation and collaboration that is more concerned with solving problems and creating public goods than with placing blame. This different kind of politics is rooted in local cultures, not only places but also cultures of institutions where people encounter each other on a regular, face-to-face basis. It is philosophical and practical, not ideological or partisan, based on values such as participation, justice, community, and plurality. And it is not owned or controlled by professional politicians or by professional activists. Everyday politics is of the citizen, in the original Greek meaning of the term, *politikos*. Interestingly, despite the rationale that the professionalization of politics is inevitable in a complex, information-saturated world, the experiences of the last generation have shown dramatically that everyday politics, when it taps and develops the public talents of ordinary citizens, can be far more effective and productive than politics dominated by experts. Everyday politics has grown under the surface of mainstream attention across lines of partisan and other differences around tough public problems, from housing shortages to environmental hazards.

It is the central argument of *Everyday Politics* that such hands-on, accessible, and community-rooted politics is an alternative to politics as usual with far ranging possibilities. Everyday politics reconnects citizens and public life. It holds the potential to re-knit the two strands of populism—progressive challenges to corporate power and conservative challenges to liberal professionals—that have bitterly divided America into blue regions and red regions on the electoral map. Across the world, everyday politics can generate the civic energy and talent to address the multiplying problems that governments alone cannot solve, but which cannot be solved without government. It is also a *democratizing* politics, the way to revitalize the public life of institutions, from schools to universities, religious congregations to public health clinics and neighborhood associations, where a narrow, meritocratic professionalism now stifles citizen creativity.

To develop and spread such a politics will require a continuing process of learning across national boundaries. But the core elements are already clear.

In the first instance, politics needs to be owned by the people, not professionals. It is rooted in everyday settings, not in government or elections or mobilization campaigns. It is thus *populist*, in the sense that Thomas Jefferson once argued, resting on the premise that the only safe repository of the powers of the society are the people themselves. Politics is the practice of power wielding to get things done in complex, heterogeneous societies.[8]

In the second instance, everyday politics is also *civic*. It weds concrete self-interests to constructive work that contributes to the life of communities and the well-being of the society. This civic aspect means understanding politics not only in distributive terms, as a fight over scarce resources—who gets what—but in productive terms as well, about problem solving and culture-creating. Everyday politics adds to as well as allocates our public wealth.

Over centuries, the public world had vitality in America largely because it was felt to be the product of the cooperative but also self-interested, practical, down to earth work of citizens. This was what David Mathews has called the "sweaty and muscular" tradition of citizenship, in which people built schools and roads, libraries and cultural festivals.[9] E. J. Dionne and Kayla Meltzer Drogosz get at this sense of citizenship in the introduction to the Brookings Institution volume, *United We Serve: National Service and the Future of Citizenship*. They propose that when service takes the form of public work, it "is the essence of the democratic project." Such public work means keeping in mind larger civic ends. "Public work entails not altruism, or not only altruism, but enlightened self-interest—a desire to build a society in which the serving citizen wants to live."[10]

Public work is central to the idea of productive, everyday politics. Such politics means change in individuals' identities and practices as well as social change. It leads to people seeing themselves as the co-creators of democracy, not simply as customers or clients, voters, protestors, or volunteers. To highlight the creative, educative, and productive dimensions of politics, public work can be best defined as sustained effort by a mix of people who solve public problems or create goods, material or cultural, of general benefit. Public work is work that is visible, open to inspection, whose significance is widely recognized, and which can be carried out by people whose interests, views, and backgrounds may be quite different.

Historically, as people saw themselves creating American democracy, they became more public people, with the habits, virtues, identities, knowledge, and public reputations needed to make and sustain the public world. James Weldon Johnson, an architect of the Harlem Renaissance, captured the way the cultural work of blacks in Harlem, expressing the interplay between public and self-creation, also forged a powerful resource for the public struggle against racial injustice. "Harlem is more than a community; it is a large-scale laboratory experiment," wrote Johnson. "Through his artistic efforts the Negro is smashing immemorial stereotypes." Johnson saw the black American as "impressing upon the national mind the conviction that he is an active and important force in American life; that he is a creator as well as a creature; that he has given as well as received; that his gifts have been not only obvious and material, but also spiritual and aesthetic." The creative contributions of African Americans expressed in the Harlem Renaissance meant that the black American was to be seen as "a contributor to the nation's common cultural store; in fine, he is helping to form American civilization."[11]

Practices of public work, everyday nonprofessional politics, and democracy as a way of life profoundly impacted the political culture of the first half of the twentieth century. They reemerged again in the civil rights movement of the late 1950s and 1960s. Stirrings of their resurfacing appear again in the twenty-first century. But in recent decades, these themes have also sharply eroded in the political culture, in ways that need elaboration.

From Producer to Consumer

Mark Ritson illustrates the erosion of public life in his study of the Minnesota State Fair, held each year at the University of Minnesota. True to the university's land grant history and its partnerships, especially through university extension, with rural farming communities, the State Fair embodied productive, work centered themes. As one example, for instance, each year young people from 4-H clubs across the state would showcase their baked goods and livestock as well as their community betterment projects. 4-H arts and theater presentations were attended by tens of thousands of people.

Using quantitative and qualitative indices, Ritson shows how the State Fair changed its focus in the 1950s from production to consumption. Ritson compared premium list data (cash prizes awarded to exhibitors for winning displays of production skill) to revenue from concession stands, food tents, and commercial stalls for the period 1883 to 1995. He also conducted a detailed thematic analysis of speeches, brochures, news reports, and other material to discover "what did the fair mean to the people who organized and attended the event, and how did these meanings change over time?"

Ritson describes three distinct periods in State Fair history. In the first, from its beginnings in the nineteenth century until 1932, the fair strongly emphasized production. It featured farmers' livestock and bountiful harvests and showcased pioneers' work building homes and towns. In 1914, the president of the State Fair described it as "the annual assembling of the best products of the fields and orchards of Minnesota for the inspection and enlightenment of the citizenship of the state." This was the era in which land grant partnerships were rooted, and communities across the state took the occasion to celebrate their inventiveness and ingenuity, not only about crops and cattle but about educational innovations, rural homemaking, parks and recreation, and in general the quality of rural life.

A transition period, from 1933 to 1946, mingled themes of production and consumption. Work done through New Deal agencies was in prominent display. The Works Progress Administration sponsored the construction of many fairground buildings, while the Civilian Conservation Corps received attention and praise for creating much of Minnesota's park system, as well as innovations like soil conservation districts and contour farming.

From 1947 on, the fair increasingly focused on consumption. "Every year the Minnesota State Fair finds as many as a million people wolfing down gastronomic novelties," ran a story in the *Minneapolis Tribune* in 1956. Concession stands came to dominate, while livestock exhibits and other displays of productive activity were radically scaled back. Even the blue ribbon, once the most prestigious symbol of the production ethos, was licensed to a private national company that buys the rights to the winning pickles and preserves and produces them under the brand name, State Fair.[12]

As both symptom and cause of the public world's collapse, a broad erosion in the public dimensions of work began to take place in the 1950s. America was once a society where citizenship was not mainly off hours "voluntarism" (a term that only came into wide use in the late 1960s) but rather was tied to work. There were citizen doctors, citizen lawyers, citizen school teachers, citizen businessmen, and also citizen truck drivers, citizen steel workers, and citizen politicians—workers in many settings who thought about the public contributions and meaning of their work.

Susan Faludi in her book, *Stiffed: The Betrayal of the American Man*, brilliantly describes the loss of the public side of work. She shows that until the 1950s men sought what she calls "publick usefulness"—borrowing an older idiom—as the defining identity of citizenship. American culture was competitive, but success was pursued in the context of cultural norms that also stressed civic values. The point of work was to make contributions to families, communities, and the larger world, not just what one did to be able to buy things.

Since World War II, popular culture increasingly defined citizens precisely in terms of what they can buy, as consumers, not contributors. It lauds go-it-alone individualism, celebrity status, and shopping. Celebrities in *People* magazine replaced CCC boys and GI Joes or public spirited but realistic journalists like Ernie Pyle as the images of success.

As a result, men who could no longer achieve "success" came to feel themselves victims, a dynamic which the modern cultural vocabulary, with its stress on individual feelings and personal remedy, makes hard to describe. Faludi explores the way men have become like the "trapped housewife" of *The Feminine Mystique.* "American housewives can be given the sense of identity, purpose, creativity, the self-realization, even the sexual joy they lack by the buying of things," Faludi quotes one housewife who wrote to Betty Friedan. The woman concluded, "My brain seems dead. I am nothing but a parasite."[13]

Many men, in very different settings, voiced similar feelings. Faludi detects immense hidden social discontents about consumerism and celebrity culture among industrial workers, veterans, evangelical husbands, media executives, porn actors, and bad boys alike. Such discontents hold explosive democratic potential. But it will take a different kind of politics to realize its promise.

The Limits of Electoral Politics

Worries about materialism and privatization, two dynamics that define the gated communities of our imaginations, have been growing below the surface of American culture for some time. In 1996, the Kettering Foundation commissioned the Harwood Group, a public issues research firm, to conduct focus groups across the country in order to better understand the "nature and extent of the disconnect between what people see as important concerns and their sense that they can address them." The focus groups picked up among both men and women themes similar to those Faludi discovered. Harwood found a nation of citizens deeply troubled about the direction of the society as a whole, even if they felt optimistic about their own personal lives and economic prospects. They saw large institutions, from government to business to education, as increasingly remote and focused on narrow gain. They worried about America becoming a greedy nation, where values such as look out for number one and get rich quick replace hard work, community and family life, and a sense of the sacred. They expressed grave concerns that people are increasingly divided by race, ideology, religion, and class. Society used to "build walls to put the bad people in," said one man in Memphis. "Now we're building walls to keep the bad people out." He also saw that as futile. "There's no sense of community anymore. Everybody is walled off from the other neighborhood."[14]

Yet people also felt largely powerless to address such trends. The Harwood study found people retreating into smaller and smaller circles of private life where they feel they have some control, even if they think retreat spells trouble. "If you look at the whole picture of everything that is wrong, it is so overwhelming," said one woman from Richmond, "You just retreat back and take care of what you know you can take care of—and you make it smaller, make it even down to just you and your unit. You know you can take care of that."[15]

Electoral politics can give voice to discontent about materialism, consumerism, and privatization in different partisan accents, but it does not by itself well address the underlying dynamic of citizen powerlessness to do much about these trends. The election of 2000 is instructive to analyze, both for the ways in which the themes of citizenship, power, the common good, and related ideas appeared and also for the ways in which they were sharply narrowed in meaning.

Al Gore, who had helped found a Populist Caucus in Congress in the 1980s, made gains—and got the plurality of the vote—with his declaration, "I'm fighting for the people, not the powerful!" Ralph Nader leveled tirades against corporate interests that eroded the common good. In a vivid example, Nader charged children's advertisers with marketing seductive apparel to five-year-old girls behind parents' backs, in clothing lines with titles like "Street Walker." "The old-model corporation never sold directly to kids, except maybe bubble gum. They let parents decide what to buy for children," Nader declared in his acceptance speech to the Greens. "Today, the corporations are electronic child molesters, subjecting children to violence and low-grade sensuality."[16]

Midway through President George W. Bush's term, Democratic candidates for president, past and present, were regularly challenging the culture of "materialism and greed," a culture they blamed on his administration. "Millions of Americans now share a feeling that something pretty basic has gone wrong in our country and that some important American values are being placed at risk," declared Al Gore on July 20, at New York University. "What we have here is a form of looting," Gore declared about the Bush administration's economic policies, quoting economist George Akerlof.[17]

Yet to the consternation of those who saw him speaking for wealth instead of for commonwealth, in the 2000 election George Walker Bush had energetically campaigned on a critique of materialist values that was notably stronger than Al Gore's. In his convention speech, George Bush declared, "we must renew our values to restore our country." These values, in Bush's terms, were not about affluence. "The vision of America's founders . . .

never saw our nation's greatness in rising wealth or advancing armies." Bush claimed the heritage of Americans who had acted in the past. "When Lewis Morris of New York was about to sign the Declaration of Independence, his brother advised against it, warning he would lose all his property. Morris, a plain-spoken Founder, responded, 'Damn the consequences, give me the pen.'"

"That is the consequence of American action," said candidate Bush, calling Americans to join in "a time for new beginnings." He argued that "who we are is more important than what we have." He posed the question, "what is asked of us?" and envisioned history's verdict: "A hundred years from now, this must not be remembered as an age rich in possessions but poor in ideals."[18]

In his first major policy address as a candidate, on July 22, 1999, Bush outlined his plans to rally the armies of compassion. Through the campaign he called this government truly by the people and for the people. After the election, Bush continued in this vein. A call to citizenship was the center of his Inaugural Address. "I ask you to seek a common good beyond your comfort," Bush proclaimed, "to be citizens, not spectators, to serve your nation, beginning with your neighborhood."[19]

In a media packaged age, it is easy to be cynical about such language. Yet the formal political process, in important respects, is reactive. Politicians of all stripes pick up, use, and amplify citizens' views and assumptions, albeit in complicated and often indirect ways. The themes struck in the 2000 campaign are likely to be strong currents in American politics for many years.

From the vantage of older traditions of citizenship, what is striking about Bush's definition of citizenship is its private and personal quality. He spoke of compassionate acts that "warm the cold of life," but neglected any collective action that might change the conditions giving rise to the cold. He defined citizenship without reference to power, the lifeblood of public life. He talked about kindness, but not public impact.

Bush's version of citizenship robbed both citizenship and community of their larger public side, turning them into an ensemble of private, individual relationships. Community, if it is to be more than a marketing slogan, is not simply made through private ties; it is created by people working together on tough public problems with an eye to the well-being and future of the community as a whole.

Yet it is a mistake to see privatized citizenship—citizenship without public power or substantial roles for citizens in the affairs of the nation—as simply a trait of Republicans. Al Gore described what *government* could do to solve the problems of the nation and the world, and what he, as president, would deliver in the way of new benefits—but citizens, as citizens, were missing. Indeed, Gore had presided over the Clinton administration's Reinventing Government initiative that redefined citizens as government's customers. Ralph Nader called for citizen action against powerful corporate interests, but his moral calculus made citizens blameless for the consumerism and materialism he excoriated, and his view of citizen action lent scarce room for productive engagement with Republicans or conservatives. Most Americans are well aware that we all are implicated in this culture. Bush, by way of contrast, appealed to millions of American citizens precisely because he called them to participate in acts of civic renewal, beyond comfort and spectatorship, however sentimental his version of citizenship.

For a number of years, scholars preceded the president in calling for citizenship and civic engagement with theories that hand over ownership of politics itself to professionals. The terms of the debate have increasingly been set by academics grounded in communitarian philosophy, who advocate community service in practice. Communitarians stress what Amitai Etzioni calls the "social dimension of human existence." They argue that America suffers from excessive individualism that overemphasizes rights and underemphasizes responsibilities. The result is moral decay.[20]

Communitarians strike a chord by decrying the decline in America's community spirit in an increasingly depersonalized world. Respect for Americans' desire for community, in a world that often tears communities apart, is powerfully resonant. As a result, it has gained important political champions—both Bill Clinton and George Bush described themselves, at various times, as communitarian.[21] Yet as a theory of citizenship, communitarianism has major flaws in that it slights the importance of politics, power, and public life.

Instead, communitarian theory draws specific attention to the moral failings of citizens. *A Call to Civil Society: Why Democracy Needs Moral Truths*, by the Council on Civil Society, had signatories from Cornel West on the left to Senator Dan Coats (R-Ind.) on the right. *A Call* argued that Americans are "deeply troubled by the character and values exhibited by young people today."[22] In response, communitarians aim to promote civic values. More than forty organizations, ranging from the American Association for Higher Education to the Council of Chief State School Officers, have created an alliance known as the "Partnering Initiative on Education and Civil Society," to "integrate civic values into virtually every aspect of the educational experience."[23] Community service is touted as a particularly effective vehicle for inculcating civic values, and has spread widely. By 1998–99, 32 percent of all public schools had service courses, including 46 percent of high schools.[24]

From this perspective, the ideal citizen is a compassionate volunteer. While better than the radical individualist ideal, the focus on helping without political dimensions has clear limits. Community service programs typically promote outcomes like self-esteem, consciousness of personal values, and a sense of personal responsibility. But they neglect to teach about root causes and power relationships, fail to stress productive impact, ignore politics, and downplay the strengths and talents of those being served.[25]

An etymology of service illustrates the problem. Service is from the Latin *servus*, meaning slave, associated with "servile" and "serf." In one of its meanings, "performing duties connected with a position," service is a useful bridge for reconnecting with the world. Yet in all meanings, service is associated with other-directedness. The service giver, in focusing on the needs of those being served, adopts a stance of selflessness or disinterestedness. Service is the paradigmatic stance of the outside expert. But interests, and people working to further their interests, are the elemental particles of politics.[26]

Liberals challenge the Bush administration and its communitarian advisors on just these grounds. Thus, Michael Schudson charges that Bush's citizenship substitutes service for justice. "There is no acknowledgement that democracy has been enlarged in our lifetimes when individuals have been driven not by a desire to serve but by an effort to overcome indignities they themselves have suffered," he argues.[27] In contrast to the communitarians, liberals see a world of clashing interests and power relationships. Thus, Seyla Benhabib argues against what she sees as communitarians' view of society "without conflict and contention." Rogers Smith, challenging idealized conceptions of American identity, calls for an unromantic liberalism attentive to exclusions and inequalities in the name of American citizenship: "We need an . . . account that gives full weight to America's pervasive ideologies of ascriptive inequality."

Liberal theorists contribute a needed focus on power and interests. Yet they also have a state-centered and professionalized view of politics as a bitter struggle over scarce resources, pithily summarized by Harold Laswell's definition of politics as"who gets what, when, and how." For Rogers Smith, "political decision-making is in reality almost always more a matter of elite bargaining than popular deliberation." To Benhabib, society is "the sedimented repository of struggles for power, symbolization, and significa-tion—in short, for cultural and political hegemony carried out among groups, classes, and genders."[28]

Real politics always involves a struggle for justice. Yet like communi-tarians, liberals narrow the orbit of politics to government and see it as a zero-sum fight in which there are inevitably winner and losers. More, they tend to neglect the theme of community.

Politicians and conventional political theory are joined by other insti-tutions in articulating a thinned out version of citizenship. Political cam-paigns and policymaking (and media coverage thereof), as well as civics classes, all position government and experts at the center of the action, the problem solvers, service providers, and agenda setters. By separating the people who "count" in public life from the people themselves, these dy-namics end up professionalizing politics and privatizing everything.

Everyday Politics

To renew public life in America will require a new politics in which citizens, acting at every level, from local community-building to national policy-making, reclaim ownership of politics. In practice such repossession of poli-tics involves citizens in diverse environments learning the skills of political work with people unlike themselves on the public tasks of communities, the society, and the world.

Here and there, intimations of a politics that puts citizens back at the center of public life appear in mainstream discussion. Thus, for instance, *A Nation of Spectators*, the report of the National Commission on Civic Re-newal co-chaired by Sam Nunn and William Bennett, explicitly used a pub-lic work definition of democracy and citizenship. In the report, chiefly au-thored by William Galston, democracy was defined as "neither a consumer good nor a spectator sport, but rather the work of free citizens engaged in shared civic enterprises."[29] Elizabeth Kautz, the highly successful mayor of the suburban city of Burnsville, Minnesota, defines politics in this way. She has overseen a process of redesigning all city agencies to facilitate the efforts of civil servants in cooperative public work with other citizens. She argues that government alone can't solve most of the public problems Burnsville faces, though they can't be solved without effective government. "Govern-ment can be a catalyst. I can work with people. But I can't pretend to fix things anymore, and neither can anybody in government."[30] In a conservative blue collar district of Milwaukee in 2002, Josh Zepnick, a former Humphrey Institute graduate student who had researched public work approaches in local government as part of his studies, won a seat in the state legislature with the campaign theme, "Everyday politics, not politics everyday!"

Professional fields, as well, show signs of change. Thus, for instance, the syndemics prevention network, a worldwide network of public health practitioners and theorists who take a systems approach to prevention science sponsored by the Centers for Disease Control in Atlanta, is incorporating public work and everyday politics as central to building "community strength." Community strength is increasingly recognized in public health as a pivotal variable in disease prevention and health promotion.[31]

More broadly, cultural trends suggest the return of pluralist populist themes in which ordinary citizens take on central roles in shaping the world and in which truth appears as multi-vocal and many-sided. Thus, for instance, *Lord of the Rings* features the unlikely everyday hero Frodo and his companion Sam. The remarkable popularity of the Hammadi texts of lost Christian traditions suggests popular interest in religious conceptions that are down-to-earth, centered more on human experience and less on doctrinal purity.[32]

Yet these are still minor currents in the dominant languages of politics.

A 1999 study of baby boomers and older adults by the Minnesota Board of Aging found that most people wanted stronger, bolder, savvier civic opportunities in the public work vein, but were well aware of the obstacles. Asking about interest in "doing more than volunteer" by participating in solving public problems, they found that both baby boomers and older adults wanted to be useful, to contribute to rebuilding a sense of community, and to be involved in decision-making. Citizens expressed the desire to learn civic skills, such how to work across divisions of ideology, race, or culture, and big picture thinking that ties specific tasks to the larger questions and challenges.

Citizens also argued that meritocratic assumptions structure the relations between citizens and institutions. Most institutions—governmental, business, educational, and civic—condescend to their intelligence and talent. Volunteer opportunities relegate them to "positions of mediocrity with the assumption that they lack the capacity to work on big issues that impact the community." Volunteers are rarely asked "what they are good at, what is important to them, and how they want to be part of shaping their communities."[33]

The point about meritocracy, developed in Chapter 2, was powerfully expressed some years ago by John Lukacs, a self-described "reactionary Catholic intellectual" who took refuge in the United States from Hungary in 1957. In *Outgrowing Democracy*, Lukacs said that he came to America believing that the country overestimated the capacities of "the democratic masses." Whether or not that was true, Lukacs argued that in the 1950s America came to vastly underestimate popular capacity, as it shifted from a democratic order to a bureaucratic state dominated by experts. Government was by no means alone; virtually every institution—the media, schools, higher education, foundations, businesses—came to downplay the talents of most people.[34]

We need a politics of respect, not of sympathy, compassion, or indignation. A politics of respect taps and also develops the intelligence and skills of American citizens for practical public action; it is a politics with both civic and populist dimensions.

Everyday politics, in its largest implications, retrieves democratic themes of the New Deal and the civil rights movement, as well as more recent feminist and environmental efforts, faith-based community organizing, and the current movement around youth civic engagement. It sees citizens as co-creators of a democratic way of life. It integrates community, the theme of communitarians, with politics, the centerpiece of liberalism. It melds practical, interest-group bargaining with civic ideals. The key to such political alchemy is a concept missing from theories of participatory democracy: "work."

Before exploring the concepts of everyday politics and public work, it is useful to analyze the kinds of citizen-involving politics that now dominate in American life. Chapter 2 describes progressive and conservative versions of populisms, arguing that both express real grievances but offer few solutions.

Chapter 3 describes the central empirical development on which this book's argument rests, the growth of everyday politics rooted in local settings. Everyday politics reflects an organizing approach rather than the mobilizing approach of partisan populisms or ideological mobilizations. In everyday politics people learn to deal with each other in much richer ways than through sound bytes and slogans. Chapter 4 argues that to integrate and spread everyday politics into highly professionalized systems requires a challenge to conventional theories that define the citizen as a volunteer and neglect the civic meanings of work. Chapters 5 and 6 describe two initiatives in which everyday politics have taken shape, one with young people and the other with new immigrants.

Chapters 7 and 8 shift the lens, to use a photographic metaphor, from an F-stop of individuals and small groups to one focused on professional cultures and culture-making institutions like higher education. Chapter 7 describes several examples (ministry, teaching, occupational therapy, family practice) in which professionals have recovered public dimensions of their work through practicing everyday politics and public work. Chapter 8 sketches a young but important effort to change the culture of the University of Minnesota, a change effort that has had an explicitly political dimension and that aims at deepening the public dimensions of every aspect of the university's work.

Chapter 9 expands the F-stop to a still larger compass. I argue that there are signs of an everyday, nonprofessional, and productive politics emerging around the world. And I lay out what we need to do to deepen and expand everyday politics as a democratic alternative.

Chapter 2
Populisms

Your mission is to subjugate to the beneficent yoke of reason the unknown beings who live on other planets, and who are perhaps still in the primitive state of freedom. If they will not understand that we are bringing them mathematically faultless happiness, our duty will be to force them to be happy.

—*Evgeny Zamyatin,* We

It will be a hard pill for many Americans to swallow—the idea of doing with less so that big business can have more. Nothing that this nation or any other nation has done in modern history compares in difficulty with the selling job that must now be done to make people accept the new reality.

—Business Week, *October 12, 1974*

For those who identify with the progressive populist tradition of challenge to corporate power in America, Bill Moyers's "Take Back America" speech to 1,000 grassroots activists at a Campaign for America's Future conference on June 9, 2003, was a bracing tonic. Moyers delivered a call to arms against "government of, by, and for the ruling corporate class." He charged that the Bush administration, if unchecked, would privatize America's public things in order to enrich corporate interests. He pointed out that White House political doyen Karl Rove's hero was Mark Hanna, the Ohio political boss who managed the campaigns and presidency of William McKinley and went on to establish an administration unabashedly the ally of the largest corporate interests. Moyers recalled the populist legacy, and declared that "the social dislocations and the meanness of the nineteenth century" are being repeated by politicians who are strangling the spirit of the American Revolution. He called for populists and progressives of the twenty-first century to "restore the balance between wealth and commonwealth," and concluded with a fiery challenge to activists to "get back in the fight." "Hear me!" he said. "Allow yourself the conceit to believe that the flame of democracy will never go out as long as there is one candle in your hand."[1]

Populist calls are appearing often in the early years of the twentieth first century, though rarely with the fire of Moyers's speech. Like politics generally, today's populism reflects larger cultural trends, the shifts in Americans' civic identities from producer to consumer and client and the bitter divisions among the people that have resulted. America's divided populist politics is emblazoned in red states versus blue states on election maps. The map dramatizes partisan approaches on the left and the right which name problems but which have few solutions. The map is also a reflection of the ways in which populisms, like politics generally, have largely become the property of professionals and intellectuals with their own categorizations of what's wrong.

If progressive populists challenge corporate power, conservative populists, from politicians such as Ronald Reagan to intellectuals such as William Schambra, Gertrude Himmelfarb, Bob Woodson, or William Bennett attack liberal professionals for being contemptuous of the values of ordinary citizens and institutions such as families, religious congregations, and ethnic groups. Indeed, protest against the culture of liberal professionalism has been the mainstay of conservatives for the last generation.

Both challenges to corporate power and challenges to liberal professionalism are rooted in real grievances. Left and right wing populists also speak languages that seem incomprehensible to the other.

Populism can be understood in very different ways, depending on whom the people are thought to include, which institutions are seen as centers of power and privilege, and what it means to return power to the people. The late Minnesota Senator Paul Wellstone called himself a populist, as did Jesse Jackson. Al Gore was a founder of the Democratic Populist Congressional Caucus in the 1980s. Ralph Nader proudly uses the label. But Ronald Reagan, on the other side of the spectrum, also was often called a populist, and the challenges he presented to liberal professional practices and culture had broad resonance with Americans. Sometimes, political leaders confound left and right divisions. Bob Riley, the conservative Republican governor of Alabama, is called a populist as well. As a U.S. Representative, Riley had a near perfect record of opposing legislation supported by liberals, but when he became governor he scrambled things up. "Governor Riley has stunned many of his conservative supporters and enraged the state's powerful farm and timber lobbies by pushing a tax reform plan through the Alabama legislature that shifts a significant amount of the state's tax burden from the poor to wealthy individuals and corporations," reported Adam Cohen in the *New York Times*.[2]

Populism crosses traditional partisan divisions because its central agent, the people, is left, right, liberal, conservative, and also much more. The great strength, as well as the limit, of electoral politics is that at heart it is always an argument about the state and future direction of a society. Who the people are is always a matter of debate, as are the structures responsible for usurping popular power and strategies about what it will take to return it.

Peoplehood conveys the concept of a historically, politically, and culturally constituted entity. As such, it is not a modern idea, but rather a concept with ancient roots. A people has a founding moment—the Muslim hegira, the birth of Christ, the Romulus and Remus story of Rome's founding, our own Declaration of Independence. It has a history. It is enacted symbolically by rituals, documents, and constituting stories. In some societies, peoplehood is strongly identified with cultural homogeneity. In the diverse cultural mix of the United States, though there has been a struggle around whether Anglo-Saxon Protestants form a cultural norm, peoplehood is identified with political symbols, events, and struggles. These include events like the Revolution, the writing of the Constitution, the Civil War and the civil rights movement, and the holidays that commemorate these, like July Fourth, Memorial Day, and Martin Luther King Day.

Historically, populism constituted a political tradition much wider than simply electoral politics or the People's Party of the 1890s. In that period, it also included groups as diverse as the Farmers Alliances cooperatives, the Knights of Labor, and leaders in the Women's Christian Temperance Union. As a political tradition, it shaped such twentieth-century efforts as the New Deal and the civil rights movement of the 1950s and 1960s.

For farmers, small business groups, and skilled and semi-skilled workers, populism was a set of organizing strategies (for instance, a focus on cooperatives), a legislative program, a lecture circuit aimed at self-education, and a vision of the cooperative commonwealth, all together. The overall thrust was an effort to bring the economic and social transformations associated with emerging industry, monopoly capital, and urbanization under popular control.

Populists never envisioned a utopia of socialized property. Rather, as populism's leading historian, Lawrence Goodwyn, has described, they sought a society based on small holdings where large-scale enterprises were subject to democratic regulation. White populists took a prophetic stance that claimed the legacy and aspirations of the American Revolution as a resource to be adapted to the challenges of a radically changing world. Blacks, Latinos, and other racial minorities had a more complicated and ambivalent relationship to American populist and democratic traditions— what Frederick Harris has called the "orderly and disorderly oppositional civic culture." For minorities, populism and related commonwealth traditions furnished resources for a complex political balancing act that included alliances and the pursuit of racial justice. But racial minorities also found in its vocabulary important resources for pressing their cause. Indeed, the very idea of "40 acres and a mule," the unrealized heart of the Reconstruction program in the American South after the civil war, was based on the commonwealth ideal, the idea that citizens needed independence and self-reliance in order to participate in public life.

Populism also built on a legacy of rough-hewn democratic practices that many immigrants of middle peasant and artisan backgrounds brought with them. These resonated with democratic themes into the twentieth century.[3]

Thus, in its broad manifestations populism had a focus on developing the power of the people ("return of power to the people") to exercise control over larger structures, both corporate and bureaucratic, that were re-shaping the United States from a nation of small towns and a largely agricultural society to an urbanized, industrialized nation. It also had a focus on building the commonwealth. As such, populism furnished a distinctive democratic alternative to conventional ideological politics of left and right by emphasizing development of democratic power and the quality of democratic civilization. The salience of particular policy plans could be judged not mainly against a particular programmatic blueprint but rather against the question, what do they contribute to civic power and learning and to the overall advance of the democracy?[4]

This focus on civic development, empowerment, and the vitality of the commonwealth had a strong tie to work and the civic identities associated with the citizen as producer. Michael Kazin's history of movements that have used populist rhetoric, *The Populist Persuasion*, demonstrated that populist politics with a tie to work and productive citizenship were relatively open and democratic. Those framed in moral terms, defending "traditional values," were likely to be reactionary.[5]

Into the 1940s the populist character of the New Deal meant that average citizens had the sense that they were helping to make it, as Lisabeth Cohen details in her book, *Making a New Deal.* The transformation in the political culture of the Chicago working class from the early 1920s (when disengagement from federal government was more severe than today) to the late 1930s (when 90 percent of unskilled workers and 81 percent of semi-skilled workers favored the New Deal) was directly tied to the sense of popular agency and contribution. Workers believed themselves to have helped make the whole enterprise in a myriad of ways, from voting to union activism to settlement houses and public work projects like the WPA and CCC. Moreover, the public works programs and civic activities of the working class furnished a vital schooling in democratic skills, habits, and sensibilities—responsible for the achievements of what is fondly remembered as "the Greatest Generation."[6]

Populist themes shaped the New Deal, and reemerged in the civil rights movement of the 1950s and 1960s, which stressed "realization of democracy's promise." But the roots of populism were eroding rapidly. As mediating institutions through which ordinary people learned everyday politics of dealing with others unlike themselves—religious groups, labor unions, political parties, schools, settlements, and many other settings—became highly professionalized and lost public dimensions, politics became increasingly strident and ideological. As citizens changed from producers to consumers and clients, politics revealed Americans' profound discontents with such roles—but offered little in the way of programs or strategies for overcoming them.

The result is that red and blue populisms both embody the deep divisions, grievances, and frustrations of our society. On the left, populism's demand has been for redistribution of the pie and a challenge to corporate power, with little hope for changing the nature of the pie itself. On the right, it has been for defense of traditional values and institutions like the family, religious congregation, and ethnic group, especially against intrusive government, with little sense of these institutions as living, dynamic social creations through which people can act with power to shape the larger world. In both cases populism has lost its essence: the idea that politics, owned by the people, is the activity through which people of diverse views and backgrounds develop their power to shape the world.

"The New Populism"

Midway through the Bush administration, open alarm about "plutocracy," an alliance of great wealth and corporate interests with the Republican Party, had spread from the left wing of the Democratic Party to the mainstream of progressive discussion. [7] Paul Krugman, the economic columnist for the *New York Times*, argued in his column, "Toward One-Party Rule," that "an unprecedented national political machine . . . is well on track to establishing one-party rule in America." Krugman pointed to a number of signs, from fliers supporting tax cuts that General Motors and Verizon mailed with dividend checks to shareholders, to pro-war rallies organized by Clear Channel radio stations across the country. Most particularly, he described a new "K-Street Project," in which Republicans are placed in key corporate and industry lobbying jobs and Democrats are excluded. "Corporations themselves are increasingly part of the party machine," he argued. "They are rewarded with policies that increase their profits: deregulation, privatization of government services, elimination of environmental rules." In "For Richer," an earlier cover story in the *New York Times Magazine*, Krugman detailed the dramatic increases in inequality in the last two decades. "We are now living in a new Gilded Age, as extravagant as the original," he said. "The man in the grey flannel suit has been replaced by the imperial C.E.O. Over the past thirty years, the average pay of the chief executives of the largest 100 companies went from $1.3 million a year—39 times the pay of the average worker—to $37.5 million, more than 1,000 times the pay." Krugman, challenging explanations for the growing inequality like globalization or technological change, traced it to cultural politics. "Much more than economists and free-market advocates like to imagine, wages—particularly at the top—are determined by social norms," he proposed. "What happened during the 1930s and 1940s was that new norms of equality were established, largely through the political process. What happened in the 1980s and 1990s was that these norms unraveled, replaced by an ethos of 'anything goes.' And a result was an explosion of income at the top of the scale."[8]

Krugman's concerns are dramatic, but not new. Since the 1970s, progressives have issued warnings about the political power and culture-shaping efforts of corporate interests. Efforts to roll back environmental and consumer protections, deregulate communications, transportation, and banking, and privatize government together constituted a broad assault on the very idea of a public world. Business commentators in the early 1970s warned of a looming "capital crisis" that would undermine business investment and productivity increases. They argued that the nation's wealth needed redistribution—upward. "It will be a hard pill for many Americans to swallow—the idea of doing with less so that big business can have more," read the lead editorial in *Business Week*, October 12, 1974. "Nothing that this nation or any other nation has done in modern history compares in difficulty with the selling job that must now be done to make people accept the new reality." Corporate leaders created lobbying groups like the Business Roundtable and launched a massive "image advertising" campaign.[9]

A new generation of large citizen action groups arose in response. Beginning in the 1970s, citizen organizing efforts achieved significant victories—from the election of labor reformers to union leadership to environmental gains like the Clean Water Act and the Superfund Bill to clean up toxic waste. Accomplishing these victories required a political language and strategy different from that of the New Left or New Politics liberalism. The "New Populism" was the name given to these citizen efforts. Progressive intellectuals added a populist dimension to progressive demands, arguing that the new left had been profoundly mistaken to scorn American democratic traditions and symbols, as well as local institutions like neighborhood groups and religious congregations.[10]

The New Populist organizers sought to reach people who didn't think of themselves as activists—people in poor, working class, and middle class communities. They combined a focus on economic, consumer, and environmental issues with new methods of citizen mobilization.

The New Populism encompassed both local groups and organizations like Citizen Action, ACORN, the Citizen Labor Energy Alliance, and Clean Water Action. The Congressional Populist Caucus had more than thirty House and Senate members. According to Byron Dorgan, a Democrat from North Dakota, the Caucus was organized because "people out there feel powerless, because they're preyed upon by bigger interests."[11]

For some years I was connected to the New Populism through my writings (including *The Backyard Revolution: Understanding the New Citizen Movement, The New Populism: The Politics of Empowerment*, a collection edited with Frank Riessman, and *Citizen Action and the New American Populism*, coauthored with Heather Booth and Steve Max), and through my work with the Citizen Action network and the Populist Vision Project of the Congressional Populist Caucus.

This history of citizen mobilization to counter the corporate agenda forms a hidden chapter in progressive politics for the last generation. It was this history that formed the background for the New Citizenship project with the White House from 1993 to 1995, aimed at developing strategies to overcome the citizen-government divide. The Camp David meeting on the Future of Democracy surfaced new populist themes. At the meeting, held on January 14, 1995 before Clinton's State of the Union address of that year, Hillary Clinton, for instance, passionately described how the fight against corporate-right wing efforts to dismantle government was the defining objective of both Clintons' entire political careers. Her words reminded me of many leaders in the New Populism whom I had known over the years.[12]

The New Populism had successes, but it had two weaknesses. Its methods of mobilization, structured by professional logic, oversimplified political issues and relations, contributing to a radically polarized political culture. Related to this oversimplification, it neglected the ways in which liberal professional culture itself was eroding the civic life of everyday settings and the authority and standing of ordinary citizens. Thus, it slighted the real and powerful grievances that give conservative populism broad appeal.

First, the New Populism defined politics as good citizens against evil big business. This perspective was reinforced by the New Populism's mobilization strategies, such as door-to-door canvassing, which depend on pushing hot-button issues.

The canvass began in 1974, when Marc Anderson, with Citizens for a Better Environment, joined with Heather Booth, founder of Midwest Academy, who was developing a network of state citizen organizations that became Citizen Action. The canvass involves paid staff going door to door on an issue, raising money and collecting signatures on a petition. Over the past generation, a number of canvass operations have developed in citizen action networks. Through the canvass, large numbers of working and middle class citizens have been mobilized to counter roll-backs in environmental, consumer, affirmative action, and other government regulations as well as shifts in the tax burden away from business. Canvass supporters believe that the canvass teaches citizens about public issues and the core principles of citizen participation on a face-to-face scale, unlike other methods like television advertising. Chris Williams, a one time environmental planner, worked with Indiana Citizen Action Coalition because he believed it provided an alternative source of information for the public. "The press simply hadn't covered the corruption that was going on around issues like utilities," he explained. "With the canvass we were able to let people in key legislative districts know that the public service commission was controlled by the utility companies themselves."[13]

More subtly, but crucial to the motivation of many who organize canvass operations, the canvass is seen as expressing a key principle: ordinary citizens are not powerless to affect the forces that otherwise overwhelm them. Larry Marx, an articulate philosopher of the canvass, said, "the canvass validates people's feelings that the rules of the game are rigged, perceptions that on their own make them feel psychologically paranoid." In his view, "The basic message is that people don't have to just take it. We're not helpless victims. We can control our own lives." Our book *Citizen Action and the New American Populism* defended the canvass on these grounds.[14]

Critics have argued that the canvass has had damaging if little explored effects on politics. In an important article in *The American Prospect*, John Judis contended that the canvass was a key element in the emergence of what he calls "advocacy group politics," politics done by groups dominated by professionals, with more tenuous connections to their members than older style interest groups.[15]

This is a useful critique, but one that missed a key element of the issue. The crucial problem with the canvass is its overly simplified theory of politics itself.

The canvass's political theory had several roots, including the organizing strategy of George Wiley, founder of the National Welfare Rights Organization, and arguments of French new leftist André Gorz, in *Strategy for Labor*.[16] Ralph Nader articulated the canvass philosophy in his "Democracy Rising" effort after the 2000 election. According to Nader, democracy is being taken over by corporate interests, which only "an aroused and active citizenry," explicitly committed to progressive politics, can counter.[17]

Citizen action groups use the canvass with the goal of activating citizens, not simply raising money. To activate citizens, the canvass strategy follows a distinct set of political principles:

- Focus on concrete, winnable issues;
- Target an enemy who can be used to dramatize and personalize the issue;
- Define issues in majoritarian ways that cross lines of class, race, and religion which were bitterly divisive in the 1960s;
- Mobilize forces for change through mass action.

The canvass crystallizes, in ideal type, widely held assumptions: politics is a zero-sum struggle over scarce resources, always tied to government. It pits the forces of good, in this case powerless citizens, against the forces of evil, powerful corporate interests.

In citizen action groups like ACORN or Clean Water Action, the canvass has become the tail that wags the dog. Narrowly scripted issue campaigns come to dominate, while the more complex, vital work of public leadership development and the creation of sustainable local cultures of civic engagement disappears. Typically, canvassers are given a prepared script to deliver along with a nightly fundraising quota; they also solicit signatures for petitions. It is extremely hard work. Canvassers talk constantly about the "burnout" that comes from such scripted, narrow, and often manipulative encounters with citizens. During the summer, tens of thousands of young people canvass, and a remarkable number of those who try it quit within a few days—at least 50 or 60 percent. Still, large numbers survive the initial experience and go on to participate in a canvass culture, with pep talks, songs, conferences, and other activities.

Though there has been no systematic analysis of the effects of the canvass on the public, the canvassers, or the broader political culture, the scale of the door-to-door canvass is so vast it seems likely to be significant. Columbia University's Dana Fisher, formerly a director of the national PIRG canvass, estimates that at least 150,000 young people, mostly college students, survive the initial cut each year. At Princeton 10 percent of the student body has canvassed. In Pennsylvania, as many as 15–20 percent of public university students may have tried it. Conservatively, over the last generation this amounts to 3.5 million people who have canvassed.[18]

In *Citizen Action and the New American Populism* we estimated that the canvass was reaching at least 12 million households year after year, more during large national campaigns. In states like Massachusetts with long-standing canvasses, more than 80 percent of the population knew the main canvass organization, Massachusetts Fair Share.

Such mobilization technologies have metastasized into many other techniques, used by left and right alike, from internet lobbying to phone canvasses. Millions of Americans are now mobilized by over-simplified approaches to politics. These all share the same features: they expect very little of the citizen; they depend upon caricatures of the enemy; and they are forms of citizen participation in which professionals craft both the message and the patterns of involvement. Kathy Magnusen, general manager of the *Minnesota Women's Press*, who backed the Greens, pointed to the thinness of this politics: "Seeing the world in terms of good and evil is seductive. Ralph Nader was great at that. But you don't deal with the motivations of those you disagree with, or where they come from, or what their constraints are. It's a lot more work to grapple with the complexity of things."[19]

If new populists have had too narrow a political language of "big business versus the little guy," the second problem has to do with the ways in which it neglected the dynamics undermining the popular authority of everyday settings and the agency of ordinary people within them. In the New Deal, ethnic neighborhoods, unions, congregations, lodges, a local press, neighborhood schools, or the YMCA were mediating institutions, places that brought people together for shared purposes. In these, people developed the political skills of dealing with people of diverse opinions. Such local political settings were the everyday nonpartisan root system for larger political systems. They developed the civic energy, attitudes, habits, and implicit understandings of politics as productive activity of citizens themselves, not mainly of professionals. These insights and habits nourished the vitality of the formal political system.

Thus, in a vivid example of the learning that could occur in nonprofessional political settings, Hubert Humphrey traced his famous political career to his father's drug store in Doland, South Dakota. "In his store there was eager talk about politics, town affairs, and religion," he said. "I've listened to some of the great parliamentary debates of our time, but have seldom heard better discussions of basic issues than I did as a boy standing on a wooden platform behind the soda fountain." His father was one of a few Democrats in a town of hundreds of Republicans. "Dad was a Democrat among friends and neighbors who took their Republicanism—along with their religion—very seriously." His drug store functioned as a kind of library, as well as public space. "A druggist in a tiny town in the middle of the continent, American history and world affairs were as real to him as they were in Washington. . . . Time after time, when he read about some political development . . . he'd say, 'You should know this, Hubert. It might affect your life someday.' "[20]

From the 1950s on, powerful forces destroyed these roots, with the result that formal, large-scale political institutions became increasingly detached from everyday life experiences of most people and new hierarchies of power became woven into the fabric of everyday life. In the early twenty-first century, progressives speculated about why George Bush retained such strong support among white blue collar workers, despite policies such as hostility to unions and tax breaks for the rich. "Ironically, the sector of American society now poised to keep [Bush] in the White House is the one which stands to lose the most from virtually all his policies—blue collar men," wrote Arlie Hochschild, a thoughtful chronicler of blue collar culture. Hochschild noted that there has been an enormous shift in political identification over the last thirty years among white blue collar workers, especially pronounced among men, toward the Republicans. Professionals, indeed, are much more likely to oppose the Republican George Bush in a historic reversal of older patterns. She speculates that the reason may be a secret Republican strategy of appealing to white working class males on the basis of their fears of social invisibility, job loss, and terrorist threats. "They felt that everyone else—women, kids, minorities . . . even the spotted owl—were moving up and they were moving down," said one man about his blue collar Republican friends in Maine. "He and his job were on the way down, and he's angry."[21]

Fears of job loss, terror, and declining relative status are doubtless factors in the political shifts. But there is another, populist element as well neglected by progressives: ordinary Americans have innumerable experiences with being made to feel powerless and stupid by liberal professionals.

Meritocracy and the Rise of Conservative Populism

Would it be dangerous to conclude that the corrupt politician himself, because he is democratic in method, is on a more ethical line of social development than the reformer who believes that the people must be made over by "good citizens" and governed by "experts"? The former at least are engaged in that great moral effort of getting the mass to express itself, and of adding this mass energy and wisdom to the community as a whole. (Jane Addams, "On Political Reform")[22]

Jane Addams, leader of the Hull House settlement that worked with new immigrants in Chicago, voiced a striking prophecy at the turn of the last century. She warned about the emergence of a class of professionals, or "experts" as she described them, who saw themselves outside the life of the people. "We are all involved in this political corruption," she argued. "None of us can stand aside; our feet are mired in the same soil, and our lungs breathe the same air."[23]

Addams's warnings about outside experts bore strong resemblance to the concerns of her colleague John Dewey about the detachment of intellectuals and professionals from public life. Dewey's prophetic insights about the structures and systems of organized knowledge power and its democratization through public professionalism are taken up in Chapter 7. Yet the irony is that Dewey himself was to suffer some similar degree of detachment from what Addams called "the common lot" when he left Chicago, went to Columbia Teachers College, and helped establish the *New Republic* magazine. Dewey became one of the architects of a new way of seeing the world. In the pages of the magazine and beyond, politics became highly professionalized and largely equated with the scientific administration of the state. Academics came to write about politics far more than they practiced it in democratic and public terms in their own environments.

As historian Daniel Rodgers has described in *Atlantic Crossings*, the roots of the academic detachment were growing rapidly before the First World War. In the late nineteenth century, American graduate students studying in Europe, fired with the same reformist zeal that moved Dewey, Addams, and others of their generation, absorbed a model of scientific objectivity and policy making in private consultation with political leadership, far removed from public involvement. Young intellectuals had a passionate desire to temper the workings of the marketplace. But, they saw this as an elite activity. As Rodgers put it, "Students of the first German-trained economists . . . establish[ed] new forms of authority by colonizing the social space between university professorships and expert government service." In Rodgers view, "their efforts came to define a central structural element of American progressive politics."[24]

The culture of private consultation among progressives had developed at the turn of the century. It found new authority with the founding of the *New Republic* in 1914. The magazine was a forum for a stunning array of literary, political, and intellectual leaders—within the first year, H. G. Wells, Theodore Dreiser, Conraid Aiken, Harold Laski, Lewis Mumford, and a host of others. However distinguished such contributors were, however, the magazine nevertheless played a significant role in marginalizing amateurs' involvement in politics.

"We all have to follow the lead of specialists," wrote Walter Lippmann, who set much of the intellectual course for the *New Republic*. In his view, a growing body of opinion "looks to the infusion of scientific method, the careful application of administrative technique." In the modern world, science was the model for modern liberal thinking, and "only those will conquer who can understand."[25] The magazine touted the outlook of engineering and the image of the state as a "machine" whose workings were best understood by the application of technique. This technical outlook gained considerable impetus from America's involvement in World War I, which the magazine enthusiastically supported.

The enemy of the war effort, in the editors' views, was inefficiency. By 1918, mobilization had made the piles of undistributed anthracite coal disappear. "It is a triumph of organized units over unorganized individuals," wrote one regular writer. An editorial elaborated, "In the last analysis, a strong, scientific organization of the sources of material and access to them is the means to the achievement of the only purposes by which this war can be justified." By the war's end, the *New Republic* was suffused with scientific triumphalism. The war had taught us, it argued, "to meet the threatened class conflict by placing scientific research at the disposal of a conscious purpose." One unsigned editorial argued the consensus: "the business of politics has become too complex to be left to the pretentious misunderstandings of the benevolent amateur."[26]

Dewey dissented from the elitist sentiments of most other progressives, including his fellow editors at the *New Republic*, in seeking to sustain some concept and practice of public life, most notably in his book, *The Public and Its Problems*. The book was written in response to Lippmann's attack on the very idea of "public." One cannot fairly blame Dewey, as Randolph Bourne did in his famous essay, "Twilight of Idols," writing as a bitter former acolyte, for being responsible for the privatizing culture of technique that prevailed among liberals. Yet Bourne's passionate statement nonetheless held insight. Bourne argued that the defect of the philosophy of "instrumentalism" (Dewey's preferred word for pragmatism) "even when it means adjustment to changing, living experience, is that there is no provision for thought or experience getting beyond itself. . . . You never transcend anything." In Bourne's critique, the "realism" of Dewey had "everything good and wise except the obstreperous vision that would drive and draw men into it."[27]

For Dewey, ordinary men and women, not simply credentialed experts, had a role to play in the creation of what he called "social [or scientific] intelligence." But Dewey also often imagined the future in terms of engineering and mechanical metaphors. "The more one loves peace . . . the more one is bound to ask himself how the machinery, the specific, concrete arrangements, exactly comparable to physical engineering devices, for maintaining peace are to be brought about." The problem with such logic, as John Jordan has observed, is that mechanical "modes of reason, no matter how democratically or generously applied, are inescapably hierarchical." This is, in part, because this way of talk privileges one discourse—technical and scientific—above other ways of talking and thinking, such as narrative voice or the wisdom gained from daily experience and "common sense." It is also "because of the hubris that held there could be only one correct logic."[28]

Engineering and scientific modes of thought, in conventional views at least, are different from politics and a public world of difference. Politics involves a constant interplay and negotiation among different and often clashing interests, values, and ways of looking at the world. There is no one precise and efficient answer. Dewey sought to resist the elite nature of American decision-making. But since conceptual maps make a difference, narrow definitions of politics took a toll. Dewey did not have a sufficiently political understanding of community or society to resist meritocratic trends woven into the heart of the rising professions and intellectual culture.

Dewey's definitional mistake can be found in his address on *Social as Social Centre*. Despite its importance—it helped spawn a movement for schools to become centers of community life across the nation—it also articulated a faulty distinction between politics and society that was widely shared among progressive intellectuals. "I mean by 'society' the less definite and freer play of the forces of the community which goes on in the daily intercourse and contact of men in an endless variety of ways that have nothing to do with politics or government," Dewey argued. He proposed that citizenship needed to be defined more broadly, "to mean all the relationships of all sorts that are involved in membership in a community," and he saw the range of school activities related to citizenship education as wide. But his definition took the political edge off of citizenship.[29]

Without seeing its political side, the idea of community becomes privatized and purified. Moreover, wide-ranging changes of the sort Dewey called for are utopian fantasies. Politics is the master language of decision-making and power wielding in complex, diverse societies. When politics becomes increasingly professionalized, the property of professional politicians, activist lobbies, or ideological mobilizers of the people, most people are shut out of the serious work of deciding about and creating the world. Citizens are reduced to righteous demands, complaints, or peripheral acts as helpers. This was increasingly to be the fate of citizens in both theory and practice.

Despite the arguments of democratic intellectuals such as Dewey, the rise of the experts about whom Jane Addams warned was shrinking explicit attention to politics, replacing it with a technical language of expertise. The growth of an expert class detached knowledge production from communal contexts, experience, and a political sensibility in field after field. It replaced public and political habits and skills with rationality, methodological processes, and a stance of disengaged objectivity. These seemed to offer to an anxious middle class ways of reimposing order on a turbulent environment.[30]

The technocratic strands of liberalism have been a consistent theme throughout the twentieth century, above all the preference for what are called "value-free" techniques that hide values, interests, and power relationships under a scientific and neutral pose that holds professional practice to be entirely absent politics. For instance, the movement for domestic science sought to make housework a profession by applying scientific management techniques adapted from the factory setting to the home environment. "Old functions of child welfare and training have passed over into the hands of sociologists, psychiatrists, physicians, home economists, and other scientists dealing with problems of human welfare," wrote two child guidance experts in 1934. "Through parent education the sum of their experiments and knowledge is given back to parents in response to the demands for help." Employing educational media that ranged from settlement house classes—Addams's warning was about her immediate environment as well as the more distant professional system—to home economics departments in many colleges, domestic science stressed scientifically planned kitchens and sanitation. The knowledge was often the product of deep research and well-tested development. But its dissemination was part of a one-way pattern of expert intervention that conveyed the image of a remade, rational, homogenized society.[31]

In the 1950s, Gunnar Myrdal, a hero of American progressive thought because of his seminal critique of racial segregation, *American Dilemma*, argued that "increasing harmony . . . [is emerging] between all citizens in the advanced welfare state. The internal political debate in those countries is becoming increasingly technical in character."[32] The triumph of technique in social relations and even social change efforts created institutional similarities across political systems. "From the standpoint of the employee," remarked Arnold Toynbee, "it is coming to make less and less practical difference to him what his country's official ideology is and whether he happens to be employed by a government or commercial corporation." State-owned businesses under social democratic regimes and, increasingly, nonprofit organizations as well produced the same patterns of efficiency-minded management and occupational fragmentation that could be found in American corporations. Meanwhile, social policies in welfare states such as Sweden, long a model for progressive intellectuals in America, were if anything further advanced toward a technical rational and radically circumscribed politics. Myrdal, drawing on Swedish experience, depicted welfare-state populations as objects, acted upon by experts and government—"like domesticated animals . . . with no conception of the wild life." All these dynamics illustrate the radical erosion of people's civic agency.[33]

Such patterns of growing professional control affected the formal political system as well. Election campaigns, with their growing reliance on consultants, advertising executives, and other experts are a vivid case in point, but the pattern extended to activists with a commitment to citizen involvement. As Alan Ehrenhalt described in *The United States of Ambition*, progressives with roots in the 1960s movements, for all their emphasis on participatory democracy, were often architects of the demise of everyday, vernacular politics. They ran for office motivated by issues like civil rights, feminism, and environmentalism, and they attacked local parties and backroom deals, but they ended up with little to connect them with the general citizenry other than their television ads. The policy-making skills of politicians may be better than ever, but gridlock and isolation await many officeholders, like Rick Knobe, who won the Sioux Falls, South Dakota, mayoral race against the establishment in 1983, only to find that "I was carrying the whole city on my back. I was an island unto myself."[34]

The ideology of the expert class, meritocracy, rule by the best and brightest, justifies removal from a diverse public life. Late twentieth-century politics dramatized meritocracy. The quote at the chapter's beginning by Zamyatin, an avant-garde Russian writer, suggested a pattern of condescension that has increasingly dominated American institutional and political life—the shift from democracy to bureaucratic state in which experts know best.

Conservatives have found endless resources for populist appeals in this development because the justification of technocracy by justice, evident in policies from busing to comparable worth, splits communities along hidden lines of power. "Decisions have been taken out of the hands of the people," declared George Wallace's campaign platform of 1968. Populism, argued Richard Darman, deputy secretary of the treasury for Ronald Reagan, "is anti-elitist, opposed to excessive concentrations of power, oriented toward fairness and toward a degree of leveling." As Hedrick Smith observed in his coverage of the 1980 election, it was Ronald Reagan who put together a remarkably successful "populist coalition." "Thousands of towns and neighborhoods have seen their peace disturbed by bureaucrats and social planners through busing, questionable educational programs, and attacks on family," said Reagan. In Reagan's words, it was a time for "an end to giantism" and "a return of power to the people."[35]

Conservative populist appeals communicate a broad set of themes about power and everyday life. When George W. Bush declared in 2000 that "I trust the people, my opponent trusts the government," or challenged Al Gore for his expert language, he brought to mind for many encounters of everyday life, from the doctors' waiting room to the teacher parent meeting at school.

Both left and right wing populisms grow from the mass protests and mobilizations of the 1960s, when every issue was posed in Manichean terms of good versus evil. By the early years of the new century, the polarized pattern had reached extremes that reflected deep structural fault lines in American culture. While raising real grievances and describing real patterns of powerlessness, populists of left and right create cardboard cutouts of their opponents based on issue stance or partisan labels or life style (for instance, Democrats are far more likely to be "unchurched"). Sloganeering politics, however satisfying in the short term, does little to address causes of powerlessness.

"Political disagreements, cultural resentment and personal antipathy blend to create a vitriol that is at once a descent of old conflicts but also different," wrote conservative columnist David Brooks in the *New York Times*, noting the unabashed and open hatred voiced by many liberals against George Bush. Brooks also acknowledged the similar pattern in the 1990s in conservatives' reactions to Bill Clinton. "I did say some of these things when it was conservatives bashing a Democrat, but not loudly enough, which I regret." In his view, "the weeds that were once on the edge of public life now threaten to choke off the whole thing."[36]

Yet there were also other strands to the sixties that points toward a different, democratic politics, beyond left and right. Charles Payne's fine book on the civil rights movement in Mississippi, *I've Got the Light of Freedom*, is helpful in thinking about the possibilities of democratic change. Payne makes the distinction between two strands of the movement, the mobilizing approach that led to marches like the March on Washington and the organizing approach of organizers in local communities.[37]

The mobilizing tradition, focused on large, relatively short-term public events, is what is best known. In popular memory, it is often taken as synonymous with the Civil Rights Movement. Civil rights mobilizing saw the world in terms of good and evil. At its best, it had considerable strengths—Martin Luther King, describing the movement as the "children of light" against the segregationist "forces of darkness," was able to connect with the majority of Americans by brilliantly framing the movement in terms of the nation's deepest aspirations for freedom and democracy.

Moreover, the philosophy of nonviolence that he espoused, taught through civil rights organizations such as the Southern Christian Leadership Conference, CORE, and the Student Nonviolent Coordinating Committee, disciplined anger at the evil of segregation, refusing to dehumanize those who espoused racist doctrines.

Yet it was the organizing tradition that led to the transformation of everyday life and interracial power relations in the South. I saw organizing at work myself, as a young field secretary for the Southern Christian Leadership Conference in Florida, Georgia, and North Carolina. By patient, sustained work in communities, organizing approaches created foundations across the South on which the whole movement built. The stories of local people—the towering strength of leaders like Rosa Parks in Montgomery, Fannie Lou Hamer in Mississippi, Thelma Craig in Southern Alabama, Vernon Dobson in Baltimore, or Robert Hayling in St. Augustine—inspired millions of others. Such leadership had developed over decades. The movement created the context in which their public talents and political vision deepened and became widely visible.

An organizing approach changes politics and empowers citizens. It deprofessionalizes politics, taking public action from the realm of soundbytes and slogans. It relocates politics primarily in face to face horizontal interactions among people. Organizing begins with the culture, history, and past work of change in any setting. It has, as its first premise, a respect for the intelligence and talents of ordinary, uncredentialed citizens. It taps diverse self-interests, understanding self-interest in terms of the passions, life histories, relationships, and core values that motivate people. It is attentive to power relationships, from positional leadership to informal networks of leaders who sustain the cultures and relationships in any particular setting.

Organizing, in the richest of cases, conveys at least implicitly an alternative, broader view of politics itself as about the activity of diverse citizens, not professional elites. For all the travails of the political culture, this conception of politics has begun to spread across the nation.

Chapter 3
The Growth of Everyday Politics

The radical is that unique person who actually believes what he says. He wants a world in which the worth of the individual is recognized. He wants the creation of a society where all of man's potentialities could be realized. . . . The American radicals were in the colonies grimly forcing the addition of the Bill of Rights to our Constitution. . . . They were in the first union strike in America and they fought for the distribution of the western lands. . . . They were everywhere, fighting and dying to free their fellow Americans regardless of their race or creed . . . in the shadows of the Underground Railroad . . . in the vanguard of the Populist Party . . . with Horace Mann fighting for the extension of educational opportunities.

—*Saul Alinsky,* Reveille for Radicals

Protest is what people normally think about when they think about citizen politics. Such protests are found on left and right: they include demonstrations against the World Trade Organization and also against abortion clinics. Yet since the 1960s far more sophisticated citizen efforts have developed beneath the radar screen of mainstream attention to protests and related strategies like the canvass, direct mail, or more recently, internet mobilization.

While populist appeals of left or right spread across the spectrum, under the surface of most political commentary a different kind of politics has grown, a politics that is, at once, neither professionally dominated nor partisan and also often more effective. Times of populist ferment create a context for such everyday politics because they raise to explicit attention the role of ordinary people in public life, but everyday politics is not partisan populist politics of left or right. Everyday politics involves people reclaiming politics as an activity owned and engaged in by citizens, in environments that reach far beyond the formal political system. These are the settings where people live, work, learn, worship, and play, social spaces such as neighborhoods, workplaces, families, schools, religious congregations, civic groups and sports clubs. Everyday politics, in the sense used and argued for here, requires learning the skills of negotiation among diverse interests among citizens of relatively equal standing, across partisan and other divisions, to accomplish tasks or to solve problems. In the process, if such settings are explicitly tied to the work of building and sustaining the broader society, people often learn what the political theorist Hannah Arendt called "care for the whole," or in the American idiom, the public good or commonwealth.

As everyday politics has grown in recent years, it begins to form a counterweight or balance with large democratic potential because it creates a dense network of thick horizontal public and political relationships that are not state-centered or based in narrow partisan or issue identities. Everyday politics is the practice necessary to move from a nation of crowds and aggrieved consumers to a nation of publics. Everyday politics will make populism productive.

Everyday politics is visible in unlikely alliances between cattle ranchers and environmentalists in Montana, in community health programs where citizens are recognized as co-producers of health, and in the best community policing efforts, which create sustained partnerships between police officers and community members to address problems like racial profiling and enhance overall neighborhood safety.[1] All such efforts, implicitly or explicitly, use a more horizontal and interactive concept of politics rooted in local cultures, a politics that places the citizen, not the formal political process, at its core, a politics that emphasizes negotiating a plurality of interests, not the mobilization of the like-minded.

The British theorist Bernard Crick's book, *In Defense of Politics*, is used widely by contemporary citizen organizing groups, and his work can be taken as an account of their understanding of politics. Crick defines politics as negotiation and compromise among diverse views and interests, the alternative to violence in complex, modern societies of great heterogeneity, and a deeply civilizing activity. Drawing on Aristotle, Crick argues that politics is about plurality, not similarity. Crick defends politics against a list of enemies including nationalism, technology, and mass democracy, as well as overzealous partisans of conservative, liberal, and socialist ideologies.[2]

Today's citizen organizing groups teach a view of the public world as full of ambiguity, diverse perspectives, and different value systems—a sense of politics that has proven crucial to their political effectiveness. Thus, Richard Wood's *Faith in Action*, a comparative analysis of congregations in the Oakland Community Organization, analyzes the efforts of a priest in one congregation that is highly effective in making change and developing public leadership. The priest educates members in a sophisticated understanding and practice of politics, using liturgy, sermons, songs and other means to convey the complexity of the public world. His message "makes no dramatic call to disobeying authority; indeed, it explicitly calls the congregation to respect the working of legitimate authority. But it does [also] call members to a complex and critical stance vis-à-vis authority, both in the church and in the wider society . . . it rejects both unquestioning subservience and unthinking rebellion. It emphasizes that authority is fallible; therefore it must be exercised responsibly by those holding it and approached critically by those subject to it."[3] In contrast, another congregation that uses a highly personalized, therapeutic, social justice approach and a third that divides the world into fundamentalist categories of good and evil are both far less able to get results or sustain relationships with people of differing views.

Reflecting their focus on plurality, such citizen organizations are highly diverse. Their memberships range from conservative Baptists to liberal Unitarians. They sometimes come from mosques and synagogues, trade unions, schools, and neighborhood groups. They have what is best called a *philosophical* orientation to politics, grounded in democratic and religious values such as respect for minorities' rights, participation, community, concern for the poor, justice, and the sacredness of human life. And they contrast their approach with ideology. "These are normal and commonsensical people . . . not activists, for the most part, not ideologues," says Mike Gecan, organizing director of Metro IAF (Industrial Areas Foundation) in New York, in *Going Public*. Their focus is on learning public skills and solving problems, not righteous posture. "They spend untold hours mastering and using the full range of public arts and skills. They learn how to argue, act, negotiate, and compromise." He calls this "the phonics of the larger language of politics."[4]

A philosophical rather than ideological approach sees democratic potentials in different religious and partisan positions. Its practitioners build relationships with citizens of diverse religious, racial, and ideological backgrounds. They also develop relationships—full of tension and also productive results—with establishment leaders that their members once saw as the enemy.

The scale, effectiveness, and accumulated learning of such citizen networks have recently sparked increasing scholarly attention in studies by Richard Wood, Mark Warren, Paul Osterman, and Dennis Shirley. These organizing networks—IAF and others that build from its approach, such as the Gamaliel Foundation, PICO, and others—include 133 local organizations, made up of approximately 4,000 member institutions, in almost every major metropolitan area. Wood estimates that more than two million families participate, addressing issues of concern to low income and lower middle class populations such as education, policing, working class wages, and medical coverage. In San Antonio, the COPS IAF affiliate group brought hundreds of millions of dollars of infrastructure improvements to the Mexican American barrios. Across Texas, citizen groups worked together to create the Alliance school education reform effort, which has dramatically improved poor children's academic performance, and created what Shirley calls "laboratories of democracy" in which students and parents learn political arts of civic engagement. In Baltimore, the BUILD IAF affiliate won living wage legislation that raised city workers' salaries. In New York, in the wake of the shooting of Amadou Diallo, Metro IAF's efforts made Rudolph Guiliani more responsive to minority community concerns.[5] Such successes make it worth exploring the origins and culture of this kind of organizing, for its strengths and also its limits.

Saul Alinsky and the Origins of Broad-Based Citizen Organizing

In the sixteenth year of the Peloponnesian War, the Greek historian Thucydides recounted, Athens sent an armada of thirty-eight ships and several thousand warriors to the island of Melos in the Aegean sea. Unlike most of the islands, Melos had allied with Athens's chief enemy, Sparta, because, said Thucydides, ancient though distant ancestral ties existed between the two. The Athenians had a simple demand: the Melians must switch sides.

As Thucydides depicted the encounter, the Athenians were unswerving. From the beginning, they spoke a language of power. "We on our side will use no fine phrases," said their envoys. "We recommend that you should try to get what it is possible for you to get, taking into consideration what we both really do think; since you know as well as we do that, when these matters are discussed by practical people, the standard of justice depends on the equality of power to compel and that in fact the strong do what they have the power to do and the weak accept what they have to accept." Thucydides' vivid account sets up an encounter between abstract ideals and power politics that resonates across time and space.

The Melians repeatedly argued on the basis of their hopes, appealing to Athenians' own ideals; a long-range understanding of Athenian concerns for honor and stability in its empire; the possibility of last minute help from Sparta or from the gods; the integrity of their 700-year history. The Athenians referred to the concrete realities of the situation: "do not be like those who, as so commonly happens, miss the chance of saving themselves in a human and practical way." Not eager to destroy or even humiliate the Melians, they suggest that their rule of power politics is to "stand up to one's equals, to behave with deference towards one's superiors, and to treat one's inferiors with moderation." They proposed that alliance need not mean abject surrender: "there is nothing disgraceful in giving way to the greatest city in Hellas when she is offering you such reasonable terms—alliance on a tribute-paying basis and liberty to enjoy your own property." But they were immovable in their demands, while the Melians remained "true to their ideals"—and blind to political reality. The Athenians laid siege. The Melians resisted for a time. Then, recounted Thucydides, "the Melians surrendered unconditionally to the Athenians, who put to death all the men of military age whom they took, and sold the women and children as slaves. Melos they took for themselves, sending out later a colony of 500 men."[6]

Saul Alinsky, dean of the community organizing tradition, used this story as a basic training document. He intended it to shock new trainees. Shock them it did. Alinsky's recruits came to community organizing out of a range of settings—civil rights, religious activism, student involvement, and other causes, flushed with zeal to advocate the cause of the powerless and poor. The eager students would, of course, side with the Melians. They suggested better arguments the Melians might have advanced. They speculated that the islanders may have lost at the moment but won in some sense as lasting martyrs to the cause of liberty. And, inevitably, when asked, they would argue with vehemence that the Melians had done the right thing in defending their autonomy and principles even at the cost of their lives. When IAF teachers called them romantics who were acting like victims, trainees were outraged.

Student outrage was precisely the IAF educators' expectation. They used Thucydides as a dramatic device to help students shift focus from what Alinsky called "the world-as-we-would-like-it-to-be" to the "world-as-it-is." The lesson: the Melians, with their all or nothing approach, failed to appreciate the messy process of conflict, power, self interest, and negotiation that always is the medium for expressing political ideals. By the end of the 1960s, the IAF was teaching about the interactive nature of power in a way that had been largely forgotten through protest politics that counterposed power elite to power to the people, with little understanding of the interaction.

Today, most students still take several days to work through the story's implications, though the staff has noticed a change in tone from the early 1970s. Then, the full ten-day training sessions would often be taken up by debates about whether the Melians should have acted differently.[7]

In those years Saul Alinsky was famous but not popular. His was a discordant note among the voices raised on behalf of or against the tempestuous currents of social change sweeping across the country. Critics were legion, on left and right. "Saul Alinsky has possibly antagonized more people regardless of race, color or creed than any other living American," declared *Time* magazine, in what was perhaps only modest hyperbole. The man was charged with being a communist, fascist, dupe of the Catholic church, racist segregationist, and integrationist determined to "mongrelize Chicago." Ironically, by the late 1960s Alinsky was also sometimes lauded by the very establishment he loved to excoriate. *Crisis in Black and White*, the best-selling book on America's racial conflict by *Fortune* magazine editor Charles Silberman, pointed to Alinksy's Woodlawn Organization in Chicago as "the most important and the most impressive experiment affecting Negroes anywhere in the United States." *Time* argued in a 1970 essay that "it is not too much to argue that American democracy is being altered by Alinsky's ideas."[8]

What Alinsky's supporters most appreciated about the man was his approach to power, which differed significantly from both the dominant culture's obliviousness toward the question and the New Left's ideological posturing and romanticism about the people, alike. As Silberman noted, Alinsky's driving passion was to help poor and minority communities develop the actual, existing resources and capacities they had available, in the face of social service bureaucracies and professionals who, in the name of doing good, infantilized lower classes. "Society stands in the same relation to [welfare recipients] as that of parent to child," said Raymond Hilliard, Director of the Chicago Department of Social Services in 1961. " 'Social uplifting' . . . cannot expect to meet with success unless it is combined with a certain amount of 'social disciplining' just as it is on the preadult levels." Alinsky not only saw views like Hilliard's as "crap"; he believed passionately that the poor could be mobilized in successful revolt against what he termed "welfare colonialism." Throughout his life, Saul Alinsky sought to develop methods that would aid poor people in getting power. This focus marked him as a pivotal figure in the history of everyday politics, the bridge between nineteenth-century movements and our own time.[9]

Saul Alinsky, born in 1909 to an lower middle income Orthodox Jewish family in Chicago, was from the beginning of his organizing career irreverent about conventions. "In little ways I've been fighting the system ever since I was seven or eight years old," he told *Playboy* magazine. "I was the kind of kid who'd never dream of walking on the grass until I'd see a KEEP OFF THE GRASS sign, and then I'd stomp all over it." Such iconoclasm emerged particularly in his fierce scorn for intellectual abstractions that seemed to impose arbitrary categories on everyday life. "Saul thought experts studied communities theoretically but that their approaches were mostly bullshit," recounts Ed Chambers. "Talk about 'social disorganization' and social pathologies with no face to face analysis he saw as irrelevant."[10]

For Alinsky, focusing on the world as it is demanded candor about power: "the power concept must be seen nakedly, without the sordid raiment which serve more as disguises for our own inability or unwillingness or timidity," he told a group of housing officials. Power became the animating principle for Alinsky. "Power is the very essence of life, the dynamic of life," he declared, in language intended to shock and unsettle middle class audiences. Reminding his public that Lord Acton's famous quote was customarily misquoted—Acton had declared that "power tends to corrupt, and absolute power corrupts absolutely"—he argued that "the word power has through time acquired overtones of sinister, corrupt evil, unhealthy immoral Machiavellianism, and a general phantasmagoria of the nether regions." Such derogation of the concept was simply paralyzing: "We prefer to keep it framed in the popular context of corruption and immorality as a defense, an excuse, to avoid entering the arena of conflict." Power was the active principle, the honest rationale for involvement in politics.[11]

For Alinsky, Americans' lack of attention to the methods and theories of practical democracy was a great frustration. "Communists are completely committed to change. They have a developed literature, organizational principles, a Communist philosophy," he complained to a class of priests in 1964. "But we have no literature on [our own theory of democratic] change whatsoever in this country." It was his life's work to rectify the absence in terms that people could understand and put into practice. In particular, he sought to adapt earlier commonwealth, populist themes to the strikingly different world of the twentieth century. Alinsky recalled the temper of the Knights of Labor, populist, and other radical movements at the turn of the century. But he was most directly a child of the 1930s, when older movements' populist themes had come alive again on a massive scale, in new ways. Then, everyday politics taught skills of cooperative action that had been weakened by the fragmented, mobile, technocratic world of the developing twentieth century. The successful movements of the 1930s reconnected politics with everyday life. Alinsky learned from them.

Where union organizing proved effective, it drew on ethnic heritages that shaped workers' identities, reintegrated workplace organizing with the community, and also created a larger public context, where different groups, often bitterly divided, could develop new, horizontal political relationships. Abstract appeals to class solidarity apart from such roots simply did not work. In New York City, for instance, an early twentieth-century generation of Jewish immigrant organizers imbued with European theories of socialism and committed to a purely secular radicalism failed to create any significant popular movement. Only when a new group arrived that was able to blend socialist language with labor organizing and Yiddish culture did Jewish workers become a leading force in the creation of industrial unionism. They led the massive strikes in the garment district of New York: the "uprising of the 20,000" in 1909 and "the uprising of the 50,000" in 1910.[12]

The unions that grew from these uprisings—the International Ladies' Garment Workers Union and the Amalgamated Clothing Workers—laid the groundwork for a new sort of unionism which was to combine large-scale, industry wide action with older themes of civic action. In particular, the wave of industrial militancy which led to the formation of the Congress of Industrial Organizations (CIO) in the mid-1930s began as an outburst of protest against deteriorating working conditions and wage cuts. In response, workers reconnected with and reinvigorated an older heritage of democracy that had largely disappeared in the 1920s. Workers demanded civil rights on the job, branding their opponents "Tories," and stressed active citizenship. Mary Heaton Vorse wrote that "There has been a social awakening through the country, the coming of democracy in towns and industrial valleys where the Bill of Rights, such things as free speech, free assembly and even the right to vote as one pleased had been unknown."[13]

Through the 1930s and 1940s, the vision of commonwealth infused popular movements in both Canada and the United States. Electoral groups like the Nonpartisan League, the Farmer-Labor Parties of the Midwest, the End Poverty in California campaign, the Washington Commonwealth Federation, and the Canadian Cooperative Commonwealth Federation all called for a "cooperative commonwealth" that advocated social control over basic physical and economic community infrastructure (capital sources, roads, bridges, transportation, energy and communications systems, and the like), while it supported voluntary action, small business, and cooperatives. Floyd Olson, Minnesota's fiery Farmer-Labor party governor, described its objectives: "We propose a co-operative commonwealth as an ideal society, under which the government would own and operate public utilities and key industries. . . . The Farmer Labor Party is no enemy of the so-called small business man. It is his champion."[14]

Such language went against the grain of twentieth-century technocracy. But the combination of local organizing with a connection to American democratic traditions lent this vision a believability even in a world of mass institutions. At both national and local levels, key organizers of the CIO had been schooled in practices that led them to combine militant, confrontational, and imaginative tactics with distinctive cultural themes particular to the groups with which they worked. "We made every effort to make the councils part of their neighborhoods," explained Steve Nelson, a leading radical, describing the accumulated lessons that radicals applied in creating Unemployed Councils to work on neighborhood issues and issues affecting the unemployed alike. "For fund raising we tried to stage events that fit into the cultural life of the community. Most councils relied on bingo, raffles, picnics, and block parties, [in Chicago] since the Catholic church was always sponsoring such affairs, they were part of the natural way of life." Harlem council meetings, organized by radicals, began with a prayer, in deference to the black community's strong religious orientation. Council events in the heavily Catholic anthracite coal areas of Pennsylvania included "Hail Marys and Our Fathers."

At the same time, progressive electoral efforts and organizing campaigns also combined particular cultures with larger themes of defense of American democracy and defeat of fascism. Progressive political groups with names like Thomas Paine and Abraham Lincoln appeared across the country. Thomas Jefferson was described as the ancestor of all those "Americans who are fighting against the tyranny of Big Business with the revolutionary spirit and boldness with which he fought the Tories of that day." The African American singer Paul Robeson produced an anthem for the movement, "Ballad for Americans," which lauded the American democratic tradition and recast it in a way that included the full range of immigrant cultures and even atheists and agnostics as "true Americans." "We used to celebrate every holiday and use all our events as ways of educating people about their heritage as Americans," recalled Terry Pettus, a leader in the political movement called the Washington Commonwealth Federation of the 1930s and 1940s. "Later I used to argue with the activists of the Sixties. Why give away symbols like the flag and the Fourth of July?"[15]

Left wing theorists and liberal professionals alike faced huge obstacles to making such practices an explicit part of their theory of social change. Left wing theory systematically eclipsed local cultures and particular identities: the vision of the "new socialist man," required what Frederick Engels called a "radical rupture" with traditions. Liberal technocracy shared with the left a view that the detached observer was the best judge of truth and the most sophisticated analyst of community politics. Saul Alinsky, however, pioneered a different point of view.

After attending the University of Chicago, where he became interested in welfare issues, Alinsky in 1931 joined the staff of the Institute for Juvenile Research, a service agency directed at problems of juvenile delinquency. He worked with its Chicago Area Project, begun by Clifford Shaw. Shaw's model of social problem solving differed notably from the conventional approach to professional service work, which defined professionals themselves as the most important actors and their knowledge as derived largely from a purportedly scientific methodology, detached from communal experience. In contrast, Shaw believed that communities held within themselves the resources and capacities to solve juvenile delinquency. The professional's best role was catalyst and facilitator, not problem solver. Thus Shaw created efforts based on local groups and leaders rather than outside case workers, and that addressed community issues as well as individual behavior. In 1938 Alinsky wrote a paper describing Shaw's approach.

Meanwhile, Alinsky had also begun to do volunteer organizing with the CIO, where he was deeply influenced by the labor leader John L. Lewis, "one of the most outstanding figures of our time," as he put it. At the CIO Alinsky saw first hand the tactics of ridicule, confrontation, and irreverence that organizers had practiced for decades.

Late in 1938, Clifford Shaw assigned Alinsky to Chicago's "Back of the Yards" community, an area of 90,000 impoverished, mostly Eastern European, Catholic immigrants in the shadow of the meat packing companies that Upton Sinclair had made legendary in his book, *The Jungle*. The CIO was working to revive unionism in Back of the Yards, which had been crushed with the defeat of an Amalgamated Meat Cutters strike in 1922. It was a complicated task. Despite academic observers' view of the community as chaotic and unorganized, in fact it had a highly elaborated, though sharply divided structure of interests and groups, based largely around nationalist identities. Working closely with Joe Meegan, a young Irish resident who had already sought to build an area-wide community group, Alinsky helped organize a wide array of groups into the Back of the Yards Neighborhood Council (BYNC) around a campaign to support the union organizing drive.

BYNC brought together priests, small business owners, housewives, youth, communist organizers, the American Legion, and labor rank and file in an unlikely, freewheeling mix. Fifty organizations were represented at the council's first community congress, held on July 14, 1939, Bastille Day, about five months after Meegan and Alinsky started organizing and two days before a scheduled strike by the packing house union. Its founding statement expressed its aspiration to become a new sort of community forum: "This organization is founded for the purpose of uniting all of the organizations within that community known as 'Back of the Yards' in order to promote the welfare of all residents of that community regardless of their race, color or creed, so that they may have the opportunity to find health, happiness and security through the democratic way of life." With community support, the union achieved a significant victory over the packing house industry. Meanwhile, the broad base of BYNC allowed it to fight effectively for a broad range of community initiatives throughout the 1940s, from hot lunch programs to recreation projects that involved teenagers directly in their planning and implementation. A byproduct was sharp decline in juvenile delinquency rates.[16]

In his first book, *Reveille for Radicals*, Alinksy sought to codify the experiences of Back of the Yards and several other communities where he had begun working under the umbrella institute, the Industrial Areas Foundation, which he founded in 1940. The book remains a fascinating compendium of organizing principles, full of psychological insight into the processes of conflict and empowerment of the dispossessed and the importance of drama, action, and participation in grassroots activity. In particular, Alinsky emphasizes the need for popular organizations to be rooted in and reinforce the local community and its institutions.

To accomplish this, Alinksy stressed the need for organizers to investigate and listen to the communities where they are working. "The foundation of a People's Organization is in the communal life of the local people," argues Alinsky. "Therefore the first stage in the building of a People's Orga-nization is the understanding of the life of a community, not only in terms of the individual's experiences, habits, values and objectives but also from the point of view of the collective habits, experiences, customs, controls and values of the whole group, the community traditions." The organizer "should have a familiarity with the most obvious parts of a people's tradi-tions." Moreover, a careful balance was necessary for organizers with a democratic aim. Organizers often disagreed with local traditions or groups, but efforts at democratic transformation and change must always be under-taken in the terms and histories given. "The starting of a People's Organiza-tion is not a matter of personal choice. You start with the people, their tra-ditions, their prejudices, their habits, their attitudes, and all of those other circumstances that make up their lives." This required careful, attentive learning. "To know a people is to know their religions. It is to know the values, objectives, customs, sanctions, and the taboos of these groups. It is to know them not only in terms of their relationships and attitudes toward one another but also in terms of what relationship all of them have toward the outside. . . . To understand the traditions of a people is . . . to ascertain those social forces which argue for constructive democratic action as well as those which obstruct democratic action."[17]

Against the background of the left wing's focus on the new socialist man and liberal technocrats' language of scientific decision-making de-tached from communities, Alinsky's advocacy of rootedness was atypical but not unique. The French theorist Simone Weil, for instance, in *The Need for Roots* made an eloquent case for attention to wellsprings of popular radi-calism. Like Weil, Alinsky's method sought to democratize modern hierar-chies of power, ways of thinking, and the value systems that legitimated such power, using a language that challenged rather than mirrored capital-ism's rootlessness.[18]

Other intellectual traditions and methods parallel his efforts to con-nect analysis to everyday life worlds and experiences. For instance, Alfred Schutz's phenomenological investigations called strong attention to "the world of cultural objects and social institutions into which we are all born, within which we have to find our bearings and with which we have to come to terms." As developed by later social theorists like Peter Berger and Thomas Luckmann, the distinguishing feature of the everyday world is its shared, taken-for-granted quality. "It is simply there, as self-evident and compelling facticity, with its own spatial and temporal dimensions—a range of rhythms, sounds, standards." The paradigmatic relationship in ev-

eryday worlds is face-to-face, multidimensional and fluid: "it is compara-
tively difficult to impose rigid patterns upon face-to-face interaction. Whatever patterns are introduced will be continuously modified through the
exceedingly variegated and subtle interchange of subjective meanings that
goes on." However, even these relations are structured through stereotypes:
"typificatory schemes," in Berger and Luckmann's frame, "in terms of
which others are apprehended and 'dealt with.'" But in concrete encounter,
there is always more opportunity to break down stereotypes and discover
other and more complex "truths": "in the face-to-face situation, the other's
subjectivity is available to me through a maximum of symptoms." Of
course, there are many sorts of relations in everyday life worlds, ranging
from those "with whom I frequently and intensively interact . . . my 'inner
circle,' as it were," to people one encounters in only public and routinized
encounters, like the traffic cop or the newspaper vender. And there are excursions beyond the experiences of everyday life; vacations, religious events,
or encounters with art, science and philosophy are some examples. But language, while it functions to bridge different zones and times and experience, always tends to reincorporate difference into everyday life with its
pragmatic motives and frameworks.[19]

Alinsky's emphasis on listening attuned his organizers to the everyday
life worlds such theorists identified. But phenomenology's theoretical formulations and its offshoot, ethno-methodology, tend to a static, given, and
conservative rendering of experience. They pay little attention to mecha-
nisms of democratic change, nor do they suggest ways of separating out
those aspects of experience which are historically and culturally relatively
static from those which express broader human predicaments reaching
across time and location, and which can be made into occasions for public
action. Though Schutz and others argue that interpretative schemes are
shared products, the result of reciprocal interactions between interpreter
and those being interpreted, in actual fact they presented themselves as detached social scientists, with the pretended value neutrality and ironic dis-
tance from everyday life that such detachment suggests. Berger's focus on
everyday life worlds—expressed in his concept of mediating structure—has
had enormous impact on American conservatism, leading to a powerful critique of abstract and decontextualized ways of thinking, but it also defined
everyday settings in very conservative ways, as buffers against the winds of
modernity. There is little sense in Berger's arguments that people might use
and adapt these settings as instruments for empowerment to shape the
larger world.[20]

Alinsky's stress throughout *Reveille* is on self-help and self-activity, confidence-building, collective success, and dramatic encounter, all for the sake of popular empowerment. "It is impossible to overemphasize the enormous importance of people's doing things themselves," Alinsky wrote in his chapter, "Psychological Observations on Mass Organization." "The objective is never an end in itself," he continued. "The efforts that are exerted in the actual earning of the objective are part and parcel of the achievement itself. This is so important that the actual definition of the objective itself is determined by the means whereby the objective was obtained. . . . What you get by your own effort is really yours. It is a part of you, bound and knit to you through the experiences that you have undergone in securing it."[21]

By the late 1950s, Alinsky had gathered a group of close associates. The group of organizers included Fred Ross, Ed Chambers, Richard Harmon, Nicholas Von Hoffman, Tom Gaudette, and Father John Egan. This group created the famed organizations for which Alinsky gained visibility, especially the Woodlawn Organization in Chicago, Community Service Organization in California, and FIGHT in Rochester.[22]

Alinsky's great talent was as a practical theorist. His approach to organizing evolved over the decades, building on the methods developed in the BYNC. In simple terms, his model divided cities into two systems, the neighborhood and the "enemy" power structure outside. Poor, minority, and working class communities, in his analysis, were victimized by the affluent, powerful, downtown-connected interests who bestowed social services and economic largess on the already privileged areas of the city. Within neighborhoods, the goal was to create an organization of existing community institutions. As for unaffiliated individuals, Alinsky pointed to pragmatic power concerns: poor communities had to start by unifying what "pockets of power" existed. Other approaches, he argued, simply didn't generate as much power. In fact, this institutionally grounded organizing has, over a period of several decades, proven far more effective in mobilizing poor communities than have competing models of citizen mobilization. For instance, the Association of Community Organizations for Reform Now, or ACORN, a network that has avoided organizing through institutions and sought out previously disconnected community residents as core leadership, has been plagued by rapid turnover in leadership and transience of affiliates.[23]

Alinsky's people's organizations generated experiences of collective success, rare in poor people's lives, which built feelings of confidence and dignity. They also led often to improvements in people's actual situations. If skillfully put together, they delivered real goods like jobs, housing, city services, and other benefits for communities that had been left behind by urban growth.[24]

Yet Alinsky's approach also had major limitations, problems that prevented it from generating larger democratic change. When pushed, Alinksy described himself exclusively as a "radical democrat" or "urban populist," never as a theorist, even a practical one. Alinsky's often professed hatred of ideology or dogma—sets of fixed principles or ideals, which he believed undermined the flexibility and practicality of those committed to serious change—was generalized to a disdain for discussion of the larger philosophy of organizing. This lack of attention to the larger discourse of political culture ironically disregarded his own contributions, embodied in his writings and lectures: namely, the power of organized ideas, or theory that generalizes from experience. It also overlooked the larger democratic culture of the 1930s on which he drew—a culture that was not simply given, but created by an array of political and organizing initiatives.

In his later years, Alinsky discounted even the democratic language he had once used, as well as the relevance of religious themes, with caustic, often sardonic quips. In a 1965 interview, Alinsky said, in what was to become a legendary quote, that he never talked to religious leaders about their values, ideals, or convictions because of the fundamental organizing precept that organizing must be grounded in people's everyday worlds: "It would be outside of their experience, because Christianity and Judeo-Christianity are outside of the experience of organized religion." When long time associate Father Egan suggested more discussion of religious values in organizing the Woodlawn Organization in Chicago, Alinsky remarked, "you take care of the religion, Jack. We'll do the organizing."[25]

His approach, drawing on the practicality, power, and realism of 1930s organizing, always preeminently stressed beginning with "the world as it is." But, in fact, the world of the 1930s included the power of a vibrant political culture, which infused his writings and arguments with energy and compelling appeal to broad audiences. By the 1960s, in reaction against what he saw as the hyperbolic rhetoric and posturing of the New Left, Alinsky's depiction of the world-as-it-is denuded political life of cultural and normative dimensions almost entirely: "Once we have moved into the world as it is then we begin to shed fallacy after fallacy." In the world-as-it-is, as he saw it, "the right things are done only for the wrong reasons," "constructive actions have usually been in reaction to a threat," "judgment among alternatives is made on the basis not of the best but of the least bad," "irrationalities play a significant part," and "morality is to a significant degree a rationalization of the position which you are occupying in the power pattern at a particular time."[26]

As a result, his groups produced local power, but did not contribute much to cultural change, either in the organizational members of community groups or in the larger society and his view of citizen politics was, overtly at least, highly instrumental. Organizations typically lasted only four or five years. Leadership was often concentrated among a few key male leaders. The "Alinskyite method" became synonymous with an "anti-ideological" tone that spurned discussion of "power for what" or the values and meanings that informed activities. Sometimes the results were deeply discouraging to Alinsky himself. By the 1950s, the BYNC had reversed its earlier commitments to fighting discrimination and championed restrictive racial covenants. This violated Alinsky's principles, to his dismay. But his approach offered no way to address the problem.[27]

Organizing After Alinsky

After Alinsky's death in 1972, organizers and local leaders in the IAF network continued to build on the "organizing tradition" (and found, over time, an affinity with this tradition in civil rights; Charles Payne's book, *I've Got the Light of Freedom*, is now widely used). Instead of emphasizing a mobilizing approach—intimated by Alinsky's last book, *Rules for Radicals* —they deepened organizing. Ed Chambers, the new IAF director, was far more relational and concerned about the long-term well-being of organizers themselves than Alinsky had been. He emphasized the idea of organizing as a democratic profession, with decent salary and benefits and time off for private life.[28]

IAF also explored new ways to ground the organizing process in more substantial and multidimensional connection with community institutions. This meant taking seriously the real beliefs of participants—first in local churches of mainstream Catholic and Protestant orientation and later in synagogues and mosques. These developments gave rise to what they called "value based organizing."

Value based organizing wedded the struggle for power to communal fabric and cultural traditions. Citizen politics acquired explicit content— the rationale for gaining power was to give clout to religious and democratic values that the dominant world marginalized—but citizen politics also differed from ideology, or a preset blueprint that divided the world into believers and nonbelievers. The IAF organizing approach reached more deeply into the community's social and institutional fabric than it ever had before. In the process, it drew in more conservatives. It also established organizations on the basis of what organizers called "moderates" through attention not only to visible public issues but also to concrete needs of institutions like religious congregations. San Antonio COPS, the organization that pioneered this approach, helped local parishes with tangible concerns such as membership roles, fund drives, liturgy, and music.

In the process organizational leadership shifted, along with the definition of leader. Leaders in community organizing had traditionally been the more visible public actors, typically male, who had championed causes like an end to racial discrimination and police brutality. In the new organizing, the key leaders were the more invisible tier of community members, most frequently women, who worked behind the scenes to keep school PTAs going, run day to day activities in churches, and the like. COPS organizers called such leaders "community sustainers" or moderates, contrasting them with activists or liberals. "COPS built on the basis of PTA leaders, parish council members, stalwarts of the church guilds," described Sister Christine Stephens, lead organizer of COPS in the early 1980s. "Not the politicos, the people who have wheeled and dealed." Stephens described this as a fundamental shift in the social basis of organizing. "This approach builds around the people who have sustained the community. For example, these are women whose lives by and large have been wrapped up in their parishes and their children." The new emphasis created wide change in both individuals and communities. "What COPS has been able to do is to give them a public life and a public visibility, to educate, to provide the tools whereby they can participate in the political process."[29] In the process politics itself became redefined to put citizens back at the center.

As these groups experienced growing successes and thought about long-range purposes, they added a more explicit emphasis on the process of teaching politics itself, suggested by Stephens. They came to describe themselves as "schools of public life." In the process, they also undertook projects, like infrastructure improvement, that benefited the whole community, while still advancing the interests of poor, minority, and working class communities. These elements together greatly strengthened the public side of organizing.

"Schools of public life," in the IAF view, are self-funded citizen organizations where people learn the arts and skills of a multidimensional and citizen-centered politics. The new IAF network forges a thoughtful, constantly evaluated political practice out of the tension between the world as it is and the world as it should be. It not only teaches specific political information and skills; it adds a strong public relationship-building dimension that helps re-center politics among citizens. IAF affiliates are legendary for not letting politicians dominate in their meetings; they hold elected leadership accountable, on their terms. Public relationship-building and understanding self-interests depend on the widespread practice of one on ones, a continual process of interviewing that builds on Alinsky's emphasis. Leaders interview each other, across lines of difference in faith, culture, and income level, to discover what passions and core concerns motivate people. This process greatly thickens citizen organizations, in comparison with older Alinsky style groups. In teaching the complexity of others from different backgrounds, it facilitates a key skill, what they call "disciplining anger," or recognizing that even in the midst of sharp conflicts it is important to keep longer term relationships in mind. The stress on core concepts also generates a dynamic intellectual life, creating a practical theory of action by constantly employing and refining concepts like power and public life, self-interest, judgment, imagination, and leadership. Such concepts, in turn, are tied to discussion of the democratic and religious values and traditions that inform and frame their efforts—justice, concern for the poor and the dignity of the person, and participation. All these emphases create a close attention to the civic cultures of the organizational members, mainly congregations.

As these groups have evolved they also stress governance. The IAF and other broad-based citizen groups believe that it is not sufficient simply to protest; to exert power on a continuing basis, citizens must also assume an important measure of responsibility for their communities' basic public goods. Gerald Taylor, IAF's southern director, describes this as "moving into power." "Moving into power means learning how to be accountable," said Taylor. Accountability involves changes in identity as well as practice. "It means being able to negotiate and compromise. It means understanding that people are not necessarily evil because they have different interests or ways of looking at the world."[30]

IAF leaders and organizers sometimes refer to this approach as "making democracy work." They also call it "standing for the whole." "We who lead and organize with the Industrial Areas Foundation may be considered presumptuous for talking about 'standing for the whole'. . . . Yet, we do presume to describe our commitment to, our knowledge of, and even our ability to stand for the whole."[31]

By building organizations self-consciously on relational leaders and giving sustained attention to developing the public and political skills of such leadership, the IAF and other networks have developed effective methods to rebuild often devastated and fragmented communities. In the last few years, leaders have sought to build on local successes to articulate—and influence—a larger politics. Thus, in 2000 IAF leaders sought to meet with and impact the issue agenda of both the Bush and Gore campaigns. Yet here the limits also become vivid.

Limits of Practice and Theory

Citizen organizing continues to work out of an old fashioned populist analysis. "Power . . . the ability to act . . . still comes in two basic forms, organized people and organized money," argues Metro IAF's Mike Gecan. By putting organized people in relationship to organized money these groups develop patterns of power far more interactive than zero-sum notions of power exchange. Yet this framework also neglects power based on control over the flow of information, communications, and professional practices—what might be summarized as "organized knowledge." Sometimes the neglect is obvious, even dramatic. Gecan's power analysis of people and money is confounded by his own stories from New York, where coverage in the *New York Times* or local network television has often proven crucial to success.[32]

Sometimes the neglect of knowledge power is subtle. Gecan lauds "relational workers," service providers such as teachers and health providers, but he sees them as "pre-political." This view ignores the power dynamics in such occupations, forgetting Alinsky's own insights about the way the helping professions disempower people by turning them into passive clients. It also ignores the deep concerns of these professionals and others in the middle class, eclipsing the hidden discontents and cultural politics of a consumer culture.[33]

Paul Osterman illustrates these limits in his new book, *Gathering Power: The Future of Progressive Politics in America.* Osterman worked closely for several years with Ernesto Cortes, director of the Southwestern IAF and a major architect of the post-Alinsky IAF organizing strategy, to understand their process and to translate what they do to other settings and to American politics broadly. He describes superbly the confidence and public capacities that working class people develop through the IAF. But he is stymied by what he sees as virtually insurmountable obstacles to suburban organizing.

Osterman writes that suburban people "seem to lack any driving self interest or anger, which are the two motivating factors for IAF." Interviewing ministers and members in suburban congregations affiliated with IAF organizations, he observes that "the same [suburban] congregation that can only generate a handful of IAF leaders sponsors outreach days when five or six hundred people turn out to volunteer at social service agencies, staff food banks, and the like." Osterman identifies two other obstacles. "One is simply that people are too busy. The pastors constantly described congregations in which parents work sixty-hour weeks and travel a good deal, and when they are in town they shuttle their children from one activity to another." The second obstacle is subtle. "The language of power turns off many middle class people." He believes that the reason is that suburbanites are powerful and happy. "The easy reply [to fear of power] is that when people already have power (even if they do not fully recognize it), and when they are comfortable and have few difficult issues to confront them, it is easy to abhor contestation and, in fact, it is in their self-interest to take this position."[34]

Such stereotypic thinking fails to apply the cultural listening approach of citizen organizing to suburban life. In particular, it neglects the dynamic that makes such organizing so successful: making private concerns into public, actionable issues. Osterman, in making the assumption that middle class suburbs are powerful, largely problem-free, and without strong self-interests, succumbs to the dominant consumer ideals that equate life success with material possessions and acquisition. Yet this is precisely the version of the American dream about which Susan Faludi and the 1997 Kettering study found such widespread cultural discontent. Osterman here reflects a key limit of citizen organizing: it has emerged from economically and racially disadvantaged communities that are angry at the economic and social injustices they experience. Indeed, anger at injustice runs as a central thread through this organizing, which makes it disciplined, directed, and constructive. In fact, one major book on the Texas IAF by Mary Beth Larkin, is called *Cold Anger*. But anger at economic and social injustice is insufficient to tap hidden discontents—the self-interests—of suburban, professional, and other middle class or upper middle class communities. Broad-based citizen organizations impose a poor and working class view of the world on a middle class reality. In so doing, they neglect the deep cultural dynamics shaping—and afflicting—middle class life.

A far different view of American middle class life and its discontents emerges from a framework of politics that emphasizes the public work of building a democratic way of life. For instance, we have found that using one on one interviews about professionals' work surfaces widespread, organizable discontent in many settings. When Edwin Fogelman and I did interviews among faculty at the University of Minnesota in 1998, we found issues similar to those that Susan Faludi discovered. Men and women alike said that the institution's public purpose is eroding, publicly engaged scholarship is devalued, departmental communities are undermined by a star system, and marketplace values are replacing liberal education.

These discontents at the University of Minnesota, like hidden discontents in suburbs and professional settings elsewhere, suggest wider possibilities for democratic renewal than simply distributive politics. Turning private issues into public questions means emphasizing and developing the public side of suburban communities and also the public dimensions of professional work. Thus, as described in Chapter 7, one dynamic that Osterman lists as an "obstacle" to politics—frenetic over-scheduling—turns out to be a potent issue for organizing.

To get to such issues and to democratize organized knowledge systems requires a reconceptualization of politics. Most particularly, it requires attention to the productive, world-building dimensions of politics—what can be called *work* with public meanings, public conditions, and public outcomes. This theme is slighted in broad-based citizen organizing, and actively opposed in participatory democratic, deliberative, and civil society theory.

Chapter 4
Citizenship as Public Work

Work: from IndoEuropean base, werg, to do, act, from which is derived in
Greek, ergon, action, work; and organon, tool or instrument.
Noun. Physical or mental effort to do or make something; purposeful ac-
tivity; labor; toil . . . something that one is making, doing or acting upon.
—Webster's New World Dictionary

If ever therefore your rights are preserved, it must be through the virtue
and integrity of the middling sort, as farmers, tradesmen, & c. who despise
venality and best know the sweets of liberty.
—"Publius," for Philadelphia artisans, 1772

Everyday politics, spread by broad-based citizen organizing into
community and civic institutions, represents an implicit challenge to theories of citizenship that neglect power and politics, and also to theories that
oversimplify cultural dynamics with accounts of dominant culture as
monochromatically oppressive. Conventional civil society theory, an approach that now shapes the civic agenda with its emphasis on citizens as
volunteers, is an example of the former. Left wing theory, which seeks to
find in civil society a space for radical opposition to cultural patterns, exem-
plifies the latter.

Civil society theory's influence vividly illustrates the power of ideas to
structure resources and define themes. Major foundations have civil society
divisions that distribute hundreds of millions of dollars to volunteer activity. Government agencies give time off to their employees so that they can
volunteer and thus do citizenship. America's living presidents gathered in
1997 at the Summit on Volunteerism to praise the idea. George W. Bush
made voluntarism a centerpiece of his 2000 presidential campaign.

In recent years, theorists and practitioners of democracy have added deliberation to voluntarism as a defining activity of civil society. The American Political Science Association made deliberation a central theme of its 1994 convention. Sheldon Hackney, chair of the National Endowment for the Humanities, took up the idea with a National Conversation project, aimed at creating space for public discussion across lines of difference. And creative and practical experiments have multiplied. The American Health Decisions network stimulates citizen deliberation about health care policy and value questions through forums held in nineteen states. The National Issues Forums, facilitated by the Kettering Foundation and the Public Agenda Foundation, bring thousands of citizens together each year to explore different perspectives on critical public issues. Public or civic journalism projects use the media to bring citizens more directly into the conversation of democracy.

Civil society's emphasis on voluntarism and deliberation adds useful dimensions to conventional liberal theory's concepts and practices. Much of the civil society agenda has merit. Volunteers' service projects often make important civic contributions. A focus on character and values frequently prompts needed public debate. Around the world, civil society provides a crucial counterweight to overweening governmental claims and power. And at its best, civic deliberation fosters public judgment, what Immanuel Kant called the *sensus communis,* or common sense of the people. This, in the richest sense, has kinship with politics: interactions with people outside our own immediate worlds.

Yet there are serious problems with the prevailing civil society approach to citizenship. Simply, the dominant civil society approach, descending from the flawed distinction made by John Dewey and other progressive intellectuals, depoliticizes citizenship while it professionalizes politics. It assigns politics to the arena of government, consultants, lobbyists, and experts, leaving ordinary citizens as helpers on the side. It also separates production, which it locates in the economic sector, from public life. As a result, citizenship is purified, stripped of power, interests, and the institutional foundations needed for serious civic work; politics is defined in distributive terms associated with government, as who gets what; and the actual process of creating the what—our public wealth—disappears from view. The world threatens to become entirely privatized and the market to spin out of control.

I begin this chapter with a discussion of the strengths and weaknesses of the theory of civil society. I then offer a third conception of citizenship, beyond the voter and protestor of liberalism or the volunteer and deliberator of civil society, or even the older participating citizen descended from Greek theory. This is the concept of citizenship based on public work, the political activity of citizens as co-creators of democracy. This concept also enriches politics by highlighting its productive, world building dimensions.

The Democratic Origins of Civil Society

In recent years, when civil society and related concepts (such as mediating structures) first reappeared widely and with significant political impact, they emerged to address power questions—dynamics that undermined the authority and the agency of citizens in modern society. This usage of civil society differed from earlier meanings.

The concept of civil society first appeared in the eighteenth century. Scottish intellectuals such as Adam Ferguson, David Hume, and Adam Smith used civil society to describe the broad social and economic changes they witnessed around themselves. For these writers, civil society consisted of egoistic commerce, specialization, and self-interested pursuits. It described a shift from aristocratic norms of courtesy, honor, and social obligations. Civil society, said Ferguson, the first writer in English to propose a history of the term, conveyed a loss of social unity. "Society is made to consist of parts, of which none is animated by the spirit of society itself." Adam Smith believed that private self-interest would advance the material well-being of all (his famous "invisible hand"); he also worried it would lead to a "society of strangers."[1]

Hegel built on such arguments. For Hegel, civil society was a kind of social space, "the stage of difference which intervenes between the family and the state." Hegel included work (commerce) as well as institutions that we now label "voluntary" in his map of civil society. In his treatment, the growth of civil society was unambiguously negative. He saw the "rush toward equality" inherent in civil society as leading to ever greater consumption.[2]

The concept has had a lively history and usage since then. It reappeared in the 1970s and 1980s with an explosive force, emblazoned on the banners of sweeping social movements—a rallying cry for strands of conservatism and populism in the United States, and for opposition to authoritarian states in Eastern Europe, Africa, Asia, and elsewhere. Several currents of democratic thought and action associated with the concept are worth noting because they need to be integrated into a critique of current usages.

First, the social terrain called civil society often fosters the creation of free spaces that are seedbeds for democratic movements and alternative ways of seeing the world, beyond the commonplaces and inequalities woven into everyday life. The concept of free spaces challenges ideas of citizenship and politics that celebrate social solidarity, social trust, and communities without conflict, but the concept also offers an alternative to intellectual fashions that view culture as simply oppressive and treat relatively power-less groups of people mainly in terms of their victimhood and their false consciousness.

Modern critical theorists have posed the question, how citizens, be-mused by the socialization dynamics of modern capitalism, can ever come to see themselves as other than free laborers or free consumers, even though their apparent free choice itself functions to hide the oppressive relations of society. Karl Marx had made the point about mystification—what he also called false consciousness—in *The German Ideology*: "Thus, in imagination, individuals seem freer under the dominance of the bourgeoisie than before, because their conditions of life seem accidental: in reality, of course, they are less free, because they are more subject to the violence of things."[3]

Prevailing intellectual fashions, updating such arguments in compara-tive and anti-colonial terms and drawing on cultural theorists of power such as Frantz Fanon, Michel Foucault, Edward Said, and Claude Lévi-Strauss, have focused on the ways in which cultural norms and practices operate in the spaces of everyday life to make oppressive assumptions seem normal and inevitable. Dominant cultural ideas, including those generated by the work of intellectuals themselves, shape, define, and circumscribe the life worlds and possibilities of ordinary people. For instance, the philoso-pher Rick Turner in South Africa keenly observed how the apartheid system dramatized the "naturalization" of oppressive racial domination. Apartheid seemed self-evidently the way things are to whites and even to many blacks, whose experiences in virtually every institution from family to church, from school to media, constantly reinforced white privilege and power.[4]

Cultural theorists of power have brought important attention to pre-viously invisible power dynamics. The problem is that, when left wing intel-lectuals develop a theory of what is to be done in response, they radically oversimplify the operations of cultural power. The result is a culturally es-tranged and alienated politics. Jean-Paul Sartre's strategy of what he called "transcendence," or the act of standing outside prescribed roles and the commonplaces of culture with a sharply critical eye, can be taken as em-blematic of the general stance of critical scholars. This stance is widely hostile toward rooted institutions such as religious congregations, ethnicity, family, and ties to place, as well as to the broader cultural traditions and symbols that constitute a sense of peoplehood. The left wing view of liberated consciousness as a process of radical separation from roots and traditions lies behind Michael Harrington's vision of a "rational, humanist moral code to replace traditional moral values." It is what Ralph Miliband meant when he argued that "the Marxist notion of a 'most radical rupture' with traditional ideas signifies a break with all forms of tradition." It is the view of social change succinctly summarized by Stanley Aronowitz in his essay entitled, appropriately enough, "The Working Class: A Break with the Past." According to Aronowitz, all particular identities of "race and nationality and sex and skill and industry" are obstacles to the development of genuinely oppositional, radical consciousness.[5]

In contrast, a new generation of social historians concerned with the actual development of popular movements—how it is that ordinary people, steeped in experiences of subordination, develop the courage, spirit, and confidence to assert themselves—has produced a rendering of the roots of democratic movements far more nuanced than the views of alienated intellectuals. Social history especially draws attention to the conflicted, contradictory quality of community settings and cultural traditions, full of oppositional currents, democratic elements, and insurgent themes as well as hierarchical and oppressive ones. Social historians have richly described the ways in which powerless groups draw inspiration from cultural elements that critical intellectuals write off as part of a monochromatically oppressive system.

Sara Evans and I, building on such social history, combined ideas of public space and freedom for democratic self-organization in the concept of free spaces, a concept we argued is a crucial dimension to any adequate theory of democratic social change. Free spaces, rooted in everyday life settings, are places in which powerless people have a measure of autonomy for self-organization and engagement with alternative ideas. Thus, for instance, the historian E. P. Thompson, especially in his great work *The Making of the English Working Class*, described places such as taverns and sectarian churches in which working people found space for intellectual life and democratic self-organization, separate from the gentry and the crown.[6] Free spaces are places where people learn political and civic skills. They are also culture-creating spaces where people generate new ways of looking at the world. In free spaces, people simultaneously draw upon and rework symbols, ideas, themes, and values in their traditions and the culture to challenge conventional beliefs. On a broad level of change, free spaces suggest the importance of what might be called the prophetic imagination as an alternative strategy to a stance of the outside, estranged critic, which finds in a society's central motifs and themes material for a radical different future than the world as it is.[7]

We argued that free spaces were at the base of every broad democratic movement in American history, from populist Farmers' Alliances of the 1880s, as Lawrence Goodwyn shows, to labor struggles of the 1930s, from women's and feminist movements to modern community organizing. They have been at the heart of the African American freedom tradition, in ways well described by Frederick Harris. Such democratic movements show how complex are the power relationships of culture within and across societies. Subterranean spaces for political agency and culture-making can be found even in settings that seem overwhelmingly oppressive. Thus, for instance, African American slaves in the American south found such space for self-definition and for insurgent cultural alternatives to conventional view of American democracy in the midst of extremely brutal circumstances. Christian religious services and practices were originally taught to slaves by slave owners in an effort to break their ties with African roots and socialize them into passive, docile roles. Yet Christianity provided rich materials for strategies for everyday resistance (for instance, work songs and Gospel music) as well as far-ranging radical democratic visions of a transformed racial and political order. Martin Luther King and others built on this insurgent heritage to claim and to transform definitions of American democracy, freedom, and citizenship.[8]

These dynamics also help throw into relief other flaws in conventional thinking about politics that revolve around the idea of the modern, progressive state as necessarily a liberating force. Civil society re-emerged in theory and practice as a popular counterweight to the power of the progressive state. Real world experiences of socialism and communism dramatized how the modernist project, when wedded to enormous state power and weak sources of alternative popular action, can have disastrous consequences. Especially, democratic movements that fought totalitarian governments in the name of civil society put the concept at the center of attention.[9]

A third root of the concept has been the effort to find alternative sources of power to simplistic assumptions that the logic of freedom entails cultural uprootedness embedded in ideas like the new socialist man, or the cosmopolitan universal or global citizen. Many theorists and advocates of civil society also use the concept of civil society to challenge the claims of overweening professional authority. They have drawn attention to the everyday, the vernacular, and the commonplace, and also to historically rooted, particular identities. They argue that the modernist imagination, reflected in many strands of post-Enlightenment politics, treats ordinary citizens' lives with disdain and condescension at best, hostility at worst.[10]

In this critique, the modernist imagination has been fed by an uncritical celebration of science and technology as the highest form of knowledge and the key to human emancipation. Scientific epistemology exults the detached, analytic observer as the highest judge of truth and the most effective problem-solver. This approach is in conflict with communal common sense, folk traditions, and craft knowledge mediated through everyday life experience. This is not to say that science is wrong and folk ways are right, but rather to stress that multiple forms of knowledge are valuable in politics. Celebrating the scientific expert as the singular actor marginalizes the amateur.[11]

The fourth root of current civil society theory, of which Jürgen Habermas is perhaps the leading theorist, stresses the idea of a public sphere of mutual communication and deliberation. Communicative theory for Habermas holds potential to "locate a gentle, but obstinate, a never silent although seldom redeemed claim to reason, a claim that must be recognized de facto whenever and where ever there is to be consensual action."[12] Habermas grounds his theory in the emergence of a deliberative public sphere.

Opinion in this sense is an integrative process. By gaining insight from the perspectives of others, individuals' views become more multidimensional and nuanced. Immanuel Kant captured this in his contrast between the *sensus privatus*—views that are only formed through privatized or narrow experience—and the *sensus communis*, common or public sense. The former he also called "cyclopean thinking," referencing the one-eyed creature of Greek mythology. For Kant, it was entirely possible to be a learned cyclops: "a cyclops of mathematics, history, natural history, philology and languages." But without the "enlarged thought," or public judgment, that comes from engagement with other viewpoints and perspectives, the learned person fails to think "philosophically": in Kant's terms, as a member of a living human community. Kant argued that the most severe insanity was that defined by *sensus privatus*, those cut off from *sensus communis*, who had radically lost touch with public conversation.[13]

In this notion of public opinion during the late eighteenth and nineteenth centuries, Habermas locates the interplay between reformers' political aspirations and far-reaching social and economic transformations in European society. Long-distance trade and commerce undermined the household economy and created market pressures that reworked political relations and created new "public knowledge" across communal and even national boundaries. A politicized and self-conscious language of public action and public opinion was closely connected, moreover, to the development of a vibrant urban culture of debate and discussion that formed in a new spatial environment of the public sphere: lecture halls, museums, public parks, theaters, meeting houses, opera houses, coffee shops and more. Changes included a social information infrastructure based on the press, publishing houses, lending libraries and literary societies.[14]

American educational and media institutions have similar roots and purposes. In the nineteenth century, the expansion of public education was justified as essential to a well-informed citizenry. Newspapers commonly described their mission as creating informed public discussion of current issues. Similarly, public libraries were seen as arsenals of democracy, providing popular information and a public space for deliberation.

The deliberative approach has generated many creative insights. Yet this version of the public sphere also has major limits, often acknowledged by its advocates. As Cornel West puts it, "gallant efforts to reconstruct public-mindedness in a balkanized society of proliferating identities and constituencies seem far-fetched, if not futile."[15] These limits flow from separating the deliberative public from questions of power, interest, and practical motive, a problem also found in contemporary civic theories.

The Limits of Civil Society

Civil society has become a bandwagon on which intellectuals and politicians of all persuasions now ride. Reports on civil society have appeared all over.[16]

Civil society as now advanced is a contraption of ironic contradictions. On the one hand, it has roots in broad democratic movements, supports democratic deliberation, and expresses concern about modern culture and the power of the colonizing state. On the other hand, as it presently functions, it is substantially drained of democratic and political content. One major flaw is that it is separated from work.

Civil society in its current usages arose as an effort to generalize from recent social movements in the West and from the democracy movements of 1989. This effort has had descriptive value in highlighting sites where democratic experiments often emerge. The problem is that it erroneously *locates* active citizenship in voluntary associations. It confuses descriptive and normative projects and implicitly opposes citizenship to work. Democratic initiatives, wherever they begin, cannot be confined by the social geography of voluntary groups or even community if they are to have much impact. Indeed, the possibility of democracy on a large scale depends on crossing such boundaries and revitalizing the public dimensions of many settings including workplaces.

Jean L. Cohen and Andrew Arato's 1992 book, *Civil Society and Political Theory*, set the pattern of taking work off the civil society map. The book has democratic aspirations. But their idea of civil society, seeking to retain for the concept a critical edge, falls short. Cohen and Arato propose to revise the classical notion of civil society descended from the Scottish Enlightenment and Hegel, which *included* large institutions and commerce and *excluded* the family. They argue for "a reconstruction [of the concept] involving a three-part model distinguishing civil society from both state and economy" as the way to "underwrite the dramatic oppositional role of this concept under authoritarian regimes and to renew its critical potential under liberal democracies." They define civil society as "a sphere of social interaction between economy and state, composed above all of the intimate sphere (especially the family), the sphere of associations (especially voluntary associations), social movements, and forms of public communication."[17]

Cohen and Arato's approach bears resemblance to that of Habermas, who seeks to wrest civic action from the bureaucratic state and commercial capitalism. By the last decades of the nineteenth century, Habermas argues, the public sphere had begun to atrophy radically. The replacement of a competitive economy with a monopolized economy dominated by large interests undermined the power and authority of the commercial and professional middle classes. The state itself increasingly began to regulate social conflicts, and the public began to break apart into myriad special interests. Finally, most important, a narrowly technical and instrumental rationality replaced interactive public dialogue. Technical rationality takes the ends— how problems are defined and what solutions are desirable—as given and concerns itself with the most efficient means to accomplish the task. Public debate and dialogue previously determined these ends. In their absence, "ends" get reduced usually to quantitative measures of economic growth.

Beyond historical treatments, Habermas has sought to create a normative ideal of procedural radicalism in the service of democratic critique. After *Transformation of the Public Sphere*, Habermas's subsequent work seeks to sustain the possibility of public deliberation in a world that undermines it—some enclave of "uncoercive interaction on the basis of communication free from domination" in theory and practice, alike.[18]

His primary strategy has been to distinguish between types of rationality. For Habermas, instrumental or practical reason—thinking directed toward problem-solving—is sharply differentiated from communicative reason directed to common understanding. Practical, "purposive-rational actions" are the province of the larger "system world" of big, impersonal institutions and bureaucracies. "Communicative actions" survive—though endangered by large institutions—in everyday experience, the "life worlds" of ordinary people and communities. Habermas has sought to distill from the latter the preconditions for "ideal speech situations" to sustain an aspiration for un-coerced and free communication.[19]

Theorists such as Cohen, Arato, and Habermas are full of democratic intentions. They want to avoid what they see as the entanglements of many nongovernmental institutions in the system worlds of government and business. Yet the separation of voluntary activity or arenas of deliberation from work and government dramatically purifies their politics, while it also erodes the power and authority that citizens can gain through work. It removes the large institutions of our world from democratic action, organizing, and transformation. How, one can ask, is it possible to challenge the lack of accountability in multinational corporations or the advertising industry through communicative rationality, or with volunteers?

Democratic movements arise to address patterns of power—not to occupy a social space or to find a home. Democratic movements subvert boundaries and cross categories. And they heavily draw on the civic authority and also civic learning that comes from work. This is a different point than that made by typical theories of workplace democracy.

In American history, democratic movements gained public power by arguing that relatively powerless groups build the commonwealth and thus merit full participation. For instance, this claim is central in the African American freedom movement. The civil rights movement built on the authority derived from making work visible and dignified. The bookend events of Martin Luther King's career were the Montgomery bus boycott, based on maids who walked to work, and the Memphis garbage workers' strike. Both embodied the spirit of Langston Hughes's great poem, "Freedom's Plow":

Out of labor—white hands and black hands—
Came the dream, the strength, the will, to build America . . .

Land created in common,
Dream nourished in common,
Keep your hand on the plow! Hold on!
If the house is not yet finished,
Don't be discouraged, builder! . . .

The plan and the pattern is here,
Woven from the beginning
Into the warp and woof of America.[20]

Similarly, women used claims based on their civic work (challenging the distinction between paid and unpaid) as the foundation for suffrage. Thus, Francis Willard, a key suffragist, populist, and leader of the largest women's "voluntary" association in the nineteenth century, the Women's Christian Temperance Union, titled her book *The Work and Workers of the Women's Christian Temperance Union.*[21]

The word "voluntarism," apart from its designation as a specialized philosophical school, does not appear in the *Oxford English Dictionary* until the 1950s. It does not come into wide usage as an "ism," as a pattern of unpaid citizen labor in social service, until only recently. For example, in 1969, the *Wall Street Journal* so labeled "Nixon's program to enlist the help of private groups in solving social problems." It is noteworthy that the term amateur then began to acquire derogatory overtones.[22]

The settings that prove seedbeds for democratic movements, free spaces, often find hospitable ground in the life of communities and voluntary associations. But freedom for self-organization, political education, and public space are not *properties* of community or voluntary groups. Throughout American history, broad democratic movements have incubated in diverse settings which people own, that have (or in which people can achieve) a significant measure of autonomy from dominant power systems, and that also have public and political qualities.

The concept of free spaces does not so much refute the idea of civil society as show its sharp limitations. Free spaces highlight the importance of work and organizations associated with work. In another example from the African American freedom struggle, the Brotherhood of Sleeping Car Porters and associated community groups (such as women's auxiliaries described by Melinda Chateauwert in *Marching Together: Women of the Brotherhood of Sleeping Car Porters*) sustained free spaces for political education and oppositional culture for generations.[23]

In recent writing, Cynthia Estlund, professor of law at Columbia University, has also sought to put work and the workplace back on the civil society map by highlighting civic learning at work. Estlund brings a wealth of theoretical perspectives on civic action and political culture together with a large body of social science literature and examples from popular culture (splendid treatments of television shows, for instance) to argue that the workplace is a resource for social integration, social capital, and deliberation in ways current theorists neglect.[24]

A virtue of Estlund's treatment is its complex, many-sided realism. She fully acknowledges the hierarchies and continuing patterns of discrimination, domination, and alienation that workers experience in most workplace environments. But she makes a compelling case that, nonetheless, workplaces are still the only environment where most people are likely to have sustained encounters with people of differing racial, cultural, and ideological backgrounds. Moreover, they have such encounters under conditions conducive to interaction and collaboration, with relative civility, and practical, goal directed tasks. These features enable people to develop enhanced respect for others, reduce their prejudices and stereotypes, build trust, develop civic skills, and create cross-group networks. For instance, Estlund observes that "It is not just the friendship potential of workplace relations that makes it a promising source of interracial contact"; the work process itself "is generally cooperative and directed toward shared objectives; much of it is sustained, personal, informal, and one-to-one." Workplaces further democratic equality by "convening strangers from diverse backgrounds and inducing them to work together toward shared objectives under the aegis of the societally imposed equality principle."[25]

Estlund also notes changes achieved through social movements such as unionization and civil rights, which interacted with changes in the law. Thus, Section 7 of the Wagner Act, in part the product of New Deal reform and organizing, created "a kind of rudimentary system of civil liberties within the workplace," which in turn allowed further organization and action by workers. The equal protection of the law provisions, enshrining in words "the notion that people should not be segregated or subordinated on the basis of their race or certain other immutable traits" was the result of civil rights efforts. Though the effort is not completed, it furthers democratic purposes.[26]

Paying attention to the workplace raises questions of power, change, and civic interaction that are absent from conventional civil society theory. Emphasizing work also has potential to reunite civic processes with civic consequences and civic creation, a connection often absent from deliberation.

Left wing critics of Habermas such as Nancy Fraser, Mary Ryan, and Geoff Eley focus on problems of power and interest. They argue that Habermas's construction of the public sphere is, simply, too nice: it embodies a notably middle class bias. Historically, it also fails to problematize the highly gendered division between bourgeois public (the arena of middle class males) and private (the household, where women "belong"). In fact, they argue, Habermas's public sphere was defined in part through the explicit exclusion of women and in opposition to both traditional elites and lower class groups. They propose that the processes Habermas describes were defined by expulsion as well as inclusion.

In a critical and left wing perspective, a more dynamic historical understanding posits a series of diverse publics rather than a singular "public sphere." Mary Ryan artfully depicts the publics of street corner and outdoor society—far removed from the reading rooms and clubs of polite society—to make the point. Similarly, as she describes, political judgment and citizenship, far from abstract and universalist categories, are always infused with interests, power relationships, and points of view. Public judgment is not the search for "truth" or "consensus" in pursuit of the "public good," which Habermas and other deliberative theorists often advance as the aim of public discussion. In real life, judgment depends on context and perspective, always suffused with power, and certainly not always with a generalized public good in mind.[27]

Yet the context-dependent, provisional, open-ended quality of public involvement and public judgment is dramatized by attention to another significant weakness in Habermas's account, a weakness that also plagues his left wing critics. All separate the public talk from the ways citizens act directly to define and solve the problems of society and create the elements of a shared public life. In making such separation, Habermas and his left critics take as given the exclusion of ordinary citizens from governance and the making of the public world. They also wrongly divide different sorts of judgment-making.

For the Greeks, public judgment was conveyed by the concept of *phronesis*, or practical wisdom, which involved the insights accumulated through action around common issues in the public sphere. For Habermas, the modern public sphere is different from that of the Greeks. "The theme of the modern (in contrast to the ancient) public sphere shifted from the properly political tasks of a citizenry acting in common (i.e., administration of law as regards internal affairs and military survival as regards external affairs) to the more properly civic tasks of a society engaged in critical public debate."[28]

Severing debate from civic action mirrors the formal structures of modern politics, where representatives make decisions about public affairs and official political authority is delegated, not practiced by the citizenry as a whole. Yet Habermas and left wing theorists take formal structures of governance too literally. Their arguments rest upon a static theory of power, ignoring the interplay between large systems and everyday life, collapsing the lumpy, interactive quality of power dynamics even in situations of sharp inequality into granite-like relationships. In the real world, power relationships resemble more an ever-changing landscape than a fixed, two-dimensional map.[29]

Severing formal systems from communicative action and life worlds purifies broad civic activity. It collapses the official world of public policy into a realm of elites, officeholders, and technocrats engaged in narrowly instrumental action and limits others to broad but ephemeral talk or marginalized helping roles. In actual practice, understanding and equality, when effectively pursued, are always combined with other purposes. Purposive and communicative aims exist in complex combinations.

The very division between life world and system world, purposive and communicative action, as natural as it first appears, obscures the agency of people who always learn to live along the borders between the everyday and the systemic. Moreover, what gets lost in either a narrowly instrumental, distributive politics or deliberation aimed at understanding and consensus is the moral ambiguity and open-ended, provisional quality of the public world. In public settings the search is not for "truth" or final vindication; rather, there are many truths, reflecting the multiplicity of experiences that bring diverse groups into politics, and their enlarged judgment is aimed at practical action. The challenge is finding provisional resolution of pressing concerns. In a problem-solving public, there are few saints or sinners but rather an interplay among people with diverse interests and values. Questions of justice arise, but no one is simply a victim or an innocent; everyone bears responsibility for solving problems pragmatically identified.

Thus deliberative democracy, though it has important insights particularly for a meritocratic culture that condescends toward popular intelligence, is not enough. Alone, it all too easily takes on a hortatory, idealized quality that separates out an abstract public sphere of communicative consensus from real world politics built upon negotiation, messy compromise, and public problem solving and creation.

To bring back a fuller account of public life and politics I argue for a third version of citizenship, beyond the voter and protestor of liberalism or the volunteer and deliberator of civil society. This conception expresses and develops the public dimensions of work and the productive dimensions of politics.

Work, in Theory and Practice

Work is absent from conventional theories of participatory democracy, not only in recent versions (such as civil society and deliberative theories) but over millennia. The western tradition to which we are heir conceives public life as the democratization of aristocracy. As Benjamin Barber has observed, "To the Greeks, labor by itself defined only mere animal existence, while leisure was the condition for freedom, politics, and truly 'human' forms of being."[30]

Contemporary political theorists continue to distinguish between the public sphere and work. Thus Hannah Arendt, the great twentieth-century philosopher, viewed work as had the Greeks, as part of the apolitical world. She saw "manual labor" as an undignified necessity, "herdlike," while "work," on the other hand, was far more creative and important, the activity of *homo faber*, or "man, the maker of things," the builder of the world. Yet Arendt still believed that work did not belong in the public arena of "deeds and action," and specifically of politics.

Rather, Arendt believed that the worker's "public realm is the exchange market, where he can show the products of his hand and receive the esteem which is due him." Producers remained "private," or isolated: "*homo faber*, the builder of the world and the producer of things, can find his proper relationship to other people only by exchanging his products with theirs because these products themselves *are always produced in isolation*" (italics added). Arendt argues that the thought and manual art which produce craft—the creation of a "model" or idea in one's mind which one then reproduces through shaping materials of the world—necessarily requires isolation. Only apprentices and helpers are needed, she argued, in relations based on inequality.[31]

In contrast with the marketplace, for Arendt the public realm of action is an environment of "innumerable perspectives and aspects in which the common world presents itself and for which no common measurement or denominator can ever be devised." It is a world of visibility and disclosure, where people's words and deeds potentially allow them to achieve immortality. "By their capacity for the immortal deed, by their ability to leave no perishable traces behind, men, their individual mortality notwithstanding, attain an immortality of their own and prove themselves to be of a 'divine' nature."[32]

The source of power in the public world, for Arendt, is its plurality, drawing on Aristotle's conception of politics. "Being seen and being heard by others derive their significance from the fact that everybody sees and hears from a different position. This is the meaning of public life, compared to which even the richest and most satisfying family life can offer only the prolongation of one's own position with its attending aspects and perspectives." Thus, Arendt argued that public experience had a weight and reality that private life lacked: "the subjectivity of privacy can be prolonged and multiplied in a family . . . but this family 'world' can never replace the reality rising out of the sum total of aspects presented by one object to a multitude of spectators."[33]

Arendt's work, especially her book, *The Human Condition*, made a significant contribution by bringing a notion of public back into intellectual discussion. In so doing, she retrieved for modern audiences the memory of the vitality of ancient Greek democracy and politics itself. Arendt was a democratic theorist: her public world was potentially open to all, regardless of race or culture or income or gender. Yet by separating politics from work, she also adds an episodic and heroic quality to the public realm. Arendt believed, for example, that public life emerged for ordinary people only at extraordinary moments—during the American Revolution, for instance, or the civil rights movement.

Arendt simply failed to grasp the public, cooperative, and deeply political qualities of much work, vividly illustrated in the American experience. In slighting this dynamic she reveals more about the academic culture in which she did her work than about the nature of work in general. Thus she also missed the wellspring of American democratic energy and possibility: the tie between everyday labor and the public world.

The living tradition of democracy in America, understood as a way of life, not simply formal institutions, confounds any opposition of work and public life. The distinctiveness of American democracy, indeed, has been especially its tie to work. From the Revolution onward, urban artisans, laborers, and farmers all stressed work as a far better source of public virtue than leisure. Thomas Paine, especially, among Revolutionary leaders, drew his inspiration from the common sense and dedication to liberty he believed resided among "middling sorts."

Democratic ideas of freedom and independence were made practical by the fact that citizens (free white men) owned their own labor. This was not a morally or socially uncomplicated process. Slavery locked most African Americans into a status of unfree labor (one of the ironies of American democratic life is that, by so doing, free labor gained dignity by way of contrast). Depredations against native peoples—their forcible removal from lands to create new towns, part of what Robert Wiebe called America's "portable democracy"—is a terrible chapter in American history. Yet, in ways that even the most astute observers of American democracy such as Alexis de Tocqueville neglected, America's civic life was marked by work and its values. Democracy had resonance because citizens helped to make it, in its social, cultural, and economic as well as governmental forms. Most Americans were self-employed farmers and artisans. They owned their tools. They determined what they produced. Out of such experiences, working people came together to create towns and town halls, schools and libraries, infrastructure and cultural celebrations.[34]

This tradition has a powerful resonance, for instance, in America's public and land grant institutions of higher education. In 1851, a People's College Association was formed in New York, emerging out of agrarian and labor activism. It supported higher education for agriculture and the useful arts. Its meetings drew an eclectic array of reformers, including abolitionists and "Women's Rights Ladies." The movement was given momentum by the Morrill Act, signed by President Lincoln in 1862, which promoted "the liberal and practical education of the industrial classes in the several pursuits and professions of life." It resulted in the founding of a number of new colleges, open to wider constituencies.

In the decades following the Civil War, most states established what were called land grant colleges, open but not limited to farmers and mechanics. A second Morrill Act, passed in 1890, increased funding for land grant colleges, stipulating that states have "a just and equitable division of the fund to be received under this act between one college for white students and one institution for colored students." Despite the grave injustices inherent in the doctrine of separate but equal, this funding led to the creation of black colleges—the so-called "1890 Land-Grant Colleges"—that would train generations of black leaders.

Land grant colleges always had a practical bent, and also, in their largest and most visionary dimensions, a clarity about their role in helping to create the larger culture and civilization. Land grants partly aimed, in specific terms, at spreading to rural areas the remarkable scientific developments of the times: artificial fertilizers, the Babcock milk test, knowledge about the transmission and control of crop and animal diseases, and new technologies like the tractor, all were shared. By the 1890s, this work was termed extension. And while extension mainly meant the spread of technical and scientific knowledge, this was not simply a one way process, nor was this the whole of its mission.

From the beginning, land grants also aimed to help make a vital democracy, broadly understood. Indeed, rhetoric about the democratic purposes of land grant colleges was widespread. For instance, the Trustees of the Ohio Agricultural and Mechanical College declared in 1873 that they desired not "to educate those confided to them simply as Farmers or Mechanics, but as men, fitted by education and attainments for the greater usefulness and higher duties of citizenship." In some states, "citizenship training" was covered simply by adding social sciences to the curriculum. In others, civic concerns were shaped by reform agitation from students and faculty involved with farmer and labor movements. Still others, like New York's Cornell University, stressed the need to teach and cultivate an ethos of public service in all students.[35]

In the twentieth century, land grant schools developed a more explicit civic agenda, to contribute to a vibrant rural civilization through research, teaching, and sustained partnerships with communities. This history of land grant institutions was full of implicit and at points explicit references to the concept and practices of public work itself.

For instance, Liberty Hyde Bailey, dean of agriculture at Cornell and chair of Theodore Roosevelt's Country Life Commission, stressed practical partnerships with communities to solve public problems and to create civic capacity. For Bailey, who imagined extension as the rural counterparts of urban settlements, these partnerships developed in public spaces grounded in community life where people could develop capacities for discourse, common work, and further learning. Bailey sometimes used the term public work to convey this ensemble of reciprocal partnerships, capacity-building, and public spaces.

Bailey's approach at Cornell was to integrate specialized knowledge into a much more comprehensive vision. "Students in agriculture are doing much more than fitting themselves to follow an occupation," he wrote. "They are to take part in a great regeneration. The student in agriculture is fitting himself for a great work." As such, Bailey challenged practices of narrow expert-led extension work. "A prevailing idea seems to be that an expert shall go into a community and give advice to the farmers on the running of their farms and on all sorts of agricultural subjects, being teacher, inspector, counselor, confessor, organizer, and guide." Bailey declared this approach was likely to fail on the face of it. Even where it effectively conveyed new information, it created dangerous dependencies, not capacities for self-action. "The re-direction of any civilization must rest primarily on the people who comprise it, rather than be imposed from persons in other conditions of life."

College-based rural workers could play pivotal roles if they helped communities develop their own problem-solving capacities, and also if they helped rural communities keep in mind the larger objective, the "commonwealth." Bailey continued, "Real leadership lies in taking hold of the first and commonest problems that present themselves and working them out. I like to say to my students that they should attack the first problem that presents itself when they alight from the train on their return from college. It may be a problem of roads; of a poor school; of tuberculosis; of ugly signs along the highways." The point was not simply or even mainly the specific problem. Rather, it was the fact that the public work of problem-solving created opportunities to develop community capacity for self-action and for creating rural democracy.[36]

The land grant and extension tradition that Bailey exemplified so well demonstrates the power of understanding citizens as co-creators of democracy, by connecting their work to public life and thus engaging them in public work. If taken seriously, this approach has wide-ranging implications, since it highlights not only individual or small group action but also culture-shaping institutions—especially higher education—as instruments of culture-making and culture change, not simply as inculcators of knowledge and virtue. It also points toward the need for a larger civic politics that carries this idea across contexts and even national boundaries.

In practical terms, a public work approach to citizenship opens up multiple terrains for everyday politics by highlighting the productive as well as the distributive dimensions of politics. As described in Chapter 7, it emphasizes the need to democratize the organized knowledge systems—professional practices—that structure institutions. It highlights the patterns of power in higher education and associated systems (like communications and culture industries) with profound culture-shaping effects, described in Chapter 8. Thus public work as a framework helps to surface the deeper discontents about American life, and provides a strategy for addressing them.

A public work approach also brings into public life constituencies otherwise not included in broad based citizen organizing. We have found that everyday politics of public work resonates with groups as diverse as young people, new immigrants, professionals, and middle class communities.

Chapter 5

Citizen Education as a Craft, Not a Program

When men know they are working on what belongs to them, they work with far greater eagerness and diligence. They learn to love the land cultivated by their own hands.

—*Pope Leo XIII, Rerum Novarum, 1891*

The reason why I did Public Achievement is because things in the world are wrong. Public Achievement and Dr. King are alike because we both made a difference in the world peacefully. We both look at the problems and solve them instead of blaming people.

—*Matt Anderson, fourth grade student, St. Bernard's*

Robert Putnam's famous argument that Americans are increasingly "bowling alone" reflects wide concern about the state of America's civic culture, especially in regard to young people. In recent years, a chorus of critics and educators has expressed alarm about the disengagement of young people generally from politics and public affairs in the United States, as well as about growing divisions among young people along class and racial lines. Bill Galston pointed out the pattern in the Annual Review of Political Science in an important overview argument. "[While] anxiety about the civic engagement of young adults is nothing new . . . there are also disturbing trends over time," Galston argued. "If we compare generations rather than cohorts—that is, if we compare today's young adults not with today's older adults but with the young adults of the past—we find evidence of diminished civic attachment."[1]

Thus, from the early 1970s to 1996, the percentage of young adults, ages eighteen to twenty-nine, voting in presidential elections declined from about 50 percent to less than one-third. The annual UCLA survey conducted since the mid-1960s, querying the political attitudes of about 250,000 entering college freshmen in a variety of kinds of higher education institutions, found decline in every major indicator of political engagement. By 2000, only 26 percent voiced the belief that keeping up with politics is important, compared with 58 percent in 1966. Only 14 percent say they regularly discuss politics—down from 30 percent. Similarly, a Pew Research Center poll of voters in their late teens and twenties found that fewer than half were thinking "a great deal" about the elections in 2000, compared to two thirds in 1992. Four in ten believed that it does not matter who is president, twice as many as in 1992.[2]

Michael Delli Carpini and Scott Keeter integrated evidence to show that civic and political knowledge is strongly correlated with other forms of knowledge and involvement in their 1996 study, *What Americans Know About Politics and Why It Matters.* Subsequent studies have shown that schools can make a difference in young people's interest in public affairs and knowledge about politics, especially through regular class discussions of current events. Yet schools have increasingly failed to accomplish these purposes. The 1998 assessment by the National Center for Education Statistics found that, while 25 percent of the nation's students performed at proficient or advanced levels of knowledge about the political system, 75 percent scored at "basic" and "below basic" levels. At the eighth grade level, while 81 percent of students were able to identify Martin Luther King, Jr., as a civic leader in fighting against segregation, only 6 percent could describe two ways societies benefit from having a constitution. At the senior level, only 9 percent of students could list two ways democratic societies benefit from citizen participation.[3]

Finally, civic knowledge and learning opportunities are increasingly dividing along racial and class lines in America, with those who most need the power derived from political skills and knowledge being those who are also least likely to gain such knowledge and skills. Two out of three of the poorest Americans cannot describe political parties' attitudes toward government spending priorities, whereas almost all the wealthiest Americans know exactly how the Democrats and Republicans differ. The National Commission on the High School Senior Year, in its 2001 report, sketched a dire scenario:

If we go along as we have been, about half our people, perhaps two thirds, will . . . be well-suited to participate in an increasingly global and multicultural world. . . . The other one-third to one-half . . . are more likely to flounder. Poorly educated, worried about their place in a rapidly changing world, they may look on the com-plexities of an interdependent world as threatening and the demands of citizenship as a burden.[4]

Such patterns of growing divisions and political disengagement among young people have prompted a movement for civic education over the last decade. In 1999 the National Association of Secretaries of State (NASS)—the organization of state officials charged with overseeing elections and civic education efforts—launched a "New Millennium Project" to analyze youth attitudes toward politics and increase young people's political involvement. The National Commission of the States created a similar effort. In 2000, more than 80 organizations launched the National Alliance for Civic Education to advance the cause of civic education, civic knowledge, and civic engagement. National Campus Compact, an organization of more than 800 presidents of colleges and universities, which advocates service learning, adopted an explicit mission aimed at citizenship in higher education.

Yet calls for civic education can conceal differences in politics as much as they clarify grounds for common action. There are now several different approaches to civic education, what the Campus Compact organization de-scribes as "frameworks [that] may share some common themes, but . . . are distinct enough to offer separate conceptions of the democratic citizen, with corresponding skills that the citizen under each model would need to develop." [5] The differing paradigms of the citizen in each hold implications for widely different politics.

Traditional citizenship education has been dominated by "liberal" theory. This has been long enshrined in American school curriculum in civ-ics courses. Here, the focus is on the state, on the one side, describing de-partments of government, processes of legislation, and the like. On the other side is the individual, who is conceived as the bearer of rights and a voter or petitioner. The role of government is to secure such rights and ensure a fair or just distribution of goods and resources, as well as to main-tain the rule of law. Politics is a distributive struggle over scarce resources—"the authoritative allocation of goods, services, and values," in Easton's classic definition, or more simply, as Harold Laswell puts it in his famous book title, "Who gets what, when, how." [6]

In the last generation, citizen participation in the liberal approach has come to mean more than voting or an occasional letter. Citizens are brought into distributive politics through widespread technologies of citi-zen mobilization such as the door-to-door canvass described in Chapter 2.

But such politics only mobilizes the righteous on one side against the enemy on the other. It teaches little or nothing in the way of everyday politics in which people learn to negotiate differences.

Two stories illustrate the contrast. The first is drawn from Public Achievement, the youth civic education initiative sponsored by the Center for Democracy and Citizenship. In Public Achievement, young people are conceived civically as co-creators of a democratic way of life. Politics is understood as an activity that negotiates diverse interests for the sake of creating things of broad public benefit. We know from multiple evaluations that it is possible to re-engage today's young people of a great range of backgrounds with such a politics.[7]

The second playground story conveys what politics is understood to be today, more generally. The story draws specific attention to citizen organizing structured by mobilization technologies like the door-to-door canvass.

A Tale of Two Playgrounds

The first story is about a group of young people at St. Bernard's school in the working class North End area of St. Paul, part of the youth civic engagement initiative called Public Achievement. In this case, Public Achievement teams of fifth, sixth, and seventh graders worked for four years to create a playground. They eventually succeeded, overcoming many obstacles. Joey Lynch, a leader in the teams, was recognized by Governor Jesse Ventura in his first State of the State address in 1999, as a "citizen prevailing against all odds."

Watching the work of the Public Achievement playground group unfold over the years, I know the rich civic and political learning that took place. Dozens of children were directly involved, and the whole school, parish, and neighborhood were affected. A number of students from James Farr's political sciences classes at the University of Minnesota were also involved as coaches and derived important learning from the experiences.

In Public Achievement, teams of young people—ranging from elementary through high school students—work over the school year on public issues they choose. They are coached by adults, who help them develop achievable goals and learn political skills and political concepts. At St. Bernard's, generations of teams continued to work on the issue. In order to succeed, teams had to turn neighborhood opinion around on the playground issue (neighbors had originally thought that a playground might be a magnet for gangs). They had to get the parish council on their side, negotiate zoning changes with city officials, and raise $60,000 from local businesses. To accomplish these feats, the children had to learn how to interview people, write letters, give speeches, call people they didn't know on the phone. They had to deliberate and come to understand the views of adults they thought were mean and oppressive, negotiate, make alliances, raise money, map power, and do research. Throughout, they enjoyed describing their efforts as public work, sentiments suggested in the name young people chose for the park, "Public Achievement Works."

Young people in the effort also learned about political concepts—power, public life, diverse interests, and politics itself. The framework we use in Public Achievement stresses this sort of effort as a different kind of politics, a public work politics of everyday public problem solving and public creation. In Public Achievement, young people are conceived as citizens today, not simply as citizens in preparation. They are co-creators of the democratic way of life in their schools, neighborhoods, and the larger society and world.

In 2003–4 about 3,000 young people were involved in Public Achievement in eighty sites in ten American communities (the Twin Cities and suburbs, Mankato, Kansas City, Missouri, Kansas City, Kansas, Northwest Missouri, Milwaukee, Denver and Fort Collins, Colorado, Manchester, New Hampshire, and Broward County, Florida), with about 400 coaches. Public Achievement had also spread to Northern Ireland (in 1999), Turkey, Palestine, and Israel, with interest expressed by educators and youth workers in South Africa, Scotland, Kenya, Japan, and Poland.

In Public Achievement young people work on a large range of issues, from teen pregnancy and school violence to environmental concerns and the curriculum of their schools. A variety of forms of evaluation have found that young people and college coaches alike develop many different political skills in such work: chairing meetings, interviewing, deliberating, negotiating interests, public speaking, writing, holding each other accountable, doing research on issues, to mention a few.

College students and children and youth of all ages in Public Achievement teams often develop a favorable view of politics itself as a result of their experiences. In 1999, Angela Matthews, a visiting young adult leader of Public Achievement in Northern Ireland, gave a speech to a Twin Cities PA conference. It included young people from third grade through college. She asked, "how many of you like politics?" Most—without any prompting—raised their hands. Then she made her point: "It's because we're doing politics; it's not simply something politicians do."

Joe Kunkel, a political science colleague at the State University of Minnesota at Mankato, each year has his students in teacher preparation coach Public Achievement teams in a local middle school, Dakota Meadows. His students are not by any stretch activists; most come from small town and rural areas. Dakota Meadows is a middle and upper middle class school, where the seventh and eighth graders choose issues much like other suburban school sites (the year 2001–2, after 9/11, there were eight teams working on teen depression and teen suicide). Kunkel uses two forms of assessment to explore their skills and views of politics. He does a survey of what he calls political and professional skills practiced by kids in the teams at Dakota Meadows. In 2001–2, 54 percent made a phone call to an adult in authority; 80 percent interviewed adults; 43 percent used a power map to identify people to contact; 50 percent chaired meetings; and 72 percent spoke in public.

Kunkel also assigns his college students a concluding essay reflecting on their experience. He asks them what the teams they coached learned, in their judgment, and also what they themselves learned about "democracy, citizenship, politics, and working in groups." A few quotes are illustrative. "Coming into PA I thought that citizenship meant to live in the United States and that politics was something only politicians were involved in," said one. "However, as the year went on everything turned into a political struggle. I could not believe how big a role politics played even in a Middle School. The kids and I had to deal with the principal, workers at Hy_vee [supermarket], and people at Echo. I am proud to say the kids handled this all themselves, but I know exactly how big of a role politics will be playing as I enter the teaching world."

One of the striking things illustrated by his students' papers is the latent political energies of this generation. "I am amazed by what I have learned," said one. "Not only did I learn to be an effective coach, I also learned about what it means to be an active citizen. We as coaches are in a sense renewing democracy for future generations. It has become clear to me through this course that the concept of democracy in America has lost much of its luster and it must be restored." "First off, I learned something fundamental about democracy. Democracy is only what we make it," said another. "No longer do I just sit back and let this crazy democracy machine roll by. If we do not like something we can take steps to make the situation better."[8]

One could continue with encouraging stories and quotes. But this sense of political possibility is not the full picture. The more typical view of politics that young people learn is illustrated by the second story.

This story is about a young friend of mine, Daniel, who worked for the affiliate of a nationwide community organizing network in a large urban area. A group of young people in the neighborhood where he was organizing told him they wanted to get a playground. Daniel, who knew about the Public Achievement experience, wanted to see what they could do.

He approached the local organizing director for the citizen group. But she was skeptical. "What does a playground have to do with power?" she asked. She feared that concentrating on a playground might detract from the upcoming mayor's race. She believed energy should go into mobilizing citizens for clearly progressive causes. Her conclusion was that Daniel could work with the teenagers on the playground only under certain conditions. He had to be able to "cut" the issue in a progressive way, which is organizing language for identifying a clear enemy and making sure most people agree. He had to figure out how it could be used to organize a protest.

As Daniel talked with the kids, this approach did not make much sense. It wasn't likely to result in a playground, even if they could find out whom in the Parks Department to target as an enemy. In any case, through the summer months, the organization became increasingly involved in the mayor's race. Daniel felt relief, and so did other staff. "Our organizing clay suddenly makes sense when poured into this mold," he commented. "Some camaraderie is really beginning to creep into walls that seemed to house folks who talked about quitting over cigarettes nearly every day. Campaigning is all about numbers, mobilizing the base and turning out the regulars. We don't even pretend to develop leaders or build anything sustaining. We just go out and get the numbers."

This episode is telling. Over the last generation, many activist citizen groups have emerged that purport to be educating citizens generally and young people specifically for political life, increasing citizen participation, and creating responsive government. Yet conventional definitions of politics, as a struggle of the forces of good against the forces of evil, offer little hope that America will see a broad revitalization of public life and democracy. Public Achievement suggests another direction, a civic education and engagement approach which is better understood as a craft than a program.

Roots and Early History

Public Achievement began shortly after the start of civic engagement work at the Humphrey Institute in partnership with the new mayor of St. Paul, Jim Scheibel, who was interested in exploring ways to engage young people in politics. Its initiating premise was that developing theory as well as practical and successful methods for re-engaging citizens in public life must include attention to creation of strategies for engaging young people in politics.

Public Achievement has its roots in the freedom movement of the 1960s, especially in the Citizenship Education Program (CEP) of the Southern Christian Leadership Conference in which I worked as a young man. CEP sponsored what were called citizenship schools—informal training and discussion groups organized in clubs, beauty parlors, church basements, and other settings. In these, often profound changes were evident in outlook and identity among children younger than myself. Moreover, when black youth in the south, suffering the abuse of generations, developed courage and hopefulness about the possibility of change, they often transformed adult patterns of fatalism and hopelessness. Taylor Branch captures this in *Pillar of Fire*, suggesting that the entire movement's very success may have turned on Martin Luther King's agreement with the arguments of field staff members James Bevel and Diane Nash to allow young people to participate in the demonstrations in Birmingham, in May 1963. Most of the African American community had become opposed to continued demonstrations for fear of retaliation. After King agreed, thousands of children began to participate, with dramatic results. "On the first day, nearly a thousand marching children converted first the Negro adults," Branch describes. "Not a few onlookers . . . were dismayed to see their own disobedient offspring in the line, and the conflicting emotions of centuries played out on their faces until some finally gave way. One elderly woman ran alongside the arrest line, shouting, Sing, children, sing!"[9]

The citizenship schools taught a philosophy of nonviolence and skills of citizen action. They were also infused with a deep, albeit critical belief in the resources of American democracy, what Frederick Harris has called the combination of "ruly and unruly" civic commitments that have historically characterized the African American freedom tradition. "We are redeemers, not revolutionaries," said the Rev. Johnny Ray Youngblood, an African American minister schooled in this tradition. "We love America. We love democracy. We are just critical lovers."[10]

In Public Achievement these themes were translated into a set of criteria for the issues young people choose to take up. Issues must be nonviolent, legal, and able to make a public contribution. The Southern Christian Leadership Conference experience also informs the framing of Public Achievement as about both developing active citizenship essential for a flourishing democracy and challenging the inadequacy of conventional meanings of political concepts such as citizenship, politics, and democracy itself.

Public Achievement from the beginning embodied the concept of free spaces and also lessons about everyday politics from the most successful community organizing. From our treatment of free spaces, we drew the importance of places in community and institutional contexts which youth "owned," where they could have wide latitude for experimentation, creation, self-definition, and democratic reflection. From community organizing, we drew our original core repertoire of concepts, and also the stress on development of public talents and public leadership, dynamic elements in networks like the Industrial Areas Foundation (IAF). Core concepts included the idea of public life as a space of practical action on common tasks and difference, connected to but different than private life (IAF conceptualizes public space in ways similar to Hannah Arendt's notion of a public work of distinctively different persons gathered around the things of a common world), power as relational and dynamic, and self-interest, broadly understood, as the driving source of passion and energy. We framed these with a notion of nonprofessional politics itself as a key dimension of the fabric of every environment, and called the framework citizen politics. The focus on public leadership development also created an emphasis on tough, unromantic engagement with young people, in contrast to youth programs that sentimentalize, marginalize, or pity youth.[11]

From its outset, Public Achievement stressed cooperative action on real world problems and issues, in which young people would themselves design and implement the bulk of the work. PA was organized in teams coached by adults (usually young adults). Young people choose projects around issues they are concerned with and develop strategies for real work on the issue, usually over the course of a school year.

Public Achievement was launched by Project Public Life (soon to be the Center for Democracy and Citizenship) in 1990, with a series of discussion groups among teenagers, organized in association with the newly elected mayor of St. Paul, Jim Scheibel. Although conventional wisdom in the United States held that youth were apathetic and unconcerned, it was soon apparent that young people—every group talked with—had deep concerns and problems they worried about. These ranged from violence, teen pregnancy, drugs, gangs, and racism, to depression, lack of recreational opportunities, school reform, and environmental degradation. Issues varied somewhat with area, class, and race; concerns with gangs were much more common in inner cities, for instance. Yet issue choices were also not simply parsed, and many crossed geographic, racial, and income lines. Young people in every setting, for instance, expressed anger at school policies they felt were unfair, or at teaching approaches that failed to recognize their interests and intelligence. What youth in all the groups said, virtually unanimously, was that adults had rarely asked the opinions of young people on such issues. Moreover, almost no adult they had met ever imagined that young people could actually do anything about the problems and issues they were concerned about.

Other key themes of Public Achievement came out of this period, such as the concept of "coach " (young people liked the idea of adults as coaches, more than any other role—advisor, teacher, mentor). Young people also responded powerfully to the idea of a public world where they can interact with different kinds of people outside their own community.

The flagship school for Public Achievement was St. Bernard's K-8 elementary school in St. Paul, Minnesota. There, the principal, Dennis Donovan, now national organizer for Public Achievement, had himself undergone what he calls a "personal transformation" through his involvement in an affiliate of the Gamaliel Foundation, a congregationally based organizing network akin to the IAF. Donovan saw Public Achievement as potentially a way to teach students who often voiced lack of purpose and even despair, new hope, courage, and skills of effective citizenship.

The Bathroom Busters

Public Achievement expanded to Andersen Open School in the low income Phillips neighborhood of Minneapolis in the fall of 1997. Fifth and sixth graders, meeting in what is called an "issue convention," identified issues and problems they wanted to work on over the course of the school year.

That year, their coaches were members of the City of Lakes AmeriCorps program.

One group of eight boys, a racial and cultural mix of Mexican immigrants, Native Americans, and European Americans, expressed fury at the state of their bathroom. The stalls had no doors. Toilet paper and other supplies were missing. The walls were covered with obscenities. They named themselves the "Bathroom Busters" and decided to take action.

Two AmeriCorps coaches helped them to understand the issue in public terms larger than the bathroom. The issue was twofold—students' disrespect for common property and the school system's disrespect for students. The coaches also helped them map the complexities of power and politics around their problem. They were dealing with a highly inefficient bureaucracy. The school principal had been unable to get the central school district to paint the bathrooms for four years. Unions had to give approval. Funds had to be found. Moreover, the group had to learn how to make themselves understood. Half its members had difficulty speaking English.

Yet, as sometimes is the case in Public Achievement, youthful determination mixed with good coaching got action that many adults thought was impossible. The team created an alliance with sympathetic administrators, teachers, and parents. They contacted district officials. And they achieved a seeming success. The walls were painted.

The next year, however, graffiti again began appearing on the walls. Cesar, a Mexican American youngster who had been involved the year before, chose to work on the problem again. His team met with other children who used the bathroom. "This is our property. What can we do to prevent graffiti?" was their question. Out of these discussions came a plan to create an art mural in the bathroom, the composite of many kids' ideas and suggestions. As the mural took shape, the bathroom became graffiti-free.

It also turned into a symbol of school pride. A string of visitors—Minneapolis U.S. Representative Martin Sabo, vice president of the Commission on National Service Jim Scheibel, and other political and civic leaders—came to see the school that year. All were taken to the bathroom. They heard the explanation by Cesar, who became known for his exuberant eloquence on the topic, and his team: "This is our property. We have to take care of it!"

A Craft, Not a Program

The story of the Bathroom Busters is interesting on a number of levels—as a tale of youthful energy and determination, latent political skills, cross-cultural cooperation, successful changes in youth cultural norms around graffiti, and the ways young people learn to connect to common things through their own activity and interests. It is also a story of the particular flavor that each group and team takes on and the discoveries made along the way. Public Achievement is not a program, though it has programmatic elements.[12] It is improvised. It raises dynamics and issues that are specific to locales and institutional cultures, as well as issues that are common across widely varying contexts. It evolves and changes as the work progresses. We sometimes say Public Achievement is like jazz.

Circe Torruellas, a Humphrey Institute student who investigated the development of Public Achievement in Turkey and Northern Ireland in the summer of 2003, found this pattern repeatedly. She recounted on the worldwide Public Achievement list serve one story from Turkey:

Near the Istanbul Bilgi University Kustepe campus, many children are sent out by the parents to the surrounding streets to beg the 'privileged' university students. Two young students of Serdar Degirmencioglu [the organizer of Public Achievement in Turkey] were bothered by the situation, from which they had many times turned their faces and ignored. Finally they stopped to talk, and learnt from the children about their situation. Serdar asked them about their interests to consider whether they would be willing to do work in a team as a coach, meet weekly, and tackle this difficult issue.

The students immediately wanted to address the vicious cycle that existed of parents sending the kids to beg, the children obeying, and the university students supplying the cash. The students power-mapped the issue and identified the points where they can have an impact. They realized that families would be the most difficult thing to change [so] they came up with the idea of communicating the issue to the university student body. They figured out that once the study body was informed about how they themselves were contributing to the problem then they will stop.

Throughout the entire project the students always went back to the children, meeting with them, and building relationships of trust. One of the kids named the student team, Gulsun Kustepeli Cocuklar (MKCS), translated as "May Kustepe Children Smile."

The team did not want to stop there. They wanted to do something for the children so they went back to the children to ask them what THEY wanted. They all came up with the idea of hosting a summer school camp. The children contributed with ideas of what they wanted to do at the camp, games, drawing, acting. The MKCS team is setting this up for mid-July.

The MKCS team met with the administration of the school that the children who beg attend, and are exploring other strategies. Hilal Kaplan, one of the coaches, put it, "When we first started I thought we would change the world overnight. But it is very difficult to do this, especially in Turkey. It's good to start small, and then see changes going from small to big." She added that "giving the children money and then looking the other way is easy. Contributing my time and work to this has been one of the most significant things I have done."[13]

Torruellas's account shows the discovery process involved in PA. It also illustrates that such everyday politics is not simple or easy work for either young people or coaches. As Robert Hildreth, an evaluator of Public Achievement over the last four years who has interviewed more than 200 coaches, put it, "being a coach is a complex balancing act of facilitating the project (getting the work done, thinking strategically, holding themselves and others accountable) and the process (building a small democratic group, learning about their focal issue, evaluating their work, and reflecting upon their learning)." This is a different role than teacher, facilitator, mentor or guide. "Coaches must co-create with team members a group and a space where all participate in making decisions, all contribute according to their abilities, and all work together on common goals." Coaches often describe the first few team meetings as chaotic, even, at moments, as "terrifying."[14]

Public Achievement also faces considerable constraints. Most sites in the United States are in schools. As the evaluation group of Michael Baizerman, Robert Hildreth, and Ross Roholt noted, "any innovative philosophies and practices [like Public Achievement] which do not fit the classroom or 'program' model rub against everyday practices, rules, procedures, policies, individual preferences, and whims." These constraints are amplified by the relatively short amount of time young people experience Public Achievement, usually from ten meetings (in schools that run on trimesters) to up to thirty meetings, in sites where Public Achievement runs the whole year. This means that each team has from ten to thirty hours to get to know each other and the coach and to get the work done. The issue choice process is usually by secret ballot, so teams organize around issues, not friendship groups, research their issue, work on and make progress on a project, learn through the process, and reflect on their work in public and political ways. It is perhaps not surprising, given the wide variation in experiences, that most teams, in the evaluations, do not use an extensive political language to name their work.

Yet evaluators have found that Public Achievement works, for all the obstacles, in a number of ways. "That it is not fully invisible, submerged, twisted out of its shape or sabotaged is a testament to its inherent soundness and to the vitality it invites in its advocates and leaders," the Baizerman team said. "We found that young people experience PA as a place where they were efficacious, had a voice, became skillful, did meaningful work, and learned." PA provided almost all participants "an invitation and an opportunity . . . to expand their everyday, small, and private worlds" and "to do something" for their schools and community. They consistently said that they found it a space where they were allowed to state their ideas and not to worry about being put down. As one said, "I can talk about things that really matter to me." "I can be myself in Public Achievement." "I can take my masks off." As Hildreth observed, this experience of "self-disclosure" in front of others can be thought of as a public sphere, in contrast to normal experiences of young people which are highly constricted by categories, expectations, norms and roles of school, grade, gender, clique-grouping, class, race, family and other contexts.[15]

Young people also describe Public Achievement as a place where they are able to work on real issues that matter to them, and a place where they learned to be efficacious. "It made me know that I can work with other people and figure out stuff," said one elementary school student." "I'm a better speaker," said another. "I know how to work with adults now."

Over four years, the Baizerman team interviewed 282 youth participants, 204 coaches, 25 teachers, 24 principals, and various others involved in seven sites. Participants vary in how much they use explicitly political language—Public Achievement's definitions are a sharp contrast to conventional usage. Most used a language of service: "I can help the community," or "I can help others while I'm helping myself" were typical. They concluded that participants' use of political language, varying with age and conceptual skill, is also strongly a direct function of how much practice teams and coaches alike have with such language.[16]

Those who learn a richer civic and political language can often be dramatic in their descriptions of politics and citizenship, as in the case of Kunkel's students, where he ties coaching to a course on citizenship and democracy. Others pick it up from their own histories or their coaches. "Citizenship is tackling problems and taking things into your own hands, not just sitting back and watching," said Chou Yang, a sixth-grade Hmong student at St. Bernard's.[17]

The experiences at Minneapolis Community and Technical College (MCTC) bear out the argument that explicit use of political concepts tied to practical public work makes a considerable difference in how young people understand what they are doing and how well they are able to generalize their learning to other settings. At MCTC Public Achievement is integrated into the core curriculum of the Urban Teacher Education Program (UTP). Student teachers take a course in Public Achievement concepts and practices, co-taught by Dennis Donovan. They do projects themselves one semester and coach at several area schools the next.

Michael Kuhne, on the UTP faculty, observes that making the concepts live is difficult. For instance, he argues, "it is not so much an issue of understanding free spaces [as a concept] as it is creating and behaving in free spaces. This is especially true in academic settings, where the force of past experiences in classrooms casts an especially powerful spell over the people in the room." He observes the setting: "the cramped desks—or even worse the chairs bolted to the floor—facing the locus of power, the teacher's desk, the teacher's podium, the blackboard or the screen. People walk into classrooms and adopt their roles almost unthinkingly. The teacher 'teaches' and the student 'learns.'" More, free spaces are not bestowed. "It is not simply a question of the instructor declaring that the classroom is a free space and circling up the desks (though that is a start) . . . free space is created and re-created collaboratively."[18] Yet for UTP and now several other disciplines (including the Police Academy and Parks and Recreation Program) the Public Achievement approach has proven a useful civic and political pedagogy with strong appeal. "I recall that in the beginning of the semester, Dennis Donovan asked me if I wanted power. I said, 'no,' because I did not know what to do with it," recounted Mona Abdel-Kerim. Her views changed. "Now I want the power because I believe I have the ability to help others who want to make a difference." Tami Ginther tied power to her future career. "As a future teacher I can't stress enough how important it is to be confident with the power one has; otherwise the students and coworkers will see that the teacher can't handle power." Lisa Staplin argued that there needs to be a realism about gaining power. "It will be good for students to learn that there are many levels of power, and that while they may have little power on their own, if they can find others with the same interests as a group they have much more power and can really affect changes in their world."

As with Kunkel's students at the University of Minnesota/Mankato, MCTC teacher education students also came to have strongly positive associations with politics. "I had to present my issue in such a manner that would make it stand apart from my other classmates' presentations, yet make my issue sound attractive," Danielle Peterson described. "The intricacies of language, public speaking capabilities, creativity, and—really—charm came into play in this political act." Many also generalized to their future careers. "It has advanced my training as a future teacher by opening up my mind to where politics takes place," said Jena Vue. "I use to think very narrowly and naively that politics only takes place in the government. Learning about this core concept has given me the understanding that politics is everywhere and that a classroom environment does explore politics."[19]

Insights and Challenges

When I was first invited to participate in Public Achievement, what impressed me was that these students believed they had the power to change the world around them. As 22 years old I didn't think that I could do that. I heard stories of murals that had ended a school's graffiti problem, campaigns against chemical abuse, playgrounds being erected. . . . Children without jobs, money, or influence proved that they could indeed have influence. Meanwhile, there I sat feeling powerless. (Joe O'Shea, Coach, Hartford Middle School)[20]

Public Achievement has been a fertile environment in which to develop methods of youth civic engagement and also to theorize civic agency. In contrast with the prevailing scholarly wisdom that young people are uninterested in public life and politics, Public Achievement demonstrated that findings of "civic apathy" are functions of the relatively weak conceptions of civic agency and professionalized politics that structure the questions. More robust conceptions illuminate the hidden political interests of a generation that, far from apathetic, is deeply worried about the public problems of our time and eager to have their energies enlisted in addressing them.

The Public Achievement initiative has helped to make clear how different traditions and frameworks of citizenship and politics lead to far different civic pedagogies: the idea of a citizen as voter, protestor, or claimant, associated with liberal political theory, produces civics classes, with perhaps a complementary focus on student government. The idea of the citizen as a volunteer, associated with communitarian theory, leads to the modern service movement, where the dominant focus is on individual helping, the concepts like power, politics, and self-interests are normally missing, and real world civic products are seldom discussed. The concept of the citizen as a civic producer or co-creator of the commonwealth leads to public work and everyday politics. None of these models is wrong. Indeed, discussing them is a way to highlight distinctive and different dimensions of citizen-

TABLE 1. MODELS OF DEMOCRACY, POLITICS, AND CITIZENSHIP

	Liberal	*Communitarian*	*Public work*
What is democracy?	Representative government, rule of law	Government and the "voluntary sector"	A democratic way of life, created through public, political work of the people
What is politics?	Who gets what?	A nasty fight to be avoided	Negotiation and work to solve problems and create public things
Who owns politics?	Professionals, specialists	Professionals, specialists	Citizens, amateurs
What is the citizen?	Voter, consumer	Volunteer	Producer, co-creator
What is civic education?	Civics classes, lobbying and advocacy skills	Community service	Public work projects
What is government's role?	To deliver services	To educate in caring, helping	To create partnerships with citizens, adding to as well as allocating public wealth
What is civic action?	Advocacy, protest	Service (e.g. soup kitchens, shelters)	Building the commonwealth

ship. But the public work approach greatly expands the roles and capacities of the citizen by retrieving a nonprofessional conception of politics, as the activity of citizens. Table 1 is the chart of models of citizenship that has been developed through the work of Public Achievement.

To return to the wellsprings of our work, this concept can be usefully linked to the sense of democracy-making that infused the citizenship schools of the civil rights movement. Then, it was evident that neither courses nor political leadership would desegregate the south—though they visibly and palpably played crucial roles in the process. A large-scale process of redefining the meaning of citizenship was necessary in order to tap the civic interests and energies of millions of ordinary African Americans and their allies. In our time, a concept of the citizen as co-creator provides resources for an analogous project, the revitalization of a civic culture and democracy as a way of life, in a time of rapid change.

There are large challenges to sustaining and expanding Public Achievement or related and similar efforts that provide public work opportunities for young people. Concepts of the citizen as co-creator, power as relational and interactive, public life as an arena of everyday politics where people learn to negotiate differences and undertake public work with others of different backgrounds and views—all go against the normal structures and culture of a commercial and technocratic society, what our colleague Mishkat Az-Zubair calls a gimme society. Moreover, the Baizerman evaluation team warned that the school environment, at least in the United States, is changing in ways that may make Public Achievement more difficult. "In the past two years teachers and other school staff have told us how they feel more and more pressured around issues of high stakes academic testing," they wrote in the summer of 2003. "We have no doubt that the federal 'No Child Left Behind' legislation with its testing imperatives will have profound impact on PA. If PA does not address the realities of testing it may only be able to survive as 'extra-curricular,' becoming even more marginalized to the central mission of the school."[21]

Thus the fate of PA and other public work youth engagement efforts is bound up with many issues of wider educational politics in the United States. Here, it is also connected to the very definition of where education and learning takes place, what they involve, and what is their aim. For those concerned with democracy's future, this means careful attention not only to invention but also to retrieval of richer, older conceptions of democratic education in the American tradition such as that found in the settlement house and adult education movements a hundred years ago.

Chapter 6
The Jane Addams School for Democracy

It is needless to say that a Settlement is a protest against a restricted view of education.

—*Jane Addams,* Twenty Years at Hull House

Jane Addams School has taught me that I have the power to help my community. There is a power when people share ideas and work together. One thing is for sure, one person can't do it alone.

—*Koua Yang Her, participant in the Jane Addams School*

It was a hot and humid day on July 26, 2003, in Parque Castillo on the West Side of Saint Paul, but the weather didn't dampen spirits as several hundred people gathered for the Fifth Annual Freedom Festival.

For more than 100 years, the West Side has been a port of entry for new immigrants, sometimes called the "Ellis Island of the Midwest." But changing colors, tones, and textures, vivid in the day's events, marked the shifting patterns of immigration in the United States. In the early twentieth century, most West Side immigrants were Jewish, escaping a wave of bloody attacks in Eastern Europe; one third of West Side children in the Riverside school listed "peddler" as their father's occupation. A multicultural event at Neighborhood House, the local settlement, would have featured Jewish matzo ball soup, prayer shawls, and yarmulkes, the food and signs of Jewish life in the shetls of Poland, Germany or Russia, ancestral homes of the immigrants. In the early twenty-first century, large numbers of Hmong immigrants from Laos, refugees from the communist takeover in the 1970s, live on the West Side. Immigrants have also arrived from Mexico, following earlier migrations, and from other Latin American countries. More recently, a wave of East African refugees, mainly Somali, have settled in the area. The Freedom Festival on July 26 featured bright Hmong dresses, colored kanga cloth from East Africa, and Latino designs—traditional Mexican attire, Guatemalan fabrics, and Andean wool—in the Fashion Show, one of the day's events. Foods included a range of dishes that would have struck earlier immigrants as amazing. Smells and sounds of Africa, Asia, and Latin America filled the air.

Yet if cultural tones testified to dramatic changes, the cultural politics of the day might have struck an observer with its similarities, a mingling of dedication to a new home and its democratic ideals with celebration of immigrant traditions that was at the heart of earlier settlement practices. On the one hand, the Fifth Annual Freedom Festival of the Jane Addams School for Democracy conveyed exuberant patriotism. Soua Yang of the JROTC led the Color Guard troupe in a presentation of colors; Margaret Post, a recent graduate of the Humphrey Institute, gave a stunning rendition of the Star Spangled Banner. The day's event recognized a long list of citizens who passed the citizenship test in the last year, while State Senator Mee Moua, the first Hmong elected state official in the nation—elected with the involvement of many in attendance—delivered a short speech in praise of freedom and democracy. On the other hand, as in earlier settlement houses, such celebrations of democratic ideals were phrased in distinct and diverse cultural accents, and included a strong embrace of immigrant heritages as well. The stage in the park was lit by a giant torch, made by the Spanish Circle from parachute fabric and poster board, with a fan giving the impression of huge flames. The torch used symbols for freedom from around the world. A Peruvian man, Eduardo Jurado, dedicated it to the idea of freedom in our world today and to the work of the late Senator Wellstone. An Ecuadorian woman, Ines Rodriguez, later dedicated a tree that was also planted in his honor. Hmong youth gave a presentation on how freedom is celebrated in their heritage. Guled Abdi and Yassin Ahmed told the story of the Somalis' departure from Somalia, their journeys, and their arrival and participation in Jane Addams School and the local community. Hmong musicians sang traditional folk songs from Southeast Asia. Shelley Quiali of Teatro del Pueblo led children in a play adapted from a Hmong folk tale, "The Tale of the Suns and Moons."

Jane Addams's Hull House and its sister settlements such as Neighborhood House, founded on the West Side by Jewish women in 1897, rested on a view of America as a commonwealth that is a work in progress, enriched by diverse traditions and immigrant cultures. One hundred years later the Jane Addams School for Democracy seeks to renew this perspective.[1]

Americans in the World, Post-9/11

The largest wave of immigration since World War II flowed into the United States in the last decade. Unlike a hundred years ago when most immigrants came from European countries, this influx is far more racially and culturally diverse. Most immigrants have come from Southeast Asia and other Asian societies; from Mexico and other Latin American countries; from the Middle East and Africa; from the Caribbean.

Celebration of immigrant heritage, or notions that new arrivals can contribute to democracy as a work in progress, are not the only public ideas about immigrants. The attacks of September 11, 2001, prompted furious debates about immigration, immigrants, and the U.S. role in the world (as well as the role of *Americans* in the world). Foreign students sometimes find it hard to get visas for study. The number of exchange students has dropped. New immigrants often are fearful. America roils with debates about what we should be doing in the world as a nation, as groups, as individuals.

Such immediate, mixed reactions to immigrants came in the context of a society that has come to see new arrivals often in terms of their needs and deficiencies. New immigrants experience most institutions—from schools to social service agencies—as unresponsive and often condescending, unaware of their cultural backgrounds and knowledge, dismissive of their ideas. The meritocracy John Lukacs described in his 1984 work, *Outgrowing Democracy*, is in full force when it comes to poor immigrants with little or no formal education. It does little good simply to bewail the pattern, however, or to conceive Hmong or Latino or Somali families as simply victimized.

"Everyone Is a Teacher, Everyone Is a Learner"

The Jane Addams School for Democracy (JAS) began in 1996 as a partnership among new immigrants on the West Side of St. Paul, the Center for Democracy and Citizenship at the Humphrey Institute, and the College of Liberal Arts at the University of Minnesota, Neighborhood House settlement, and the College of St. Catherine. JAS reflects an approach unlike that of those who saw immigrants as threats, but also different from that of those who call for tolerance, pity, or solicitude. It is a learning and public work network that works, in significant measure, because it involves a different pattern of interaction. JAS is a creative, fluid public space where people's talents and contributions are valued and developed; where the question, "what is citizenship?" is a constant topic of discussion and debate; where people who are marginalized develop the political savvy to be otherwise; and where power dynamics change from expert-dominated interactions (which treat immigrants as clients or customers) to public interactions where people learn and work together, and in the process create power. Such public spaces occasion conversation about issues that range from the personal to the global. For instance, recent conversations in the East African Circle have talked about conditions of refugee life, family dynamics, the local transportation system, and transportation systems (formal and informal) in other parts of the world. They also provide spaces for people to learn political skills and habits, which they use in making government more accountable, interactive, and transparent.

"When a diverse mix of people really engage each other, you can see everyone in the room getting smarter," Dudley Cocke, Director of Roadside Theater at Appalshop, Kentucky, once put it. Similar perspectives are often voiced by participants in JAS.[2]

JAS has grown rapidly since its beginning in 1996. By the end of 2003, on Monday and Wednesday evenings seven learning circles gather, mingling new immigrants and American born English speakers. The circles include Hmong circles, one Spanish circle, one East African circle, one organizing circle, one homework group for high school students, and one children's circle. Most nights, nearly two hundred participate. Ongoing projects and actions also meet outside the evening circles.

The overall philosophy stresses that "everyone is a teacher, everyone is a learner," and the reciprocal, interactive quality of the space often has strong impact on participants. Exchange and learning also mean different things to different people. For immigrant youth, for instance, JAS often provides resources for forming more complex identities, balancing ethnic traditions with American culture. "I came to the states when I was very little, and my parents don't talk about the tragedies they experienced in Laos," said one college student active in JAS for five years, since the beginning of her high school experience. The Jane Addams School "was an opportunity not only to help create something but also learn about myself, who I am and where I came from. It's been very interesting to listen to the women and to hear the stories. I needed to take time to learn about my Hmongness . . . where I came from, what my language is like, what my people have been through. It's been a journey of self-discovery. It has given me confidence to know at that place we can all be equal."[3]

For older immigrants, JAS meets practical, often pressing needs—studying for and passing the citizenship test to become a naturalized citizen; learning English; making personal connections with native-born U.S. citizens. It also serves for many as a schooling in American public life. When I went regularly in the first year, I was often struck by how many older Hmong women voiced the desire to "learn how to act in public" in the United States. "My life has changed [because of coming here]," a middle aged woman told one evaluator. "I can communicate, understand English, and communicate with whites." "I am becoming an important person to the rest of the community, going to Jane Addams," said another.[4]

For students from the University of Minnesota and other area colleges, whose orientation includes an intense emphasis that they are group *members*, learning as well as educating and not there to provide community service, JAS often provides a first time encounter on a relatively equal basis with people from far different cultural backgrounds. "Jane Addams is a public space where ordinary people are valued for who they are, where they can let their voices be heard even if they disagree with others, and where they are able to let their talents and abilities show through," said Mary Harrison, a Humphrey Institute graduate student. Harrison participated in the "Hmong Learning Circle" at JAS in the spring of 2003. "At the Jane Addams School, everyone is a teacher and everyone is a learner," Harrison said, voicing JAS's stated philosophy. "I found that even while I was primarily a 'teacher' as we studied for the [naturalization] test, I still learned a lot. I mostly learned by trying to teach the concepts of freedom and democracy. Having to find ways to illustrate showed me how contextual they are, and challenged me to think of what they meant to me. . . . I had always thought of citizenship and democracy in a very formal way. Now I see that it has at least as much if not more to do with empowering ordinary people."[5]

For instance, in preparation for the fashion show at this year's Freedom Festival, immigrants and non-immigrants from different circles discussed clothing from different places and also the meaning of clothing. At the Fashion Show itself, participants walked together to the music of different countries. The Fashion Show culminated with immigrants and non-immigrants all on the stage together in clothing from Laos, Thailand, Mexico, Guatemala, Peru, Colombia, Somalia, and several European countries. In another instance at the Freedom Festival, the Freedom Quilt, dedicated at the Freedom Festival, involved participants from all of the circles who created squares.

As Harrison suggests, Jane Addams School is also a school for politics, in multiple ways that teach politics as an ongoing activity, not given away by proxy to elected representatives. Learning citizenship means not only studying for the test but also making its questions about branches of government and their functions, political events in American history, or names of elected officials seem relevant. Events in 2003 included meetings with three Minnesota state representatives with large immigrant populations; visits by Senator Mee Moua, Judge and First Lady Mary Pawlenty, wife of the Republican governor of Minnesota, to hear about the workings of the judicial system; excursions to the state capital; visits in July by Democratic and Republican chairs of state senate and house committees on health and human services and education to discuss budget cuts and a number of other events. All involved careful preparation, training, follow-up debriefing, and often a mix of learning and political debate and challenge, especially in a climate where new immigrants were acutely affected by huge pending budget cuts. "I think Democrats and Republicans should stop trying to blame each other and work together," said one man, in the July public forum.[6]

JAS represents a conscious effort to retrieve and adapt for a new age the older, practical, work-centered view of immigrants. This was the view of Jane Addams, co-founder of Hull House, who sought to create public space where people of diverse views, skills, and life histories were not simply valued but could contribute to democracy.

The Settlement House Tradition

In the Hull House philosophy, democracy was a work in progress to which new immigrants as well as established residents and citizens could contribute. Jane Addams and her colleagues worked with immigrants from Eastern and Southern Europe and Mexico. Addams saw immigrant education as about "freeing the powers" of people for contribution.[7]

Gioia Diliberto's biography of Jane Addams, *A Useful Woman*, makes vivid the public spaces such a philosophy created, describing the "civic community" of Toynbee Hall, in the East End of London, on which Hull House was modeled. Diverse people worked and learned together. "The distinctive reform spirit of the Victorian era—an earnest combination of self-improvement and duty toward others . . . a conviction that all people, regardless of class, birth, or wealth, have the capacity and indeed the duty to 'evolve' into their best' selves . . . was epitomized by Toynbee Hall," argued Diliberto.

"Toynbee Hall teemed with courses, projects, meetings." In one month, she described, there were "classes for writing, math, chemistry, drawing, music, sewing, nursing, hygiene, composition, geography, book-keeping, citizenship, and evening courses in geology, physiology, botany, chemistry, Hebrew, Latin and Greek, European and English history, and literary subjects from Dante to Shakespeare to Moliere."[8]

Addams's Victorian language of "uplift" can sound condescending to modern ears. But from another angle, compared to our era in which most poor and immigrant populations are seen as needy and deficient by professional service providers, what is remarkable is the underlying conviction that ordinary people—poor and working class people, without money, of varied backgrounds, with little social status—had talents to contribute to the public conversation. "She was throwing in her 'lot' with the rest of the population," writes Diliberto, "struggling with them toward salvation that was in the self-interest of college educated settlement workers as it was of poor immigrants."[9]

Gertrude Himmelfarb argued that "civic community . . . implied no denial or even denigration of the distinctions of wealth, occupation, class or talent." Its premise, in Himmelfarb's view, was different. "It was rather meant to be a civic community based upon a common denominator of citizenship in the largest sense of the word . . . that made tolerable all these other social distinctions . . . which should not be exacerbated and should not be permitted to obscure the common humanity of individuals."[10]

Himmelfarb does not have it entirely right. Invocations of "common humanity" in Hull House, sentiments which by themselves could obscure real world differences in background, power resources, status, and opportunities, were not enough for Addams. She was a reformer, not simply a maker of meeting grounds. "Civic community"—public spaces—led to many gritty projects for social change, from trash collection to unionization. Addams believed civic community was a transformative space that would democratize and equalize relations and structures. Further, the work-centered philosophy of Hull House conveyed a view of power relations not simply as static, but as dynamic and open. Power was not simply "struggled over" but also created.

Simone Weil, the French philosopher of popular radicalism, observed this power relationship based on her actual experiences of work. "A . . . free life would be one wherein all real difficulties presented themselves as kinds of problems, wherein all successes were as solutions carried into action," wrote Weil. She argued that work and problem-solving, involving both reflective thought and action, entailed practical relationships that could disrupt hierarchies of power and status which otherwise operate unquestioned:

[In a "free"] society] social relations would be directly modeled upon the organization of labour; men would group themselves in small working collectivities . . . it is a fine sight to see a handful of workmen in the building trade, checked by some difficulty, [who] ponder the problem each for himself, make various suggestions for dealing with it, and then apply unanimously the method conceived by one, who may or may not have any official authority . . . at such moments, the image of a free community appears."[11]

Hull House created multiple opportunities for public work and the relationships that formed around such work. It also created strong partnerships with higher education, pioneering in extension classes, helping to shape the scholarship at leading academic centers like the philosophy and sociology departments at the University of Chicago. An aspect all these efforts was their public, open, diverse quality. This public quality included recognition of the need for political range: "The Settlement recognizes the need of cooperation, both with the radical and the conservative, and . . . cannot limit its friends to any one political party or economic school." Contrasting the Settlement philosophy with cloistered colleges, Addams argued that residents of Hull House "feel that they should promote a culture which will not set its possessor aside in a class with others like himself, but which will . . . connect him with all sorts of people by his ability to understand them as well as by his power to supplement their present surroundings."[12]

Against the background of growing discussions at the University of Minnesota about how to reinvigorate the land grant heritage for a new century, the settlement house philosophy of public spaces seemed appropriate to revive.

The Jane Addams School as Public Space

The Jane Addams School is not a program—it takes seriously the philosophy of Canon Barnett, founder of the first settlement, who argued the essence of the tradition was "the absence of program and the presence of men and women who recognize the obligations of citizenship." Nor is it a formal school. Rather, it is best described as a public space, or a network of public spaces. It stands in the tradition of the diverse "civic community" of Hull House or Toynbee Hall, and other American movements, such as the "School as Social Centre" effort inspired by Hull House, which sought to spread concepts and practices of community based education and public work across the country. The founding vision of JAS was "to free and cultivate the talents, cultures, and interests of people from diverse backgrounds to the commonwealth."[13]

In the JAS learning circles, immigrants teach college students, as well as get help in studying for the citizenship test. Teenagers learn internet and journalism skills, which they employ to make visible stories of young people's public work projects. Many projects resemble Public Achievement work, also taking place at Humboldt High School. A list of activities and projects in the adult circles in 2003 included bilingual discussions to teach civics, language, and culture; college student weekly training; citizenship test preparation; language literacy; civic training by Minnesota legislators and other public officials; a tour of the Minnesota state capital; civic training by staff; viewing of the Declaration of Independence and immigrant panel discussion; trainings for parents for gaining power in school governance structures; intergenerational field trips; computer skills work; University of Minnesota tour; and the Freedom Festival. The children's circle activities included reading; creative writing; creation of a newsletter; the theater group; skits and other activities for the Freedom Festival; bike maintenance and repair; and the creation of a political organizing group by teen boys and adults to address issues including gangs and violence, the war in Iraq, the importance of preserving immigrant cultures, language and identity. JAS had also proven a catalyst for a larger West Side effort called the Neighborhood Learning Community, an alliance of a number of groups (local schools, Riverview Library, Hmong Methodist Church, La Puerta Albierta Church, Guadalupe Church, Hubbs Center, Children's Literacy Initiative, La Clinica, the West Side Citizens Organization, the West Side Farm and Market Project, and Neighborhood House). The Neighborhood Learning Community's goal is to create a "culture of learning" on the West Side by tapping diverse experiences, traditions, and interests, using a variety of strategies.

More immediately in American history, JAS draws from the nonprofessional literacy learning of the citizenship schools in the civil rights movement. The citizenship schools avoided titles and formalities. "People with teaching experiences would likely impose their schooling methodology on the students and be judgmental," as Myles Horton, founder of Highlander Folk School—the first sponsor of the citizenship schools—described. Bernice Robinson, an early teacher in the citizenship schools, would say on the first day, "I am not a teacher. We're here to learn together. You're going to teach me as much as I'm going to teach you."[14]

Literacy work includes language acquisition—a challenge with a largely non-literate population such as the Hmong adults; civic literacy, revolving not only around the citizenship test but also around learning skills to practice democratic citizenship; and work literacy. The latter included a West Side Youth Apprenticeship Project for twenty-five teenagers working with twelve West Side businesses and nonprofits. Fourteen adult mentors and four coaches were involved, and the summer effort included weekly reflection groups to help young people "see" how work contributes to the community.

Literacy philosophy draws on adult and citizenship school traditions, stressing intergenerational learning and reciprocal pairs. In particular, JAS has created a philosophy of reciprocal learning relationships in which a college student pairs with a new immigrant and each serves as both a teacher and a learner. The pairing has an emphasis on coming to understand each other as multidimensional human beings, much like the IAF one-on-one process teaches the fluid, complex, dynamic qualities of everyday life. Partners are encouraged to learn each other's stories, interests, history, talents, and learning style. Immigrants and American born participants, often college students, often can be seen in intense conversation about marriage traditions, clothing, family patterns, foods, or other topics of everyday life from radically different cultural backgrounds.

Kathleen Winters, a French teacher from the Roseville school system, described her shift from disbelief to conviction. "As a language teacher, if I would have been in on the planning of JAS I would have said, 'You're crazy, this will never work.' I would have said all I was taught: you need scope and sequence, common materials, structured activities." Over time, however, Winters changed her view. "I've never seen learning as one-on-one before. I now believe that one-on-one supersedes any other teaching strategy." One-on-one learning is more interactive, personal, and relational. "You are able to get mutual understanding in one-on-one learning. People get lost in large group exchanges. In the one-on-one, there is an urgency to understand because you can't turn it over to someone else. You are forced to invent (together) ways to say things."[15]

Public cultural work has been an important part of the learning culture in JAS as well. JAS joined with Las Mujeras, a group of Mexican American women, to create an *ofrenda*, an altar, in celebration of the Day of the Dead. Women in Las Mujeras saw the event as a way to share their culture with non-Hispanic women, and each organizing meeting the women would describe different traditions associated with Day of the Dead, as well as their own personal stories. Each year since 1998, JAS participants have created the West Side Freedom Festival, highlighting the contributions of new immigrants and recognizing those who passed the citizenship test, featuring plays, skits, music and other cultural activities. One summer, young people in the Youth Farm, associated with the JAS, created a mural; in the summer of 2003, they worked with a local artist to create public art in the neighborhood park.

Political action and public leadership training have also been dimensions of JAS from the beginning. The JAS has created a working relationship with the Bureau of Citizenship and Immigration Services (BCIS), which allows participants to bring their learning partner to the test as a nonparticipant observer and has also involved immigration service staff in a variety of community projects. JAS played a key role in mobilizing political action among Hmong communities and college students across the country in support of the Hmong Veterans Recognition Bill passed by Congress in 2000. Immigrant parents have developed many strategies to access local schools as well. "Some of the people in this community were leaders in Laos, in Thailand, and in Latin America," argues Nan Skelton, a co-founder of the JAS. "But many have not been able to translate that into leadership in relation to the incredibly complex world of the St. Paul school system." Skelton observes that most institutions, including schools, discourage people from displaying their cultures and languages. "They want people to be proficient in the dominant culture." But the philosophy of the JAS is that "communities cannot build a future if they don't bring their past with them. [Public] leadership training [is essential] to help community leaders interact with and influence that world." The expectation of the JAS approach is that increased parent power will increase the capacity of the schools to teach. "We expect teachers and administrators of neighborhood schools will also seek ways to increase shared ownership in children's learning."

In the summers of 2002 and 2003, a teacher training program in civic and political skills, organized by Nan Kari, another co-founder of JAS, began to parallel immigrant parent training. It quickly spawned a number of projects in which teachers work with community members. Kari also directed the Youth Apprenticeship Project.[16]

Sandy Fuller, a third co-founder, describes the democratizing power dynamics that comes from the mix of immigrants, students, faculty, and others. "I have heard Hmong students say, 'I was Hmong and I was running away from being Hmong and wanted to be American. I turned my back on everything that reflected backward people. At JAS I saw the college professors with people like my parents and learning from them. That was the same stuff my parents told me and I didn't listen to them. Now these smart people are learning from my parents.'" Or, as Cindy Xiong, a high school sophomore active in JAS since the fifth grade (one of a group who raised money and organized a trip to Washington to lobby for the Veterans bill), described her interest in the Homeland Project, which organized a trip back to Laos. "We want to take a trip to our parents' homeland . . . to be in their shoes and see why they push us so much . . . we don't understand them, and there is a lot of miscommunication. We want to take this trip to understand our parents better, and to come back with this knowledge to explain it to other youth."[17]

The Jane Addams School includes a strong emphasis on productive work with civic impact. In the summer of 1998, JAS organized a Farm Project, feeding into the Twin Cities Youth Farm and Market Project, to involve young people in productive work roles. More than forty young people were involved the first year in an intergenerational public work effort with their parents, college students and faculty, and AmeriCorps members that brought young people from the Twin Cities to work on the Philadelphia Community Farm in Osceola, Wisconsin. Support from the Bonner Foundation allowed JAS to purchase eight shares of the farm, which meant that a portion of the produce was donated to the Neighborhood House food shelf, serving hundreds of families. "The produce from Jane Addams School is very helpful for the people on the West Side," said Seng Yang, a leader in the Hmong community and also one of the founders of JAS. "We usually don't have fresh vegetables, so this really benefits the community. But the best part is that the food comes from the children of the West Side, coming together to provide for the West Side." "Farming is hard work but it's fun," said nine-year-old Chor Yang about her experiences. "I'm learning a lot. I'm learning to plant vegetables, pick peas, and move and feed animals."[18]

The Farm Project was envisioned as a reinvigoration of older traditions in which young people had multiple opportunities for productive contribution. "[JAS] sees young people as producers and contributors to democracy," Nan Skelton explained. "We also believed that children should engage in serious and visible work, not simply be entertained for a few hours each night." Aleida Benitez included cultural activities as part of the summer effort. "We see kids for their potential and give them the opportunity to express themselves creatively," she described.[19]

JAS suggests something of what democratizing culture change and civic learning can look like, in which faculty and well-educated American-born students interact on an ongoing basis with new immigrants. Faculty from many departments and many hundreds of university students have been involved in different ways, and JAS has been widely recognized as an outstanding example of reciprocal, sustained university-community partnership. See Moua became active in the beginning of JAS while a student at St. Catherine's. She described what she learned. "JAS and the community on the West Side made me realize there is more to studying . . . something larger. I've been able to leave my role as student and no longer worry that I am in a particular box." As in Public Achievement, the experiences led her to rethink politics as well. "Before coming to Jane Addams I didn't like politics at all. I hated politics. I didn't realize it's not the politicians, but the people who have power. If we don't like how things are done we have the power to change it."[20]

JAS has proven a resource for larger discussion of the "engaged university" at Minnesota, described in more detail in Chapter 8. As Craig Swan, vice provost for undergraduate education at the University of Minnesota, told a group of Harvard researchers, "This is a partnership with people from the university helping immigrant populations understand our democratic traditions, but also getting new perspectives about what citizenship and democracy mean to people who haven't been born in the U.S." Swan sees "learning on both sides."[21]

The different learning circles involve times for "cultural exchange" as well as study. Bina Nikrin, another Humphrey student who took part in JAS in the spring of 2003, described her experiences working with Hmong elders who study English. "Evidently this Hmong language group comes to JAS not just to practice for the citizenship test or to learn English," Nikrin observed. "They come for a broader purpose: to learn to get along in this country and to express themselves and explore new ideas with other Hmong people and with Americans from a variety of backgrounds." New immigrants and native born citizens, in Nikrin's view, "together . . . comprise the space that is Jane Addams School."[22]

TABLE 2. TWO APPROACHES TO CIVIC LEARNING

	Service	*Organizing*
Discourse	Innocence	Politics
Goal	To fix problems (or people)	To build democratic power
Definition of citizenship	Voluntarism	Public work
Motive	Altruism	Self-interest
Method	Programs	Public leadership development
Site	Departments	Public spaces
Outcomes	Reports, proposals	Culture change, human change

The work on the West Side has brought home a contrast between two modes of educational practice: service and organizing (see Table 2). Organizing, from the Greek root *ergon*, meaning work, involves understanding education as about transformation, the reworking of ourselves and our contexts. An organizing approach is what JAS seeks to develop, as people learn to think and act in public ways.[23]

Student encounters with new immigrants at the Jane Addams School often are powerful experiences in politics through the work of teaching and learning, as Mary Harrison described. New immigrants most often come to the United States with enthusiasm about ideas like democracy or freedom or citizenship that are often unreflected upon and taken for granted here. "America is in the making," said Mai Neng Moua, a Jane Addams School participant and editor of the first Hmong anthology of writings. "It isn't a complete picture, and whoever comes adds to it." Students who encounter the freshness and excitement about ideas like democracy, freedom, or citizenship can be strongly impacted. "I'm no longer taking democracy for granted," said Meghen Kelley, a student at the University of Minnesota. "I'm authoring it. To help someone learn about freedom forces me to think about my relationship to democracy."[24]

Experiences in the Jane Addams School and its spin-offs can generate public learning for themselves for new immigrants. Indeed, as Bina Nikrin observed, this is often a powerful motivation for immigrant participation.

One of the most dramatic stories rooted in the JAS and sponsored by the Youth Farm and Market Project involved the return of a group of Hmong girls to their ancestral homeland in Laos. The Homeland Project illustrated both the public learning that takes place as immigrants negotiate the complex cultural environment of the United States and the impact that immigrants can have on broader publics. Five Hmong teenage girls and three chaperons went to Laos in December 2002, returning on January 7, 2003. The group included Sheng Ly (18), Shau Ly (17), Soua Yang (17), Cindy Xiong (16), and Mai Xiong (14), along with three young adults, Jeff Bauer, and Gunnar and Kate Liden. All had been active in the JAS and also with the Youth Farm and Market Project on the West Side. The trip was the result of more than a year and a half of intense organizing, fundraising, planning, and interaction with diverse audiences and groups across the Twin Cities. They raised thousands of dollars and gained support from groups across the political spectrum. "Some of our best fundraisers were in Republican suburbs," Bauer described. The trip also gained an enormous amount of local publicity, with interviews in the *Star Tribune, St. Paul Pioneer Press*, and *Hmong Times* as well as a chronicle of their experiences on Minnesota Public Radio.

The original mission of the Homeland Project described it as "a cultural education and community organizing initiative, created by and for Hmong youth, both to reclaim their own cultural identities and to help non-Hmong Minnesotans better understand the culture and history of the Hmong people." The project description recognized addressing the cultural tensions of being both "Hmong" and "American" as a central issue. "The Homeland Project" is a direct response to the daily, lived reality of Hmong teenagers—a reality filled with the tension between honoring and preserving one culture, while trying to grow and thrive in another." The mission also included an explicit democracy emphasis, taking note of the changed context after 9/11. "It is also a grassroots effort to strengthen our democracy in Minnesota through cultural exchange and understanding, especially during this critical time when our collective commitment to the democratic ideals of diversity and freedom must be renewed." A project fundraising proposal drafted in January 2002 described public and political skills as a central objective. "Implicit in the design and implementation of all Homeland Project activities is the development of lifelong public work skills like designing and conducting research projects, speaking publicly, facilitating meetings, writing grant proposals, forming multicultural and intergenerational relationships, engaging with schools and organizations in the community and teaching through a variety of experiential means."[25]

The political challenges were sometimes daunting, but learning to meet them created extensive political education and lessons. Thus, while families were skeptical about Hmong girls undertaking such a trip, the girls met with many elders and leaders in the Hmong community to make their case and hear advice. "We sat through countless meetings while elders told us what to do and what not to do, nodding all the time," described Bauer. To raise the considerable funds needed, the girls sold thousands of Hmong egg rolls at community and school gatherings, organized concession stands, and put out coin jars across the West Side. They also made fundraising appeals to many groups in both cities and suburbs. Before each meeting, the girls researched group interests and membership, discussed the self-interests of members in possibly contributing, and role-played questions and answers.[26]

Another sustained effort, lasting five years and involving more than forty young people, the Citizenship Test project, grew out of Hmong and Latino teenagers in Public Achievement teams at Humboldt High School who were angry about their parents' experiences in studying for the naturalization test. Coached by Jennifer O'Donoghue—a Humphrey Institute graduate student who had spent two years herself working in Hmong refugee camps— the students were also partly inspired by the widespread organizing to win passage of the Hmong Veteran Recognition Bill, an effort that involved many at JAS. Many were angry at what they considered its unfairness, especially to those, such as Hmong adults, who were not literate in their native language and for whom learning to pass the test in English seemed an often immense task. The test was also expensive. "It was really hard for my mom," said Kong Her. "And it cost my family about $600," after test costs were added to preparation classes, before Kong's mother started going to JAS (where learning is free). "My dad worked very hard but still struggled on his English," said Yang Yang, a Humboldt student.[27]

Team members were also dismayed by what they thought was the test's shallowness. Citizenship Test questions are drawn from a list of 100, 77 of which are concerned with details of government (a sample: "Who is the Chief Justice of the Supreme Court?" "What was the 49th state?" "What were the 13 original colonies?" "How many amendments are there to the Constitution?"). It also presupposes a particular theory of citizenship. "What is the most important right?" has one correct answer—"the right to vote," reducing enormously complex and debatable issues to a narrow definition of what citizenship means. "Our mom has been through these citizenship classes for the last two years and it's just memorizing," said Nicole Ly, adding that teaching about citizenship rights and responsibilities and the real workings of government was much more important. But there was no consensus on these questions, and PA teams had to negotiate a number of differences among themselves. Some thought the English language requirement was not a bad idea; others thought it was unfair; some agreed there should be a test of some kind; some thought an interactive conversation with citizens, or sustained community service, would be a better citizenship requirement.

The project evolved through stages, including visits with the Immigration and Naturalization Service to discuss the history and purpose of the test, and research on how citizenship tests had been administered in the past. In 1998, the Public Achievement group working on the issue decided to make a video on the test. The result, "Citizenship: Would You Pass?" became a highly visible project in the Twin Cities and beyond.

Judy Ly, the interviewer for the video, asked people in four settings— Humboldt High School, the state capitol building, a shopping mall, and JAS—five questions from the Citizenship Test list. Respondents were judged to have passed if they answered three out of five right. Out of 25 people interviewed, one American-born citizen passed and two immigrants studying for the citizenship test passed. Judy Ly then asked interviewees whether they thought the test is fair, and if it is an accurate measure of what it means to be a citizen—a question that solicited wide ranging answers, along with no little embarrassment.

After the video was made, the teams of teenagers presented it to a number of audiences in the Twin Cities, as well as in Denver and Washington, D.C. The Washington trip required fundraising—the team raised more than $7,000 to make the journey. Coached by Nick Longo, they made the rounds of the Minnesota delegation in Washington to express their views on the test, a first experience in some of the lessons of Washington lobbying. They found sympathy and skepticism about their arguments, but a also good deal of responsiveness. They also learned some lessons.

Senator Paul Wellstone, a critic of high stakes testing based on his own bad school experiences, spoke about his life as a son of Russian immigrants. But the meeting was shortened when he had to leave for a Senate vote, and the students never got a commitment for how he might help. "We should all remember that," said Longo, in the debriefing. "We shouldn't let them leave without getting some kind of commitment." Representative Betty Mc-Collum defended the idea of questions about the colonies. "I think it is important that we know how we got to where we are today," she told them. But she also agreed that "probably we could do a much better job" with the test.[28]

In 2003, a representative of JAS was invited to participate on a national panel to review and revise the test. Though no direct connection was made to the students' project, its visibility and student lobbying may well have been factors. There were also more intangible results. "We learned a lot of skills, like public speaking and how to evaluate our actions. The team members got a sense of working an issue through, and also the multiple sides of an issue," said Longo. He also said it taught a much more nuanced strategy. "The Citizenship Test connects to different institutions. There are many ways to approach an issue, many places to impact. But change doesn't just happen because you want it to. We also learned that change on a big scale is very hard, and takes a lot of time." Lasting friendships also developed through the work. Two members of the PA Citizenship teams came to the wedding of Nick Longo and Aleida Benitez in Providence, Rhode Island, in the summer of 2003.[29]

In JAS, as well as in Public Achievement, concepts of public life, politics, power, citizenship, and democracy take on new meanings and possibilities. This is a rare experience in our time for new immigrants, but also for college students and faculty as well. Terri Wilson, a former student at the University of Minnesota, now a graduate student in philosophy at Columbia, reflected on her several years involvement at JAS.

When I first came to Jane Addams [School] I thought of it as a place to connect the political philosophy I was studying to real and meaningful experiences. This experience—connecting ideas to work—is still so important. But [other] qualities of this experience are what have captured my time, commitment [and] passion.

The structure of Jane Addams has given me space and the responsibility to do things I never thought I could do, like be a leader and facilitator, share laughter with a 74-year-old woman across language and culture. . . .

The space of Jane Addams is a space where my contributions are seen as valuable; a space that recognizes rather than overlooks people's diverse talents and creativity.[30]

Public space is a quality of human interaction among diverse individuals, and also a cultural dynamic, as Wilson's comments suggest. It also requires politics. "With such immense diversity in JAS, the only way it works is for people to learn a different kind of politics, to negotiate different interests and perspectives," said Nan Kari.[31]

How such experiences might be more than oases of public life in our highly privatized, technocratic society requires attention to politics on a different scale: the potential of public work to alter and democratize professional practices which now render groups such as new immigrants, and many others, as helpless, needy, and deficient.

Chapter 7
Professions as Public Work

Public work involves the experience of working effectively with others about the things you care about, becoming visible, having power to make change. It is hard work, but tremendously rewarding and motivating. Public life is a source of hope.
—Nan Kari

It is in the long-range self-interest of many professionals to become more interactive with citizens in order to accomplish the broader public purposes of their craft. Nevertheless, in their normal training, professionals learn to see ordinary citizens in a particular fashion that greatly limits such interactions—as needy, victimized, and requiring rescue by educated elites. Incorporating the concept and practice of public work into professional cultures, using concepts and practices of everyday politics, unleashes the democratic potential of knowledge power and thus points toward a different sort of professional practice. Public professional work frees the powers not only of ordinary citizens but also of professionals as well. But changing professional practices and cultures is difficult, because the process entails changing identities and

ll as adding public concepts.

ucture much of American life, from

n. In dominant approaches today,

nt, while the people are reduced to

professionals are public figures, but

l from Jane Addams's common lot.

m

who "free the powers" of people,

esents a subterranean tradition of

public professional practice. This tradition has a new relevance in the knowledge-based world of the twenty-first century.

Addams's approach to settlement house work was part of a rich but largely forgotten alternative, democratic tradition of professional practice. Settlement house public workers had parallels in K-12 education, community colleges, land grant and public universities, and the cooperative extension system of cooperative agents. Their approach was also to be found in a broad array of adult and continuing education efforts that fed cultural and political movements like the Harlem Renaissance (indeed, there were strong connections; Alain Locke, with James Weldon Johnson a leading architect of the Harlem Renaissance, was also a founder of many adult education groups). Public professional work had offshoots in health fields like occupational therapy, described later in this chapter, in community practice of law, in the "beat reporter" in journalism, in youth work that emphasized young people's productive contributions to community life. I saw powerful examples as a young man in the American civil rights movement of the 1960s, in the practice of black clergy, teachers, beauticians, and others who organized communities.

Such understandings of public professional work adapted populist themes of the nineteenth century to the new world of urban life, modern communications and transportation systems, and rapid scientific advances of the twentieth century. At points, they also found broader theoretical articulation. The work and writings of John Dewey are an illustration.

As James Farr has recently demonstrated, John Dewey was arguably the most important architect of the concept of "social capital," perhaps the leading concept in the broad camp of communitarianism, a branch of political theory espoused by both Bill Clinton and George W. Bush. But for Dewey, social capital had a critical edge lacking in current usage. Dewey's deployment of the term was associated with his challenges to racism, poverty, and rural backwardness, and his advocacy of radical changes in education. Perhaps most dramatic in contrast with current uses, Dewey drew on a long line of economic reformers and radicals, from Karl Marx to Edward Bellamy, to challenge the logic and dynamic of private capital and the deification of the marketplace. As Farr summarizes, "the political economists of the nineteenth century" on which Dewey drew for his critical stance, "took capital—and its associations—from the social point of view. It might be said that today's social capitalists take 'the social'—and its associations— from capital's point of view."[1]

To return to the formative period in Dewey's intellectual life is to go back to young intellectuals involved in what Lewis Feuer called the "back to the people" movement. "The depression of the 1880s, the riots, the waves of immigrants accumulating in the new slums, and the stark drama of the Haymarket anarchists, shook America out of its complacency," as Feuer put it.[2]

Henry Demarest Lloyd called the mood "the New Conscience." Proponents of far ranging economic reform like Edward Bellamy and Henry George were held in high regard. Articulating the sentiments of young intellectuals such as Jane Addams and John Dewey, Lloyd expressed widespread views when he said, "I am on the side of the underdog. The agitators on that side make mistakes, commit crimes, no doubt, but for all that theirs is the right side." There was, in Lloyd's view, a "renaissance of moral inventions."[3]

John Dewey, coming to the University of Michigan in 1884, had been shaped in his own self-description "from persons and from situations more than from books." His youthful experiences in Vermont can be taken, in important respects, as emblematic of the social background that was the seedbed of American populism, an outlook he brought with him to Michigan.[4]

What made Dewey's populism prophetic is that he understood, far better than most of his contemporaries, the dynamics of power in an information society, where power is not simply a scarce good that requires a bitter struggle in which gains on one side are matched by losses on the other side. Rather, knowledge power is increased through sharing transactions. Dewey believed, in particular, in what he called the "social" quality of knowledge production and dissemination through education. He argued that recognition of knowledge's social quality was key to the future of democracy itself.

A passion for the relevance of ideas, for intellectual work that actually makes a difference in the real world, was a constant theme for Dewey. "The work of history," he argued, "was to free the truth—to break down the walls of isolation and of class interest which hold it in and under." But truth only becomes free, he added, when it "distributes itself to all so that it becomes the Commonwealth."[5]

Such a perspective on knowledge made Dewey a sharp critic of knowledge "for its own sake," removed from consideration of human ends. Thus, he contrasted religious evangelists (whom he did not hold in high regard) to detached scientists, "The evangelist, ignorant though he is, who is in constant contact with the needs, the sins, the desires, and the aspirations of actual human nature is a better judge of religious truth than the man of science, if a truly speculative life has shut him off from sympathy and living intimacy with the fundamental truths of the common nature of man."[6]

There was, throughout Dewey's career, a democratic respect for ordinary people's values, their activities, and their intelligence. Dewey believed, with Thomas Jefferson, that ordinary people were the "only safe repository of the powers of the society," whose judgments, however flawed they may be, were likely to be sounder than those of any elite. Thus, in his introduction to a collection on *The Living Thoughts of Thomas Jefferson*, Dewey extolled Jefferson on the ground that "His faith in the right of the people to govern themselves in their own way and in their ability to exercise the right wisely, provided they were enlightened by education and by free discussion, was stronger than his faith in any article of his own political creed—except this one." He praised Jefferson's plans for local ward government where people were to exercise power with respect to their own affairs (such as care of the poor, roads, police and the like) on the grounds, as he paraphrased Jefferson, that "every man would then share in the government of affairs not merely on election day but every day."[7]

Dewey sought to ground intellectual life in the activities and work of common people. In his view, the entire tradition of philosophy had made an invidious—and invalid—distinction between thought and action, intellect and work. "The depreciation of action, of doing and making, has been cultivated by philosophers," Dewey wrote in *The Quest for Certainty*, his attack on the idea that inquiry can be separated from the social context in which it functions. "After a distinctively intellectual class had arisen, a class having leisure and in a large degree protected against the more serious perils which afflict the mass of humanity, its members proceeded to glorify their own office." Glorifying their office meant epistemological arrogance. "Since no amount of pains and care in action can ensure complete certainty, certainty in knowledge was worshipped as a substitute . . . the ideal of a cognitive certainty and truth having no connection with practice, and [even] prized because of its lack of connection, developed."[8]

Dewey's basic argument, deeply democratic in its implications, is that all knowledge—"academic" no less than "practical"—is social knowledge, the product of an interplay of experience, testing and experiment, observation, reflection, and conversation. All have the capacity and right to participate in knowledge-creation. Recognizing the social nature of knowledge is essential to an accurate account. "Consider the development of the power of guiding ships across trackless wastes from the day when they hugged the shore," wrote Dewey. "The record would be an account of a vast multitude of cooperative efforts, in which one individual uses the results provided for him by a countless number of other individuals . . . so as to add to the common and public store. A survey of such facts brings home the actual social character of intelligence as it actually develops and makes its way."[9]

Dewey's view of knowledge as a "public and common store" shaped his view of democracy. Dewey is sometimes charged with a naïve or idealistic view of democracy. There is an element of truth in this criticism. As I argued in Chapter 2, Dewey's removal of politics from community life made his proposals for reform often highly idealized. Yet what critics overlook is that Dewey was getting at a particular dynamic of knowledge power, different from zero-sum distributive conflicts in which one's loss is another's gain. Dewey did not ignore coercion or violence in public life. His creed was based on the urgency of challenging coercion with what he called "social intelligence" as an alternative. He argued that liberals see intelligence "as an individual possession and its exercise as an individual right." In fact, he argues, "It is false that freedom of inquiry and of expression are not modes of [collective] action. They are exceedingly potent modes of action. The reactionary grasps this fact, in practice if not in express idea, more quickly than the liberal, who is too much given to holding that this freedom is innocent of consequences, as well as being a merely individual right." In Dewey's view, liberals must recognize the social power of knowledge. They must "assume the responsibility for making it clear that intelligence is a social asset and is clothed with a function as public as is its origin in the concrete, in social cooperation."[10]

Building on these premises about the social and practical nature of knowledge as well as his democratic faith in the values and capacities of ordinary people, Dewey developed a dynamic vision of democracy as built on abundance, not scarcity. Democracy was "a way of life" (using a formulation by T. V. Smith), not simply a form of government or a distributive mechanism, about which he spoke with passion. In his famous address, "The School as a Social Centre," before the National Council of Education, Dewey called upon education to be at the heart of the new civilization. "Everywhere we see the growing recognition that the community life is defective and distorted excepting as it does care for all its constituent parts. This is no longer viewed as a matter of charity, but as a matter of justice— nay, even of something higher and better than justice—a necessary phase of developing and growing life." In stressing social intelligence as different than justice, Dewey intimated deep insights about the information age and its power dynamics. "Men will long dispute about material socialism, about socialism considered as a matter of distribution of the material resources of the community," he argued. But he saw social intelligence as about a non-scarce resource, knowledge: "There is a socialism . . . of the intelligence and the spirit. To extend the range and the fullness of sharing in the intellectual and spiritual resources of the community is the very meaning of the community."[11]

In Dewey's view, a commonwealth or socialism of knowledge comes into being when all work is understood in terms of its educative capacities and human and social properties. It is, in short, a mistake to separate "work" from "education." "In the democracy of the future, goods will be made not primarily as a means to private profit, but because of their service to enriched living. . . . Not only the value of the product for those who use it, but the process of production itself will be appraised in terms of its contribution to human welfare." Challenging those who focused simply on reducing the work week, Dewey argued in the essay, "A Free Teacher in a Free Society," that "the quality of the work experience" rather than the number of hours worked was the key question. "If work were made a more effective part of the democratic social life . . . the demand for shorter hours would be far less insistent."[12]

Dewey stressed the educative dimensions "of all callings [and] occupations." He especially focused on professions, doubtless having in mind the examples of popular citizenship education and educators such as Jane Addams and others at Hull House, who saw their work in catalytic and energizing terms. Thus professionals, he said, needed to become more conscious of their educative roles and responsibilities. "The professions . . . not merely require education in those who practise them but help to form the attitudes and understanding of those who consult their practitioners," Dewey wrote. "As far as science is humanized, it educates all the laymen. Artists, painters, musicians, architects, and writers are also an immense educative force," in potential, though "at the present time . . . this educative function is hampered and distorted."[13]

Education should be practiced as a dynamic engagement with the world, its problems, and its work. Education for democracy—education's highest and most important goal—had self-consciously to cultivate the habits that once were generated through young people's involvement in the life and work of families and communities. "There was always something which really needed to be done, and a real necessity that each member of the household should do his own part faithfully in co-operation with others," Dewey argued. Everyday productive work taught habits of cooperation, responsibility, productive outlook. It also meant a deep connection with the world. "We cannot overlook the importance for educational purposes of the close and intimate acquaintance got with nature at first hand." Everyday work had once connected young people "with real things and materials, with the actual processes of their manipulation and the knowledge of their social necessities and uses. In all this there was continual training of observation, of ingenuity, constructive imagination, of logical thought, and of the sense of reality acquired through first-hand contact with actualities."[14]

John Dewey's theory of knowledge as a nonfinite resource increased through sharing represents a vital legacy for democratization. To make it come to life requires close attention to the public and political dimensions of professional work, in several senses of public. Public work entails learning the skills of interactive everyday politics, in which professionals put themselves back into the mix of interests and views that comprise a diverse group of people. It means attending to the larger public meanings and purposes of the discipline or profession. Finally, it means creating settings for interactive civic learning, treating organizing as a kind of civic laboratory.

Partnerships in Education

These dimensions of public professional practice are dramatized in some of the most innovative experiments with contemporary education in recent years, for instance, the pioneering work of Deborah Meier and her associates in Central Park East schools and now Mission Hill School in Boston. These educators have developed concepts such as "habits"—rather than knowledge transmission—and "education for democracy," by creating strong partnerships in learning with parents and communities.

Meier defines education itself as "work," with real consequences, about real problems. Students engage the world around them constantly, learning through multi-dimensional projects inside and outside the school buildings. At the foundation of her philosophy is a respect for young people. "It all fit in with my feeling that one of the reasons the country was in the shape it was had to do with the fact that people who spent years in such schools didn't have a sense of their intellectual competence," says Meier about her observations of the impact of schools. "No one had ever honored their ideas. No one had ever said, 'you're a person with ideas and you're capable and intellectual,' at least in the public sphere, no one representing the larger world." She named her first book, *The Power of Their Ideas*, to convey the energy and creativity young people have when they start school, often lost as they progress.

To bring an educational philosophy based on respect for young people's talents and capacities to life requires strong partnerships with parents and other "nonexperts" in the broader community. In her schools' philosophy, parents as well as young people deserve respect as key partners in learning. Meier got her educational start in the 1950s, during the civil rights movement, and noticed a sharp contrast. "Here we [in the movement] were saying that ordinary citizens could change the world but they were too stupid to raise their children. [That was the view of many educators] in Chicago. Even progressive-minded teachers felt that way. I saw the degree to which schools made parents feel that they were inept. Even middle class parents came to feel when their children were in a very early age, 'I can't teach my child this.'" Meier believed that partnerships with parents were far more important than any teaching method. "While it's true that I wish I could teach [parents] to teach their kid to add my way, the worst thing I could do was teach their kid to look at their parent and think, 'my parents are too stupid to add. I'm not allowed to ask my mother. I have to wait until the teacher can teach me.'"

Respect for parents means honest recognition that parents are by no means innocent in this dynamic. The night after a school parent meeting on how her current school, Mission Hill in Boston, teaches writing, Meier observed that "a lot of the questions directed at us were, in essence, 'when my kid does X at home, what should I do?' I told teachers, 'I don't want you to tell the parents what they should do. I want you to say, 'Listen, you're probably capable of figuring that out.'"

Meier has always been interested in the politics of schools. "I thought about the power relations partly in terms of how disrespectful it was, and how insulted I felt when some young teachers started giving me advice about having a table for my children's homework," she described. "I thought, 'Do you really think I haven't heard that before? I need you to tell me they need a space?' I felt deeply insulted by teachers giving me advice in places where I thought they had no business." She also thought of the contrasts. "I felt, 'My God, I have so many things going for me [in terms of status and prestige] and I feel humiliated. What must it be like for people who are not so sure that they are important? What does it do to their kids to see them treated that way?' Teachers get mad at them for not coming to family conferences or to school, but why would they come to school if family conferences were so humiliating?" Meier borrowed from the work of Seymour Saranson, who argued schools often reflect the tensions and negotiations between two groups of women, women teachers and women parents, both of whom feel vulnerable to being attacked and blamed. Interacting with upper middle class parents, teachers "fall back on 'my professionalism' even more. It's the only part of the relationship that makes them equal to parents, the identity they have as professionals."

Meier thinks these dynamics must be addressed as political questions. "If teachers had more confidence in their relationships with each other and the work they do, if they didn't feel so powerless, and they were expected to have authority about the work they do it, it would help." But the dynamic needs to be open and reciprocal. "At the same time, when they get respect, they also have to give it. They have to assume that parents have a domain. You need some domains; each needs a place where they have some authority. Some of it has to be by rules, where you recognize certain jurisdictional power."

The heart of the learning process, in Meier's view, is the development of habits, a concept she developed from Dewey. Central Park East and Mission Hill schools stress five habits that students learn to "think with" as they engage any problem or topic. They include relevance (so what?); viewpoint (where does this come from?); connection (how is this knowledge connected to other things?); evidence (what are the sources?); and conjecture (suppose something else?). She argues that "each of them serves some democratic as well as academic purpose. Conjecture teaches the world could be different. If your response to everything is 'it has to be that way,' you can't take responsibility." Each of these habits is learned in a community context, as well as the classroom.

Habits are also vital traits, in Meier's view, for public life. As with the IAF stress on leadership development, they also take work to learn. "Neither are innate human characteristics. It takes schooling of some sort to develop habits. You need habits when it isn't natural." Meier sees this as a broad challenge for democratic renewal. "Democratic culture needs citizens with very strong habits."[15]

Clergy as Public Workers

Meier's success in creating dynamic public cultures in the schools she had organized was one important inspiration for the early civic engagement work at the Humphrey Institute. Another inspiration was one rarely noted feature of the broad-based citizen organizing: in significant measure, it has proven so effective because organizers have challenged ministers to make their work more public.

In 1981, the Black Caucus of the IAF, led by Johnny Youngblood, Gerald Taylor, and others, produced a new document, *The Tent of the Presence*, based on the passage from Numbers that tells the story of Moses' "heavy burden," carrying on his own shoulders the weight of leadership in the passage through the wilderness. God instructed Moses to gather a group of elders at "the tent of meeting," the center of the Jewish community. God shared the power and responsibility for leadership with a larger group.

Moses said to the Lord, "Why hast thou dealt ill with thy servant? . . . Where am I to get meat to give to all this people? I am not able to carry all this people alone, the burden is to heavy for me. . . ."

And the Lord said to Moses, "Gather for me seventy men of the elders of Israel . . . and I will take some of the spirit which is upon you and put it upon them; and they shall bear the burden of the people with you, that you may not bear it alone." (Numbers 11: 10–18)

Tent of the Presence, rich with biblical symbolism and exegesis, included the developing IAF themes of a public life. The document argued that the black community in America, and the black church in particular, stood at a crossroads. Facing a dangerous movement away from social justice concerns in American politics, 1960s-style movement leaders were dependent on charismatic appeals and moral exhortations, and increasingly unlikely to succeed in gaining much power for African American communities. For the black community to avoid an increasingly dangerous isolation and marginality, a new style of leadership would be needed, along with new organizational forms. Like Moses, the black clergy had to choose people with promising talents and abilities and "share some of the spirit" with them. A new form of collaborative leadership needed to emerge, spreading leadership and developing congregation members' public talents and skills. New mediating institutions, "broad based citizen organizations," were needed as well, owned by members, racially and culturally diverse, aimed at gathering power over time. Baltimore, where ministers with great standing from civil rights days such as Vernon Dobson had helped draft the statement, proved a test case to put the new style of ministry into practice.[16]

Since then, IAF has given sustained and intensive attention to adding public dimensions to the work of the clergy. Helping clergy to make their work more public is a challenge. "I sometimes say that clergy and cops are alike," observed Moriba Karamoko, an IAF organizer now with the ABLE organization in Atlanta. "I know of no other two professions where the psyche and the persona that come with the profession are so much the same. People carry their work persona with them even to bed. For the average cop, everybody is a suspect. Clergy are always in the position of nurturing and giving and counseling and saving. They become fixers." Karamoko said that IAF organizing requires clergy to be more relational and reciprocal, and to "engage in the public square." This is often hard. "It's not the way they're socialized. The struggle is to help them to envision their role and their life and their contribution being also outside the church. They also have a civic voice. They have issues that are important to them as a pastor, as a voter, as a father, as an uncle, as a godfather." It takes "struggle," Karamoko put it, "to get inside their self-interests and their imagination and their vision and their anger and their hopes. What do they want to be in a city? What do they want to be in their donomination? How can this work help them in that regard?"

IAF organizers in training are taught to "agitate clergy" about what brought them into the ministry, what makes them angry, what larger public purposes they want to accomplish. Many IAF affliates have a "Clergy Caucus," which provides a regular space for philosophical, theological, and practical reflection on faith, scripture, theology—all tied to their own roles. The point is to enrich the work of clergy by adding dimensions of political education and organizing to the private, often therapeutic, pastoral practices which they were taught in seminars.[17]

Politics of Health

Nan Kari showed that the sort of political and professional change pioneered by Deborah Meier and the broad-based citizen organizing with clergy was possible in health professions. Kari taught occupational therapy at the College of St. Catherine's for many years, and then became director of faculty development, a position she shifted from a "service" orientation to what she called an "organizing" approach. In that position, she organized a group of faculty, using the "citizen politics" framework of the CDC, to help create a more public culture on the campus.[18] She subsequently was a co-founder of the Jane Addams School for Democracy.

Kari went into occupational therapy as a profession because of its philosophy of work. "Occupational therapy includes in its core philosophy the idea that meaningful work has generative power and that people have the capacity to learn from experience," she described. "When this ability is combined with the cultivation of imagination and creativity, human beings can shape their environments to create healthy, balanced, and meaningful lives." Kari was inspired by Mary Reilly, one of the profession's leaders, who argued for a work-centered philosophy of occupational therapy in her 1961 Slagle lecture, the most prominent talk in the profession given each year:

American society in general and medicine in particular has need of a profession which has as its unique concern the nurturing of the spirit in man for action. [Occupational therapy] should have as a special contribution a profound understanding of the nature of work. . . . Man through the use of his hand can creatively deploy his thinking, feeling, and purposes to make himself at home in the world and to make the world his home.[19]

Kari believed occupational therapy would be a way to make a difference. "The acknowledgement of human agency and our capacity to become whole people, regardless of mental or physical disability; the idea that the act of creating can unleash a sense of power; and the expression of human hope—all this resonated with my beliefs," she said.

The roots of occupational therapy were in the "moral movement" developed in Europe and brought to the United States in the later nineteenth century as "treatment for the insane." "Occupations," or meaningful activities, were key to its philosophy. In the early twentieth century, as occupational therapy emerged as a health profession, it retained the emphasis on occupation, or purposeful work, as a way to achieve health. The profession gained public recognition after World War I, especially through its rehabilitative and vocational work with wounded veterans. Interestingly, several key leaders had been active in Hull House settlement in Chicago.

Occupational therapy, a profession predominantly of women, competes for status within the medical hierarchy. "As it allied more with the medical model, the profession shifted away from a holistic understanding of work to a focus on smaller components of activity like coordination, strength, and endurance," said Kari. Today, the concept of work has become narrowed to two areas. Ergonomics focuses on the motions required for work tasks and the requisite physical environment. Work hardening, the other treatment modality, involves a series of graded physical exercises designed to strengthen weakened muscles. "Both have value," in Kari's view, "but the profession lost the larger significance of work. For me, it created a disconnection between the luminous philosophy and the day to day practice."

Involvement with Project Public Life led Kari to try out a number of experiments in integrating political concepts and practices into her profession. She came directly up against the therapeutic culture of the profession, which in her judgment used a language of helping and nurturing that could conceal or mystify interests and power relationships. To address this dynamic, Kari introduced concepts of power and interests in a course on group dynamics. She put a piece of tape on the floor in the hallway and asked the students to line up from the most to the least powerful in the class. "Students vied for position from the middle to the low end. Only one or two would place themselves at the high power end."

Another insight came when she did interviews with 45 students at the College of St. Catherine newly admitted to the occupational therapy program. She asked each what her self-interests were. Some were shocked at the question. Most said they simply wanted to help others. Some used religious language of a calling. One young woman declared, "If I could just save one life from misery, then my whole education would be worth it."

Kari believed that there were unseen consequences to the apolitical language of the profession. "I could see we were socializing professionals who would carry with them in their position a great deal of power that could influence people's lives. There was little if any critical reflection about it. The core identity of 'helper' hides patterns of power."

Partly to create opportunities for students to practice a different approach to the profession, partly to explore how public and political concepts could be used as tools of cultural transformation, Kari teamed up with Peg Michels, an organizer, and Pam Hayle, director of therapeutic activities at the Augustana Home of Minneapolis. Augustana was a large Lutheran nursing home in Minneapolis. The purpose of the project was to introduce a set of public skills and concepts to create a more public environment— what they called a "public community"—that would tap the talents and energies of residents, families, and staff in new ways. The four-year effort was called the Lazarus Project. Kari and Michels wrote an article on the Lazarus Project for the *American Journal of Occupational Therapy*, the main journal in the field, which won the annual award for the best article.[20]

There are large barriers to individual and collective agency within the therapeutic cultures of long term care institutions. Nursing homes vary according to size, location, or affiliation, but they often have a starkly institutional quality that reinforces regimentation and dependency. Providers' function is to provide service. Residents are recipients—often described today as clients or even customers. Their role is to express satisfaction.

Augustana Home is a Lutheran Minneapolis nursing home that at the time of the project employed five hundred staff members for 370 residents. It is associated with a larger campus of 400 apartments in adjoining high rise buildings. Augustana is a not for profit organization whose revenue sources were largely Medicare and Medicaid. The project itself was funded through a capital campaign in 1989 that had, as one goal, creating a "more empowering community."

For many residents, Augustana was the first experience of institutional living and being served, after a life of serving others. About 85 percent of the residents were women during the project, many from working class backgrounds who had been active in church activities or homemaking. For residents the most basic struggle was to learn how to live in and negotiate a radically different environment.

For staff, a rhetorical goal was to "empower clients," but empowerment was conceived in individual and psychological terms. The paradox was that as caregivers seek to establish nurturing relationships, the very intensity could easily reinforce control. Hierarchies were visible among staff about who cared the most. Staff often talked about needing to be appreciated. The intimate quality of such relationships in the absence of more public life generated expectations for residents to respond with constant signs of appreciation. At the same time staff members often expressed frustration with their inability to deal effectively with increasing demands. Their burden bore strong resemblance to Moses' complaints.

The Lazarus Project focused on intensive public leadership development, adapted from broad-based citizen organizing. The approach involved ongoing discussion of several key political ideas—power, diversity of self-interests, understood broadly not as selfishness, and public space, different from private or therapeutic space. It also included an overall language of citizen politics. However much such language went against the grain of a focus on care, nurture, and rehabilitation, instead of work on common problems, all involved were surprised by the changes this process worked. It suggested that whatever the intensity of a language of care, staff, residents, and family all desired a more open, public, honest process of interaction, conversation, and work.

A striking example of the power of political ideas occurred early in the Lazarus Project, when a chaplain intern remarked to a joint committee of residents and staff that it was hard for her to see so many people die. Augustana, like most nursing homes, avoided open discussion of death because staff were convinced the topic would upset residents. In this case, however, an earlier discussion of the concept of public spaces as arenas for working on difficult problems led Pam Hayle to ask the residents their view of the young woman's remarks. Residents responded, "We know the topic is hard for the staff; that's why we don't talk about it. But to us it seems a natural part of the process of moving into a nursing home."

The event led to a public forum, considerable conversation, and ultimately change in the norms and rituals at Augustana. Residents talked about wishing to be in charge of the process of dying, even if this meant not always complying with staff expectations. In response, staff spoke of their anxiety when what they thought of "best possible care" conflicted with residents' wishes. Ways to develop rituals and richer conservation about death and dying were incorporated into Augustana's culture.

In other instances, as well, people at Augustana gathered power in situations that otherwise rendered them as helpless complainers or overburdened service providers. For instance, residents and staff addressed a near universal nursing home complaint—slow staff response to resident call lights—through public forums on each of the floors. The forums provided space to air varying points of view and to generate solutions that neither staff nor residents had imagined. Most important, they dealt with issues for which there are no easy solutions such as feelings of dependency and overwhelming responsibilities.

Augustana did not undergo a radical transformation as the result of Lazarus Project, but it saw notable changes. Departments such as nursing and therapeutic activities developed much more open negotiation about issues like staffing and hours. Supervisors reported higher morale. Managers sought to develop a less personalized pattern of interaction.

This project pointed to the power of more open, visible, boundary-crossing professional practice even in the most therapeutic of settings. Kari took three lessons from this experience that she brought into organizing work at the College of St. Catherine and later into the Jane Addams School. First, language itself is a constituting feature of cultures and reflects as well as shapes everyday life. Second, the introduction of political language and public concepts can begin to shift identities and practices, even in seemingly apolitical cultures. Third, this kind of organizing can be a civic learning laboratory. In the case of the Lazarus Project, the experiences prompted thought about what politics means. They also highlighted the importance of making work and work roles more public—interactive, visible, infused with larger purposes—as a central element in change. For all the differences, Nan Kari also found some similar patterns in settings such as higher education and work with new immigrants.

Public practices move beyond talk. "You can learn how to be an effective actor. You have the experience of working effectively with others about the things you care about, becoming visible, having a sense of power to make change." Kari sees public work as "hard work, but it's tremendously rewarding and motivating. Public life is a source of hope." Soon, a new partnership developed in another therapeutic setting, family therapy.

Family Therapy as Public Work

"Psychotherapy in its various manifestations would appear to be the quintessentially private profession," wrote William Doherty and Jason Carroll, in their introduction to a new section of the main journal in the family professions, *Family Process*, launched at the end of 2002. "People go to therapists to deal with personal problems, and many therapists are drawn to this work because they enjoy intimate psychological dialogue." Norms and regulations stress privacy and confidentiality. Therapists are expected not to be involved with clients outside the therapy room itself. "It seems a big leap, then, to think of therapists as public citizens engaging in the work of building community and creating social change." But encouragement of such work is the point of the new section, entitled the Citizen Therapist and Family-Centered Community Building. The mission of the section is to surface and develop "new forms of public practice alongside traditional forms of clinical practice, forms of practice for citizen therapists who are, or may be, involved in their communities while still earning a living as a clinician." To accomplish this, they declared, "we have to confront head on the historic mistake made by the helping professions in the last century—the disconnecting of the work of personal healing from the work of citizenship and democratic action."[21]

It is an open question, as Doherty and Carroll acknowledged, whether the family professions will develop public dimensions in the coming years. "Time will tell whether the work we want to document and promote here will be a temporary blip in the history of family therapy and psychotherapy," they said. But the creation of the new section is itself a striking milestone, a sign of civic and public life in professional fields that seem, on the face of it, paradigmatically private.

Doherty, professor of family social science at the University of Minnesota and past president of the National Council on Family Relations, is one of the nation's leading theorists and practitioners of family studies and family therapy. Since 1996 he has been engaged in action research projects to develop examples of family practice as democratic public work. Doherty and his students and colleagues organized a group affiliated with the Family Social Science Department called the Families and Democracy Project. They are involved in a number of partnerships, including Putting Family First, a movement started by parents, community members, and school leaders in Wayzata, Minnesota, in 1999 to restore balance in families' hectic and overscheduled lives; Community Engaged Parent Education, a project with the Early Childhood Family Education network in Minnesota to develop the capacity of family educators to stimulate public work by parents of young children on the issues facing families; Marriage Matters, a public support project for married couples; and Partners in Diabetes, a groundbreaking effort with HealthPartners, a health cooperative, to create a network for support and collective work on problems associated with diabetes, in which diabetics and their families are co-producers of outcomes.

Doherty discovered Amitai Etzioni, Alan Wolfe, and other communitarian thinkers while writing his book *Soul Searching*, about the need for therapists to think about and work with the larger moral questions and dilemmas involved in individuals' personal struggles.[22] First he and colleagues created "salons" or "Networker Forums" outside Minnesota, in association with the family therapy journal, in an effort to create a collective way for therapists to think about these issues. "Communitarianism was a good model to start from in the 1980s, a both/and, private/public philosophy," he recounts. "These groups tapped the idealism of therapists who had entered the field in the sixties. At the initial organizing meetings, people talked in an agonized way about wanting to change the world. They would say, 'then I settled into private practice. I wanted to put my kids through college. I'm so exhausted at the end of the week I don't have time to volunteer. Now managed care is boxing me in.' The frustrated idealism was palpable."

Yet options seemed limited. "Therapists would write letters to public officials, and say to themselves, 'I should do more. I should do some more pro bono work. I should volunteer more.' But when they did volunteer, they felt like they were neglecting their families. And they didn't have as much energy." Doherty said. "I didn't have the words for it, but I knew something was missing from how we were all thinking about ourselves as citizens and professionals. Communitarianism was a good beginning, but not a guide to action, at least for me." They began to read about public work and it made sense. Public work is "a very big critique of the consumer culture, the passivity of citizens, that I resonated with. Public work is also action oriented. There was a craft of social change that we needed to retrieve." Doherty saw the biggest thing as the idea of change through work. "What I was hearing from therapists was, 'I have to volunteer more. I have to work outside of my profession.' So this whole idea of re-conceptualizing professions as public activities, of seeing professions as groups that have a stake in the public welfare, was very powerful."

Doherty sought to reconstruct family practice in public work terms. As he puts it, "Therapists and other family professionals, through an allegiance to a top-down expert model, unintentionally perpetuate a professional versus consumer dichotomy with families."[23] The problem with such an approach is its one-way, hierarchical understanding of knowledge production. "Knowledge and resources are centered in the professions whose job is to get out the word to families. Families' job is to listen well and practice what we preach. This approach is endemic in twentieth century professions, not just in the family field."

Doherty and his graduate students began to theorize and develop in practice an alternative model for family/professional/community partnerships that "aims to unleash the expertise of families in community, with professionals serving as consultants and catalysts instead of just service providers." Put differently, in this work, family professionals play a key role, but they are on tap, not on top. Doherty's recent book on the consumer culture of childhood and the therapeutic culture of parenthood argues that the consumer culture's invasion of family life leads many parents to see themselves mainly as providers of services to entitled children. Children's responsibilities as citizens of families and communities become invisible. Parents lose confidence in their ability to set limits and create expectations for their children. Associated with the consumer model of childhood, the trend for contemporary families is to be hyperactive in filling children's schedules, which leads to a decrease in commitment to family rituals. Further, consumer dynamics are exacerbated by the influence of a cultural therapeutic model of parenting that stresses the fragility of children and the importance of parents not showing anger.

Doherty recounts the story of what happened when he worked on these themes,[24]

After I developed a conceptual framework for action as a therapist, public work, I was giving talks to a variety of community groups about strengthening family life. I would ask, "How come you don't do family rituals?" This was the subject of my book for parents, *The Intentional Family*. I kept hearing back, "It's a great idea, but we don't have time to do anything. We're involved with taking our kids in their sports and other activities."

I would then ask, "How come you can't change that?"

"How could we possibly change that?" they would say. "We want our kids to succeed, and everyone else's kids are doing these things."

I was picking up the themes that I folded into my next book, *Take Back Your Kids*, about the frenetic pace and about insecure parenting in a competitive consumer culture.

The action breakthrough was in Wayzata in April 1998. I talked with a large group of parents at a parent fair. The parents were lit up over the problem of feeling out of control of their time but afraid to get off the treadmill. A middle school principal said, "We're part of this problem. We offer so many activities to kids that if parents agree to half of them, they're not going to have much of a family life left."

That was the dawning for me that this issue of over-scheduling was not just an individual family issue and a cultural issue. It was a structural issue as well. I talked to other people. Light bulbs started coming on for them and me both. Family time is a public issue.

A couple of months later, the organizer of the original parent fair, Barbara Carlson, called. She said, "People loved your talk. Would you come back next year and give that talk again?"

I said, "no." That was the moment that I decided to go for it. I said, "I don't want to give Doherty's greatest hits. But if you want to take on this problem as a community, I've been learning a model to do this, and I'd be willing to come back and work with you to figure out how to do it."

Barbara and I proceeded to cook up a plan for the next spring. I would give a brief talk and then there would be a town meeting.

About seventy came to the town meeting. Barbara had invited parent leaders, school board people, plus parents who were at the first talk. These people were ready. I began by asking, "Are these things we are talking about here, overscheduled kids and under-connected families, only individual family problems or are they also community problems? Are the solutions only individual family solutions, or are they also community solutions? What can we do about the problems as a community?"

It was an electrifying experience.

A mother said, "I could use something like a Good Housekeeping Seal of Approval when I'm signing up my kids. Something that would show that this organization will work with me in my efforts to have a balanced family life."

There were people from the YMCA, the head of community education, and other people who scheduled kids and families. They said, "I agree with what is being said here, but I don't get any complaints about having a facility too available. Or having too many games. I get complaints like "why are you closing the swimming pool at 11 on Sunday night?"

One activity leader told a small group, "I could leverage a Seal of Approval for change in my organization." It took somebody who was involved in scheduling to have that perspective.

I said, "I don't think anybody is setting out to hurt kids, but there are a lot of constraints people work under. We are all part of this problem, and we can all be part of the solution."

Another important moment came when I heard the classic deflators of energy in a public meeting. One woman sitting in the front declared, "This is all well and good but we're preaching to the choir. It's the parents who are not here who are the problem."

Then somebody added, "There should have been three times as many people here tonight." That's another deflator.

This is where my family therapy experience came in. I'm used to working with families where somebody in the room pulls the plug on something positive that is happening, and I am prepared to head it off. So I responded, "Margaret Mead once said, 'it only takes a small group of people to change the world, and it's never been changed in any other way.' Every social movement begins with a choir. We have a lot of people in this choir."

I could feel the energy coming back into the room. We had sign-ups, including a community activation team. That became the steering group for Family Life First.

The Putting Family First partnership has generated considerable community activation crossing traditional partisan lines, as well as an enormous amount of publicity, around the theme of families regaining power over their time, threatened by the frenetic pace and consumer pressures present in middle class life. Putting Family First argues that a hyperactive, consumer culture leads families to lose their rituals and their mindfulness about family bonds. The group's founding statement declared itself "committed to reversing the deleterious effects of the consumer culture on childhood. Today, parents see themselves as competitive providers of services to children, while children are overscheduled in a frantic pursuit of experiences and opportunities for personal enrichment and advantage over peers." Actions have ranged from developing a Family Life Seal of Approval for family friendly sports, religious, and cultural programs to a consumer guide that evaluates the impact of different children's programs on family life. Putting Family First has been reported in a large range of print and broadcast media, from the *New York Times* and a series on National Public Radio to mainstream publications like *Ladies' Home Journal* and *Better Homes and Gardens*.

Doherty's work is also an example of the democratic refashioning of the relationships between higher education faculty and staff and communities in ways that already suggest possible impact on the larger professional world. It highlights the forms of power—for democratic change or for its opposite—lodged in higher education, in ways that Dewey's focus on the democratic potentials of knowledge creation anticipated.

Focus on professions and their cultures through the work of colleagues like Kari and Doherty brought our attention to higher education and the importance in civic engagement efforts of developing the public dimensions of professional work. Higher education is the formative institution in the construction of professional identities and practices in our age, as well as in the generation of professional and disciplinary knowledge.

This attention coincided with evidence that higher education is an environment ripe for change. A growing discussion of civic engagement has developed in higher education institutions faced with declining public support.

Relevance is not only about institutional needs and survivals. At the more elemental level, it is about rediscovery of a public life and politics in fields which have become fragmented and, in explicit terms, extremely apolitical. The promise of making public the work we do in the world is the promise of a new and deeper political engagement with the world.

Chapter 8
"Architects of Democracy"

We believe that our institutions serve not only as agents of democracy but also as its architects.

—Renewing the Covenant, *signed by 24 land grant presidents, 1999*

In 2003 the American Association of State Colleges and Universities (AASCU) and the *New York Times* joined together to create the American Democracy Project, to foster institutional change at more than 150 AASCU member schools. AASCU is an association of 430 public institutions in the United States, representing more than 3.4 million students. Many of its member schools are regional colleges and universities—sometimes called the "American Dream" colleges, since many of their students are the first in their families to go to college. The AASCU commitment to the civic education of its students prompted its interest in the project.

The *Times* interest came from its concerns about long-term readership projections and surprising evidence about students' interests. The newspaper's long-term trend analysis suggests that American culture is becoming more segmented into insulated subgroups of viewpoint, ideology, and culture—while the *Times* depends on a readership that welcomes a diversity of viewpoints and vantages. It is clearly in the newspaper's self-interest to support a culture that values multiple, shared perspectives on events of the day. A recent study by the paper's marketing department suggested that civic engagement could be the key.[1]

In 2000 the *Times* sponsored a competition among advertising and marketing students to develop a theme to attract more student readers. The paper expected many different ideas; yet the majority of submissions focused on a common theme: students want to explore the world outside their bubble. They see college as a time to be stimulated, to be challenged, and to make better sense of the world.

The campaign that most clearly captured this concept was developed by students at Indiana University-Bloomington. The team coined the phrase "Understand Why," and positioned the phrase against photographic images from the *Times* that illustrated compelling and often disturbing issues. Other campaigns used similar phrases, such as "Know More, Explore the World: It's Right Outside Your Bubble."

These themes were so much at odds with colleges' own marketing approaches—which stress career advancement and competitive success—that the paper conducted its own focus groups with students all across the country. Large schools and small, North, South, East, and West, the results were the same: students either failed to respond to or explicitly rejected a campaign built on the idea, "Advance your career! The *New York Times* helps you achieve professional success." Overwhelmingly they liked the theme, "Understand Why."

The good news was that students saw the *Times* as an important resource to help them do this. The ad campaign ran and exceeded expectations in its successful recruitment of new college readers. The bad news is that most college students do not have many experiences of deep engagement with diverse cultures, ways of thinking, and real world challenges. The newspaper's other finding, which led it to participate in the American Democracy Project, was that if students do not escape their "bubbles" in college or shortly afterward, they are likely to settle into patterns of relatively homogeneous social and friendship circles that will persist through their lifetimes.

Civic Engagement in Higher Education

In the last several years, a growing number of voices in higher education have expressed sentiments similar to those of the *Times*: trend lines have to be reversed. This chorus points to the culture-shaping power that higher education wields in a knowledge-based society. It also points to the challenges to making higher education institutions "agents and architects of democracy."

In recent years, state legislatures, governing boards, community groups, and others have challenged these institutions to justify their purposes and practices. For public research universities, this debate has political urgency. As Mark Yudof, then president of the University of Minnesota, said to the Regents in 2001, "I see across America a gradual withering of the covenant or understanding that the work of public research universities is a public good."[2]

Against this background, concepts such as "public scholarship" and "the civic mission of higher education" have become part of the lexicon at an increasing number of institutions. They are frequently compartmentalized into particular centers and discrete activities, or translated into a focus on educating students in civic values. Yet a network of leaders such as Yolanda Moses, Elizabeth Hollander, Nancy Kantor, Tom Ehrlich, George Mehaffy, Ira Harkavy, Julie Ellison, Lorraine Gutierrez, and Barry Checkoway, and groups like Campus Compact, AACU, AAHE, and the AASCU have emerged with a broad vision of institutional cultural transformation. This network uses an explicit language of colleges and universities as agents and architects of democracy that indicates awareness of the formative cultural power of higher education in today's world.

At the University of Minnesota, a high-level, cross-campus Civic Engagement Task Force was charged in 2000 by then provost Robert Bruininks with clarifying the meaning of civic engagement and recommending practical measures for renewing the land grant mission—making the topic a basic question of identity throughout the entire institution. The charge aimed at incorporating civic engagement across the full range of university activities including research, teaching, and work with communities. Task Force chair Edwin Fogelman, with Jim Farr and others, crafted a definition that stressed civic engagement as "an institutional commitment to public purposes and responsibilities intended to strengthen a democratic way of life in the rapidly changing Information Age of the 21st century." The definition subsequently informed the Council on Public Engagement (COPE) established in 2002 to further this work. It highlights public engagement as a constituting dimension of professional work identities. It also stresses culture change within the institution, and promotes an expansive understanding of democracy and what higher education can contribute to it.[3]

The work at the University of Minnesota has brought home multiple dimensions of nonprofessional, democratic politics. First, to build support for civic engagement requires "thinking politically," that is, creating a broad alliance, engaging diverse interests, within the university and in the external environment. For some of us, this has involved adapting the lessons of citizen organizing to the institutional change process. For others, especially administrative leaders, alliance-building has marked their careers.

The importance of administrators like Robert Bruininks and others who believe strongly in participatory decision making cannot be overemphasized.

Second, the politics of civic engagement at a place like the University of Minnesota involves complex, boundary crossing institutional politics. Attention to institutional politics adds to the literature of organizational change by explicitly attending to the way politics shapes public ends and purposes. A public work understanding of institutional politics also highlights the fact that power and public goods in environments like higher education are not zero-sum transactions, but are created and thus expandable.

Third, thinking politically in higher education means accenting the broad dimensions of politics to draw attention to the culture-shaping power of large, diverse institutions where many different interests, cultures, and ways of knowing can interact. It means understanding politics as the complex, multidimensional process of negotiating diverse interests, perpectives, and power relations to create a way of life. This theme is taken up in more detail in Chapter 9. Here, it is worth noting how quickly the largest questions—especially, how to renew the public side of our society—emerge when public research institutions seriously take up civic engagement. This dynamic suggests another lesson. In an information society, higher education potentially plays a role as a particular kind of mediating space. Democratization of higher education, its processes of producing and diffusing knowledge, and its culture shaping activities are essential to building democracy.

Discontents, Open and Hidden

At public research universities, the immediate crisis of politics appears in declining revenues from state legislators and eroding support in many public constituencies. More broadly, and for some years, higher education has faced growing questions of legitimacy. In 1986, the nation's governors issued a report declaring that their states' students were not as well educated as students of earlier years. The Association of American Colleges charged that "America's colleges and universities no longer have a 'firm grasp of their goals and missions.'" In 1988, the Pew Higher Education Roundtable argued that "fundamental questions about the quality, content, and cost of colleges and universities are rife, both within and without the academy." A series of harsh polemics followed. On the right, Allan Bloom's *The Closing of the American Mind*, warning of "politicized" universities, sold 800,000 copies. On the left, Page Smith, founder of the experimental University of California at Santa Cruz, charged in *Killing the Spirit* that faculty members neglected teaching for research, while research itself had deteriorated. "The routine and pedestrian far outweighs the brilliant and original," Page said. "Routine and pedestrian research is not merely a very expensive nullity but a moral and spiritual drag on the institutions in which it takes place and a serious distortion of the nature of both the intellectual and the scholarly life."[4]

In the midst of budget battles across the country, it was clear that higher education would have to take dramatic steps to adjust to the new environment. In response, an increasing number of institutions and associations of higher education have come to focus on civic engagement as a matter of practical politics.

Yet there are also internal, often invisible wellsprings of discontent, even among the most successful scholars. We discovered this at the University of Minnesota in 1997, when the Kellogg Foundation asked the Center for Democracy and Citizenship to investigate the possibilities for "renewing the public service mission" of the University. Edwin Fogelman, chair of the Political Science Department and then CDC co-director, and I conducted dozens of interviews with faculty across the university, using the Center's public work framework. A focus on the public nature of work gave us a way to see the potential of civic engagement to address issues of professional identity, tied to self-interest, prestige, institutional incentive structures, professional cultures and the like.

We interviewed people who were widely respected in different departments and colleges, who were seen to embody the ethos or culture of their disciplines and the University, and who were knowledgeable about its history and operations. Far more than we expected, the interviews surfaced a strong and often painful sense of loss of public purposes in individual jobs, professions and disciplines, and the whole institution. There was widespread alarm at turf wars and the "star system." Faculty voiced desire for public engagement to be constitutive of professional work. Interest in the public relevance of teaching and research was not simply an individual desire but was also framed in disciplinary terms. "Our whole department feels too cloistered," said one department chair in the College of Liberal Arts. She expressed the department desire to engage more deeply the urban scene and the public world.[5]

In subsequent visits to other campuses, including the University of

Michigan, Brown, Duke, Cornell, and other research universities, I found similar patterns, though I have been constantly struck by how much academic cultures reinforce silence about these issues, as well.

The problem is that higher education's disengagement reflects deep norms, rituals of socialization, and other cultural patterns that make it hard to overcome. William Sullivan, who directs a project on the civic dimensions of disciplines and professions for the Carnegie Foundation, found that, "despite its great size and prestige, much of American higher education today suffers from a sense of demoralization and decline." He discovered "much talk of reform, but mostly of an administrative and financial nature, with little attention to content and purpose." The problem is that discussion of purposes is what is most important. "It is precisely the neglect of the question of purpose that has robbed the academy of collective self-confidence at just the moment it most needs to defend itself in increasingly bitter arguments about educational policy and finance."

Sullivan argues that "much of higher education has come to operate on a sort of default program of instrumental individualism." This means, he says, "that the academy exists to research and disseminate knowledge and skills as tools for economic development and the upward mobility of individuals." In his view, the "'default program' of instrumental individualism leaves the larger questions of social, political, and moral purpose out of explicit consideration." Not only does this pattern contribute to higher education's detachment from the larger society but it also has contagion effects, since graduates of higher education go on to shape much of the larger culture. Higher education's "knowledge workforce," according to Sullivan, "has in fact if not in intent abdicated social responsibility for a narrow careerism and private self-interest." Using Robert Reich's idea of the "secession" of knowledge workers, Sullivan argues that college graduates increasingly live in gated communities—of mind and identity no less than geography. "It is as if they have forgotten that they are members, and highly privileged ones at that, of the national society."[6]

Insight into the difficult personal and professional changes involved in becoming more public comes from academics who have developed strong public dimensions in their work. John Saltmarsh, formerly professor of history at Northeastern University, now directs the Project on Integrating Service with Academic Study as scholar in residence at Campus Compact.[7] "The transition from academia helped me to see academic culture in ways that I hadn't so clearly before," Saltmarsh describes. "I never quite appreciated the degree to which an academic lives in a world of their own—they show up if they want to, are available if they want to be, return phone calls if they want to—if they have a publication they are working on they can and do drop all obligations to work on their scholarship—and resurface when they please. I never quite appreciated how we are socialized to be accountable only to ourselves." Saltmarsh says this was the way he was trained. "I was socialized to believe that my first loyalty was to my profession (a loyalty that was fairly undefined but meant something about my scholarship adhering to the standards of the craft) and after that there were no loyalties, not to institution, department, colleagues, or students. This deep socialization fostering the privatization of the faculty role led to inherent disengagement in social and political affairs."

Work in the larger public world changed his views and practices. "My work at the Compact has public accountability. What I say reflects on Campus Compact. I have shifted to a more public role. I am much more conscious of an audience. I write not for a small group of academics but for as wide a group as possible." His work with Campus Compact also has changed his view of the effects of his work. "There is also a shift in the realm of impact, from my home institution and a few students and the neighborhood to working with colleagues around the country to try to shape the future, to build a democracy." He learned an entirely different language than the one in which he was trained. "If I talked about how to use education to build a democracy when I was on the faculty at Northeastern there would have been an empty room. I am now thinking and acting in much more political and public ways."

For all the ways in which private norms are entrenched in academia, discontent about them has begun to surface publicly in the mainstream disciplines. For instance, the most dramatic feature of the American Political Science Association's 2001 convention was something called the *perestroika caucus*, organized by a number of senior scholars who argued for widespread changes in the research culture and protocols of the discipline. One result was the important new journal of the association, *Perspectives on Politics*, launched in 2003 with an explicit intention to engage with broader intellectual publics in discussions of pressing political issues. Similarly, the second edition of *The Blackwell Companion to Social Theory*, published in 2000 and including many luminaries of social science, reads as a sustained attack on both positivism, the "detached scientist" model of social science, and also its postmodern antagonists in cultural studies. "My dissatisfaction with modern social theory is based upon the assumption that it is decorative—an activity of spectators who are not committed to politics or to social change, apart from complaints about distorted representations," writes Bryan Turner, professor of sociology at Cambridge, in his preface to the volume. In his concluding essay on "Social Theory and the Public Sphere," Craig Calhoun—the new director of the Social Science Research Council—goes farther. "A certain philistinism has grown within universities themselves," argues Calhoun, tracing it to norms of detachment and insularity. Ironically, "in the spirit of professionalism [intellectuals] betray the calling truly and openly to explore the world."[8]

Such dramatic sentiments from strategically positioned leaders in American higher education could be multiplied across many disciplines and fields, including the natural sciences and humanities. The question is how raw discontent can be translated into effective action for change. Lessons of both community organizing and public work theory-building at the CDC have proven relevant.

Thinking Politically

Thinking politically in higher education is difficult for both practical and conceptual reasons. As a practical matter, it runs against the grain of academic cultures. Conceptually, thinking politically differs from other approaches to cultural and institutional change. Indeed, conventional approaches disdain politics.

Practically, thinking politically means building political coalitions or alliances, and this requires recognizing what different political perspectives, interests, and disciplines have to offer. It means building extensive relationships across silo cultures. It means turning hidden, privately felt discontents into objects for public discussion. It means developing public leadership through experiences of public work, cooperative, successful effort with others. It means learning to share credit and public recognition. It means creating space for reflection and collective evaluation. Yet all these steps go directly against the grain of the free-wheeling individual entrepreneurship, disciplinary turf wars, argument culture, hierarchies, and competitiveness that both structure and fragment academia.

Conceptually, scholars and practitioners of institutional cultural change, in the main, hate politics. For instance, Peter Senge, director of organizational learning at MIT, is famous for developing the concept of the "learning organization," in which people "expand their capacity to create the results they truly desire, where new and expansive patterns of thinking are nurtured, where collective aspiration is set free, and where people are continually learning how to learn together." All this is to occur without politics, which Senge sees as entirely destructive. "Organizational politics is such a perversion of truth and honesty that most organizations reek with its odor," he wrote in his best-seller, *The Fifth Discipline: The Art and Practice of the Learning Organization.* For Senge "a political environment is one in which . . . there are always 'winners' and 'losers,' people who are building their power and people who are losing power." If organizations are to become "learning organizations," they must "transcend politics."⁹

Higher education reformers write in a similar vein. "Intellectual work that is driven by political forces is not intellectual at all," wrote William Massy, president of the Jackson Hole Higher Education Group, in his *Honoring the Trust: Quality and Cost Containment in Higher Education.* Such politicized work, in his view, "seeks simply to win arguments and influence the distribution of power." He calls on the academy "to rise above politics," based on its "professionalism, internal discipline, and tradition."¹⁰

Even reformers who recognize the necessity of politics describe it in narrow fashion. Thus Lee Bolman and Terrence Deal see politics as an indispensable frame for understanding organizational dynamics, along with three others (the structural frame, the human resources frame, and the symbolic-cultural frame). But politics offers only the bleakest view of human connection and interaction. They argue that a political frame

sees organizations as arenas, contests, or jungles. Different interests compete for power and scarce resources. Conflict is rampant because of enduring differences in needs, perspectives, and lifestyles among various individuals and groups. Bargaining, negotiation, coercion, and compromise are part of everyday life. Coalitions form around specific interests and change as issues come and go. Problems arise when power is concentrated in the wrong places or is so broadly dispersed that nothing gets done.¹¹

Yet if politics is bleak, so is their depiction of modern organizational life and culture. Bolman and Deal argue for leadership based on artistry, inspiration, meaning-making and attention to cultural metaphors, rituals, ceremonies, and stories, yet they describe organizations whose leaders are silent on the deepest and broadest of questions. They describe a seminar with corporate executives who sound much like the academics we have interviewed in recent years. "We learned how the privatization of moral discourse in our society has created a deep sense of moral loneliness and moral illiteracy," they report. "The absence of a common language prevents people from talking about and reading the moral issues they face. We learned how the isolation of individuals—the taboo against talking about spiritual matters in the public sphere—robs people of the courage, of the strength, of heart to do what deep down they believe to be right."[12]

To address these human pains, anger, and discontents requires a different kind of politics, politics not organized simply around distributive battles, and politics not dominated by professionals or by ideological prescriptions that divide the world into believers and unbelievers.

Translating Everyday Politics to Professional Settings

As described in Chapter 3, everyday politics in broad based citizen groups involves an on-going process of meetings, called one-on-ones, where people interview each other to discover cultural backgrounds, interests, and talents. One-on-ones shatter stereotypes. They also produce connections across lines of difference. Finally, they are a schooling in public life, teaching engagement with people who see the world in different ways. Rom Coles, political scientist at Duke University, recounted the recentering of politics in horizontal relationships that he saw as he became active in CAN, an organizing effort in Durham affiliated with the Industrial Areas Foundation. "Through hundreds of dialogues in pairs, stories circulate which would be difficult or impossible to surface in larger settings, and they begin to weave together a complex variegated fabric of democratic knowledges about an urban area and its people. In this more responsive and receptive context, relationships are formed and deepened in which a rich complex critical vision of a community develops along with the gradual articulation of alternative possibilities." The process develops skills of public interaction and public view. "As different positions, problems, passions, interests, traditions, and yearnings are shared through careful practices of listening, participants begin to develop an increasingly relational sense of their interests and orientations in ways that often transfigure the senses with which they began."[13]

To date, we have not found examples of such intense public relationship building in professional settings, and creating such experiences is especially difficult in higher education. Faculty are famous for being cantakerous individualists—"organizing faculty is like herding cats," the saying goes. The individualism in higher education bears similarities to that in the arts.

This is not to say that relationship building will not be an essential part of the political change process in higher education. Maria Avila, for many years an organizer with the Industrial Areas Foundation who now directs the Center for Community Based Learning at Occidential College, describes vividly what she thinks a sustained translation of organizing approaches to higher education will entail. "The medicine for our predicament [in both society generally and higher education] requires efforts to restructure the way we think, act, behave toward each other, and the way we act as a collective to restructure power and resources." Avila argues that organizing focuses on culture change before structural change. "Culture changes [come] first, leading to structural changes later."[14] Mainly, in her view, change is a profoundly relational process, tied to organizing and power. "For academic institutions to partner with community groups, institutions and organizations for a better society [will require] countless opportunities for conversations and organizing campaigns with community partners engaged in power restructuring." Such conversations shatter norms of silence and isolation in work. It is extremely difficult, she argues, in academic settings, "to be real with each other, to show our vulnerabilities, our real passions, fears, pain and anger, to put all this into a societal context, to create spaces where we can feel, learn, reflect and act together to create change." In Avila's organizing approach, higher education will have to translate civic engagement rhetoric into the hard work of "creating spaces where [diverse] groups can engage in conversations about the role of the college in society, the role of various disciplines, the connection between civic engagement and the reason [faculty members] chose their professions."

Though this deeper organizing approach remains to be generated at the University of Minnesota, we have found important motivators. For instance, the public work lens has highlighted how important making distinctive, individual, unique contributions is to faculty, as a source of creativity and energy. Moreover, practices other than one-on-ones, more familiar to higher education, have been central features of theory-building and learning. We regularly debriefed civic engagement leaders after major events. Academics form connections around ideas, so our civic engagement work has included a mix of public events—workshops, forums, visits from other universities, reports, seminars with groups like the Kettering Foundation, and a nationwide conference with the Kellogg Forum—that build on this cultural norm. The working group structure of the Task Force also promoted discussion. In the first year there were working groups on definitions; scholarship; institutional incentives; community partnerships; teaching; and institutional connections. Each group, in turn, had advisory panels of citizens beyond the University.

We have found that organizing around ideas such as higher education's contributions to a democratic way of life, or making the work of different disciplines public, is possible. This bears resemblance to the experiences of artists and intellectuals who came together in the Federal Writers Project during the Great Depression, inspired by the ideas of the New Deal for all their cantakerous disagreements and personalities, and thereby created a public culture.[15]

Civic engagement work at the University has been informed by partners in other settings. In the early 1990s, faculty at the College of St. Catherine sought to translate everyday politics from community organizing into higher education. A faculty group was organized by Nan Kari, director of faculty development, who shifted her position from service provider to organizer for civic change. Over several years, the group made changes to the school's core curriculum, created public spaces for dialogue and discussion, and developed a seed grant program to encourage civic innovation. The University of Minnesota learned from these strategies, as well as those developed by others experimenting with a public work approach at Minneapolis Community and Technical College, the University of Missouri at Kansas City, Cornell, and the University of Michigan.

Minnesota's Civic Engagement Task Force and allied efforts used an explicitly political approach to promote institutional change in the sense of building a broad, nonpartisan alliance around a vision of the engaged university. Thus, the final report of the Task Force, delivered to the provost on May 2002, outlined four dimensions to institutionalizing civic engagement at the University: an intellectual dimension, a cultural dimension, a structural dimension, and a political dimension. The latter was defined as

A political process to involve stakeholders and constituencies without whose support the effort falters. Strategies for enlisting support vary according to circumstances in each university, but the active support and leadership of key senior administrators and faculty leaders is critical everywhere. Civic engagement cannot succeed without positive support from institutional leaders and diverse publics.[16]

Building alliances and engaging diverse interests in the work of civic engagement can appear as nothing more than common sense. Yet a political approach is in fact very different from customary approaches to civic change in higher education. Most efforts locate civic engagement in discrete activities, like service learning, or in specific administrative portfolios, like community relations. The dominant approach to civic engagement in higher education is a moral one, emphasizing service obligations to society.

Politics, in the sense needed for serious higher education change, requires efforts inside and across boundaries of the University of Minnesota to build alliances among diverse stakeholders around their distinctive, sometimes clashing interests. It demands attentiveness to multiple sources of power (including awareness of norms and practices of everyday culture, and the power of status and career dynamics). It recognizes the importance of visibility and recognition, what the provost, Robert Bruininks, emphasized early in the culture change process. It develops a vision of change capacious enough to encompass diverse perspectives, captured in the Task Force's stress on democracy as a way of life. From the University's work we can draw several broadly relevant lessons about the politics of civic engagement in higher education.

The Importance of Self-Interest

Our initial interviews built on the organizing principle that deep change always comes from within a setting: It is built upon the diverse self-interests and concerns of constituencies. Over the last several years, I have continually been impressed with the importance of this principle. For instance, the Senate Committee on Educational Policy, the main faculty governance group on the curriculum, proved receptive to civic engagement ideas when it was queried about its interests in civic learning for students. Under the leadership of Bert Ahern and Martin Sampson, it established a subcommittee to develop strategies for expanding civic learning opportunities across the University. The subcommittee's single most important initiative directly tapped the self interests of deans, colleges, and departments. Rather than argue for a generic set of best practices, we asked the deans of different colleges to identify their own distinctive, unique interests in students' civic learning. The College of Architecture and Landscape Architecture emphasizes teaching students how to work with communities in designing sustainable "built environments." The College of Biological Sciences has a growing emphasis on helping communities address issues raised by the rapid developments in biological research.

The Importance of a Public Process

Change needs to be rooted within institutional cultures but also must create a larger stage and new alliances with the wider world. Higher education cultures, especially at research universities, are insular and inward-looking. Avila's longer term challenge to create innumerable conversations crossing various boundaries is essential for deep and lasting change. But even at the beginning stages, it is necessary to involve external constituencies; the conversation is notably different when community or civic leaders are present.

The University of Minnesota Task Force developed ties to sympathetic regents, supporters in the business community, rural communities, the local press, state legislators, the African American community, and other institutions of higher education. Its different working groups involved advisors from across the state and the nation. A diversity of other voices and experiences emerged in the process. One striking discovery was the way people reframe their conceptions of higher education if asked about its larger meaning.

For example, the working group on definitions drew on the intellectual legacy of John Dewey and this made a key difference. The working group cast civic engagement in expansive terms, using a definition of democracy as a way of life that descends from Dewey and other early twentieth-century progressives. This definition shifts the emphasis from off hours pro bono work or voluntarism to questions of core identity. The Task Force's first report, in addition to its definition, made the point that civic engagement is better defined in comprehensive terms that differentiate it from efforts that assign civic engagement to specific departments, discrete sets of activities, centers, or programs. In contrast, at the University of Minnesota, the working assumption is that

The university does not do civic engagement; the university is a civically engaged institution. The challenge is to spell out how civic engagement makes a difference in our research, scholarship, teaching, community outreach, and other professional work. The practical question boils down to this: how is professional work different in a civically engaged university compared to other institutions of higher education that produce instructional products for their customers and marketable research for their clients?[17]

Broad, visionary language is crucial to focus the attention on larger public purposes. In interviews with local business leaders, I found that when I asked "What should the university do?" they responded out of their culture—better customer service, more direct benefit to economic growth. But if I asked a different question, "What is the role of a great university in a great democracy?" the answers were different. Even the most successful chief executives and those who represented them in large business organizations like the Minnesota Partnership responded with worry about the increasingly narrow definitions of success and achievement in our society ("everyone in our organization now thinks of themselves as a customer, not a producer," said one). They recalled the poetry classes, or the arguments about philosophy, or the discussions of the meaning of democracy that they had had as undergraduates. And they talked about the older civic traditions of Minnesota businesses, like the practice of giving back five or ten percent of corporate profit to the community infrastructure of parks, museums, art galleries, and other public goods, that have been sharply eroded in recent years as a consequence of corporate mergers and frequent relocation of top management.

Over the three years of civic engagement work at the University of Minnesota, from 2000 to 2003, a variety of groups and constituencies beyond faculty and administrators discussed the possibilities and meanings of civic engagement. Hundreds of students took part in forums and discussions, including roundtables in all the dorms on the meaning of citizenship. University civic engagement leaders held discussions with leaders in the Hennepin County African-American Men and Boys' Project. A number participated extensively in the moderated internet discussion and later town hall meeting organized by Minnesota Public Radio on the Future of the University. The Institutional Connections Committee organized roundtables in 2000–2002 with the advisory committees on three occasions (a cross section of leaders in the state); roundtables with political, business, and civic leaders; and several meetings at Tom's Salon, a monthly neighborhood political discussion group at the Schneider Drug Store on University Avenue, where Tom Gupta, the druggist, carries on the tradition of drug store politics blazed by Hubert Humphrey, Sr., described in Chapter 2. The College of Agriculture organized six focus groups with rural Minnesotans as part of the process, as well.

Voices were sometimes supportive of the University's civic engagement process and sometimes skeptical. Moreover, many criticisms surfaced, reflecting the views of some that the University has acted in arrogant fashion. Surfacing these criticisms in the University itself often proved highly controversial; some leaders among the faculty and elsewhere argued that airing criticisms contributed to the public relations problems that the University already faced.

In one illustrative forum in early 2001, the Civic Engagement Task Force organized a meeting with several state legislators to get their views on civic engagement.[18] Representative Peggy Leppik, chair of the House Higher Education Finance committee; Senators Steve Kelley and Richard Cohen, both of the Higher Education Budget Division committee; and Senator Sheila Kiscaden of the Finance Committee participated, along with senior administrators and leaders of the Civic Engagement Task Force.

Peggy Leppik, a Republican, said that there is "a big gap between academic culture and the average Joe." She believed the University has a real problem with perceived arrogance, which the work of the Civic Engagement Task Force could perhaps address. Steve Kelley, a supporter of the idea of citizenship as public work, pointed out that "the language of citizenship has atrophied." In his view, "people think it means only voting, or being a good person." He argued for the need for "broad education efforts to get out language widely about citizenship as serious work (paid or unpaid) on tough public problems." Kelley said many of the items listed in the definition of civic engagement (access, preparing leadership, creating knowledge, being a trusted voice, etc.) have to do with the University's external role. The Task Force, if it is serious, needs to be involved in internal change as well. "There is an important difference between marketing what the University is already doing, and changing the culture so that people at the University listen better to the citizenry of the state. Both are important, but they should not be confused."

Sheila Kiscaden talked about the need for the university to be "more accessible," transparent, and locally involved in visible ways. She argued for what is an excellent description of the historic land grant mission: the university needs to be involved among the people across the state, interactive, and working with people in partnership. She suggested that we look into developing a "technology extension" like the agricultural version to help citizens and communities use new technologies. She also argued that students in professional programs and technical and scientific fields need experience with community work and cultural diversity, "in order to function effectively in the world they are going to live in." Richard Cohen said that the University needs to learn to listen to people "below the level of institutions, like schools." He argued that it needs to relate to people in less formal networks and settings, as well as through institutions. He also pointed out that one possible benefit of the current budget debate could be a renewed understanding of the University's public role.

Legislators said that the University might help develop leadership "tools" for elected officials to use to more productively handle disputes, and find ways to get the voice of local citizens better heard within government.

Within the university, more than a dozen colleges held civic engagement discussions. In 2003, the University of Minnesota's Regional Partnerships in Central Minnesota held another set of public forums on civic engagement. All these discussions lent a public cast to the process. Beyond the specific ideas and strategies, the forums provided evidence that civic engagement, broadly understood as about real work to address public problems, holds potential to galvanize various audiences. One effect of the interactions was subtle but striking: I observed repeatedly that when faculty members are engaged with external audiences or with students on these topics, their hope for change notably increases.

Building on Committed Constituencies

A key part of any change effort is identifying and enlisting constituencies commited to civic and public engagement. The Task Force accomplished this through members from four groups.

Administrators. Those in administration often have especially keen political insights and a broad overview of the institution. While it has been politically indispensable for faculty to take key leadership roles—the stigma of "administration-led change" is a sure formula for massive resistance—administrators' political savvy became apparent when Ed Fogelman and I began interviewing administrators, faculty, and staff. Julie Ellison, a professor of English at the University of Michigan who became associate vice provost for research, described her insights. "For humanists administration can be liberating. There is such a sense of paranoia around administrators at the departmental level; nobody knows what deans do," Ellison argued. Faculty work is simply different from administrators'. "The kind of work we do as faculty involves individual work. You read, then you write. The only things you need are a computer and books and time." The environment looked far different from the administrative side. When she became an administrator, "I could see how ineffectual and apolitical the institutional stance was. There was a deliberate self-limitation, almost a self-wounding around institutional agendas in departmental life."[19]

At the University, political interests, broadly understood—the desire to get things done effectively and the pleasure that comes from practicing politics—often lead faculty into administration. Thus, for instance, when I asked Victor Bloomfield, Minnesota's vice provost for research and interim dean of the Graduate School, a key leader in the civic engagement effort, why he had accepted his position in central administration after a distinguished career as a biochemist, he responded, "I was able to accomplish things that I thought were worthwhile. I had a gift for thinking up new ways to do things and for convincing other people. Most administrators think politically. If you want to get things done, you can't be a bean counter." In Bloomfield's judgment, the picture faculty have of administrators, as bean counters, is wrong and far too narrow. "If you want to get things done you have got to make alliances between people, organizations, departments. You've got to get a sense of the key players who can make a deal happen. You have to trade favors. I put a certain amount of Grad School money on the table, if college deans will also contribute, and collect resources that benefit both graduate programs and the colleges. Doing academic administration is very much developing and fostering alliances." Bloomfield sees these as the essence of politics. "A good politician is reading people's interest, how much they care. You don't push them too far. All that's political."[20]

The civic engagement work drew on the political insights of a diverse group of administrators. In addition to Robert Bruininks himself, a highly collaborative administrator who has led the overall effort, these include Kenneth Keller, a former president; Victor Bloomfield; Craig Swan, vice provost for undergraduate education; Robert Jones, vice president; Sallye McKee, associate vice provost for multicultural and academic affairs; Chris Mazier, former dean of the Graduate School and now provost; and Billie Wahlstrom, vice provost for distributed learning. Staff such as Sue Engelmann from the provost's office and Gerry Melandra, chief of staff for the president during the Task Force years, are full of insight about invisible norms, codes, and knowledge about allies and strategies.

Champions of curricular reform. Beyond his administrative title, Craig Swan illustrates a second important political resource in today's higher education landscape: leaders who champion curricular and pedagogical reforms. Swan, working with faculty leaders such as Bert Ahern, Martin Sampson, and John Wallace, service learning staff such as Carl Brandt and Laurel Hirt, and student leaders like Christine Frazier and Roudy Hildreth, has long supported community-based, service-learning, and learning community efforts. Achieving curricular reforms on these fronts depends on political skills. Students themselves are potentially a crucial resource for civic change through curricular reform.

Examples abound of learning that connects students to the life of communities and the world. The University's civic engagement work uncovered dozens of examples and helped to create others. This work also dramatized how much students want such experiences.

Diversity leaders. In June 2004, the Supreme Court upheld the University of Michigan Law School's affirmative action approach, allowing the school to consider race in admissions. What was distinctive about the case was Michigan's rationale. It explicitly connected affirmative action to the need for an educationally diverse environment, in order to prepare citizen leaders for the twenty-first century, a connection justified by the overall concept of "education for a diverse democracy." Justice O'Connor, writing for the majority, argued that "in order to cultivate a set of leaders with legitimacy in the eyes of the citizenry, it is necessary that the path to leadership be visibly open to talented and qualified individuals of every race and ethnicity." She also recognized a "compelling state interest" in diversity. "Student body diversity promotes learner outcomes and better prepares students for an increasingly diverse workforce and society," she argued. "Classroom discussion is livelier, more spirited, and simply more enlightening and interesting when the students have 'the greatest possible variety of backgrounds.'"[21]

Diversity leaders at the University of Minnesota, like those at the University of Michigan, have been at the forefront of a broad movement to support diverse educational environments as crucial for student education. Robert Jones and Sallye McKee, leaders in multicultural and academic affairs efforts to champion a more diverse faculty and student body, illustrate a third vital resource in higher education—the diversity networks that have developed in the last two decades. At the University, as elsewhere, progress toward greater access and equity requires strong political skills.

Community partnerships. A fourth group of politically savvy leaders are those who have forged strong, diverse, and reciprocal relationships and partnerships between units of the University and communities and outside groups. These include efforts like the Families and Democracy partnerships in the College of Human Ecology and the wider Consortium on Families, Youth, and Children of which it is a part, and the Jane Addams School for Democracy. The Phillips Healthy Housing Collaborative, a multi-year partnership between the Phillips neighborhood and the Academic Health Center, has helped create new relationships between medical school faculty and community leaders and traditional healers in minority communities. The Minnesota Regional Partnerships, a statewide initiative that has generated more than 180 collaborative projects involving more than 60,000 citizens, working with faculty, staff, and students from many colleges. The Regional Partnerships have helped put the question of sustainable rural development on the state policy agenda. "I'm really interested in the *making* of projects, rather than having the citizens knocking on the university door and saying 'fix it,' or the university coming out and saying, 'we're going to fix you,'" says Mary Vogel, director. "The most interesting projects are those where community and university people make a project together around a community need and the discovery of knowledge. What happens then is a mutual exploration. It energizes people on both sides."The number and variety of partnerships is extensive and includes many strong organizers for public engagement.[22]

These listings are by no means exhaustive nor sufficient. A fifth key constituency that the University had not extensively engaged as of 2002–3 were the public humanities networks and projects. Yet such work in schools like the University of Michigan has proven to be a vital force for civic change. Public humanities work, bringing academic humanists and artists into sustained, reciprocal partnership with communities and cultural institutions, holds dual potentials. It connects humanities scholars, who are now often dispirited and isolated, with creative partners in other, nonacademic cultural institutions. Public humanities work, I believe, will also be at the cutting edge of broad democratic cultural change in the society as a whole—change which is urgently needed, and within the reach of higher education to help catalyze. In 2003–4, the second year of the presidency of Robert Bruininks, all seven of his new high profile presidential initiatives (including arts and humanities) were developing explicit attention to the public engagement dimensions of their programs and priorities.

A sixth constituency, even more submerged to date but of central importance for long range, deep transformation, are nonacademic employees. They have more extensive ties to community life than most faculty at research universities, and are often partisans of its public mission.

This gives some sense of the range of leaders thinking and working politically on large-scale civic change at the Unversity of Minnesota. They represent an often invisible but crucial resource: people in higher education who want to get things done, in Bloomfield's phrase, and who do so in collaborative, public fashion.

Democratizing Culture

A popular government, without popular information or the means of acquiring it, is but a prologue to a farce or a tragedy, or perhaps both. Knowledge will forever govern ignorance, and a people that mean to be their own governors must arm themselves with the power that knowledge brings. (James Madison)[23]

The largest promise of civic engagement in higher education is its potential to help make the culture as a whole more public, open, and democratic. This involves understanding that culture itself is made, not simply given. It also requires, at a place like the University of Minnesota, sustained attention to public scholarship.

The work at the College of St. Catherine and in other educational and service settings helped clarify the differences between democratizing power in higher education and in community organizing. Put simply, while there are some similarities, the foundations of power are different. Community organizing addresses power relations that are by and large based on scarce resources, especially money. Power in educational, professional, and service institutions is largely structured around organized knowledge. In practical terms, they have enormous influence over communications, technologies, and the creation and dissemination of knowledge. Hierarchies and asymmetries in knowledge power are often extreme and closely guarded, especially in our highly meritocratic society where, as Occidental's Ted Mitchel has observed, one percent of Americans or less produces the knowledge that counts, in conventional measures. This is, especially, the knowledge generated in research universities. Further, knowledge power systems are elusive and difficult to see.

Yet knowledge is not a scarce resource. It is not used up when shared. Indeed, the more it is shared, in many cases, the more effective and power-generating it becomes. Knowledge power is fundamentally a social intelligence, in John Dewey's words. As a result, though power relations in knowledge-based systems are often difficult to change, it is in the long-run self-interest of diverse actors that they change. Effecting change requires not only everyday politics but a bold rationale.

The deeply rooted citizen organizing that inspired our beginnings at the Humphrey Institute has been successful in developing the public leadership of large numbers of everyday citizens. But as powerful as it often is, such organizing also neglects the challenges of broader culture change. One result is that even in cities where the organizing tradition is strongest, conventional definitions of politics, power, and public life prevail. That community organizing groups, despite the core involvement of religious congregations, have had scarcely any impact on seminary teaching further shows their limits.

The promise of substantial, institutionally grounded civic change in higher education, in contrast, is its potential to affect democratic change in the overall culture. Higher education's best values, such as engagement of different points of view and careful sifting of evidence, are crucial democratic habits, as Deborah Meier's K-12 schools show. Moreover, as it begins to shift hierarchical relationships in which experts are on top to more egalitarian relationships where experts are on tap, higher education has potential to spread this change throughout society.

Even in its early stages, the University of Minnesota's civic engagement process has pointed to the potential for broad culture change, where uncredentialed citizens reclaim standing in public life. This involves seeing culture itself as a dynamic and ongoing process of creating shared meaning.

Richard Wood, drawing on his participant observations of PICO network congregations, makes a broader point about cultural life in contemporary congregations as itself a political, active process. "We do not usually think of politics as a cultural enterprise, but rather in terms of voting, raising campaign contributions, convincing others of a certain point of view, accumulating power, and using that power to win future power struggles," he writes. Yet culture is profoundly political, in the sense of creating "shared meanings." The constant negotiation and creation of shared meanings, Wood observes, is a richer way to talk about politics than "values," which suggest stable, internally socialized preferences over which individuals have little control. In contrast, "the focus here on *meanings* emphasizes the contingent, often temporary quality of political commitments," Wood observes. "[Such] commitments . . . are constantly being restructured."[24]

Though leaders in civic engagement efforts recognize the importance of using a variety of approaches, serious partnership efforts have begun to significantly reshape relationships between the University and communities. It is now official University policy to shift from one-way service delivery to sustained, interactive, mutually beneficial community partnerships. To be serious, this requires that scholarship and research be made more public.

The University's civic engagement process has supported ongoing theoretical and practical discussion of public scholarship, involving both faculty and administrators. Victor Bloomfield, vice provost for research and interim dean of the Graduate School, himself an eminent scientist, proved a major voice for conceiving research in public terms. Involving him as a leader has been key to its success. When Ed Fogelman first asked Bloomfield to chair the committee on public scholarship, he demurred. "Why don't you get someone who has thought about public scholarship a lot, like a philosopher," was his response. Fogelman persisted. "We want you precisely because you're not a philosopher; we want a practicing scientist who has thought about the public dimensions of his work and can talk in these terms to other faculty about scholarship and research." Bloomfield's committees on public scholarship and on assessment—on what the University will look like in five years as a more "engaged institution"—were vital resources.[25] Another dimension of public scholarship has been to conduct interviews with intellectual leaders at the University and elsewhere, while a third dimension involved making more visible strong examples of public scholarship.

A recent study of citizen views toward the University found that people highly value the University's contribution to the state's overall "quality of life," and see the University as a "source of pride." The efforts of partnerships and scholarship that engage citizens and communities may help to explain why.

The discussion about public scholarship at the university has drawn from and contributed to a larger discussion in higher education about public scholarship, an emerging topic across institutions, disciplines, and fields. It reflects, in part, the desire by many academics to lead work lives that are more integrated, hopeful, and politically engaged, combining critical reason with commitment. This desire is especially poignant in public scholarship in the humanities. In a lecture, the University of Michigan's Julie Ellison directly addressed these themes.[26] She used a recent conference on the future of theory sponsored by the journal *Critical Inquiry* as an example. Ellison described the melancholia that grows from the unmooring of academic theory and scholarship from public life. "The tone of this gathering [as reported in the *Boston Globe*, the *New York Times*, and elsewhere], is the most disturbing thing about it," she observed. Ellison quoted participants like Catherine Stimpson, dean of the Graduate School of Arts and Sciences at New York University, who said, "This group of intellectuals has a terror of being irrelevant," She described participants' "resolute conviction that theory can't come into a productive relationship with politics, even though theorists have a passion for the foreseeable political future." She traced the problem to the fact that academic theory, in conventional terms, "is not in the room with other kinds of knowledge, theorists not in the room with other kinds of knowers and institutions engaged in the making of ideas, concepts, and other forms of knowledge and culture. . . . A world of myriad organizations, groups, professions, and institutions with which to collaborate was missing from the whole event."

In contrast to detachment, Ellison described efforts like the international "cultural democracy movement" which involves people from the academy, museums, art galleries, community historical societies, musical groups, poetry associations, and others in an explicit theory-building process. She pointed to the "City of Learning," a design and planning process in Paterson, New Jersey, which has created ten small academies through the city. These include a performing arts academy in a former Lutheran church; a health professions academy in a former downtown mall; an international studies and language academy in an old synagogue; and a transportation academy in an abandoned locomotive factory—an entire framework of curriculum, research, and seeing schools as community centers. Ellison also had a number of specific proposals to strengthen public scholarship, including creation of learning networks connecting humanists with K-12 teachers, museum curators, performing artists, archivists, librarians, radio reporters, landscape architects, board members of state arts and humanities councils, and community leaders; project based learning that integrates disciplines and diverse groups; summer field schools; and work with disciplinary associations and learned societies to strengthen emphasis on public scholarship. Ellison's strategic ideas, such as "proximate partners" of academics with intellectuals working on similar themes in nonacademic settings, had a major impact.

Toward a New Politics

The essential aim of . . . the most democratic movements we have is to train ourselves, to learn how to use the work of experts, to find our will, to educate our will, to integrate our wills . . . It is of equal importance with the discovery of facts to know what to do with them . . . In politics we do not keep these different kinds of information apart. (Mary Parker Follett, *Creative Experience*, 1924)[27]

As we have worked on civic engagement at the University of Minnesota over the past several years, the larger implications of this work for democratic renewal have become increasingly clear. Higher education is the

premier information institution of modern society. It socializes professionals. It creates credentialed knowledge. It generates and diffuses conceptual
frameworks that structure practices and institutional cultures of all sorts,
from global finance to parent education. It educates students for occupations. If higher education becomes infused with what Harvard president
Charles Eliot called, long ago, the democratic spirit, it will contribute powerfully to the development of public life across the whole society.

Democratic knowledge politics in the twenty-first century—the politics that higher education must help generate—requires democratizing the
creation, diffusion, and adoption of knowledge itself. Such efforts have a
deeply populist flavor, in the sense of a belief that everyone has the capacity
to contribute to social intelligence. As John Dewey observed, knowledge is
always the product of social and public interaction. Such a pattern was once
widely perceived among America's great intellectuals such as John Dewey,
Jane Addams, William James, Alaine Locke, Zora Neale Hurston, Ralph Ellison, and others, but was eroded by meritocratic practices.

The politics of civic engagement holds potential to empower communities and citizens in a variety of ways. In their most visionary moments,
leaders in higher education have sensed its public power. "We believe that
our institutions serve not only as agents of democracy but also as its architects," declared *Renewing the Covenant*, a statement by 24 land grant university presidents, including Mark Yudof, then president of the University
of Minnesota, issued in 2000.[28] The *Covenant* pointed to disturbing trends
in American society and education—growing economic inequalities and
educational disparities; the spread of marketplace thinking in higher education that defines students as customers and judges research only by its commercial utility; and declining levels of civic participation in the democracy—that public universities have a responsibility to help address. In their
words, public universities provide the "bridge between the aims and aspirations of individuals and the public work of the larger world."

Leaders of private schools have issued similar statements. Thus, in a
full page ad in the *New York Times* in September 2002, entitled "Civic and
Social Engagement: Now More than Ever," Michael McPherson, president
of Macalester College, presented the college's response to the spate of corporate scandals. McPherson, an economist by training, called attention to
Adam Smith's argument that "the social environment shaped [citizens'] indispensable moral sense." He argued that there had been "a failure in
American higher education to build education for civic and social responsibility into the basic college curriculum." Furthermore, higher education

had the power to make a serious difference. "A determined effort by colleges and universities to promote civic and social responsibility among their students could do much to improve the quality of civic life in America."[29]

The latent democratic power of higher education is understood in the larger society. In public forums that the University of Minnesota organized in 2000 and 2001, citizens discussed the creation of socially useful knowledge, the importance of engaging with people of differing views, the education of students as civic leaders, and the building partnerships with communities for problem solving. Repeatedly people said that civic change at the University would have a large impact. As one put it, "The whole future of the state of Minnesota is bound up with the University. If the University recovers its public purposes, it will have an impact everywhere." Or as the *Star Tribune* remarked, in calling for "a statewide conversation about the university's needs and its role in the state" as part of the search for a new president, "The University [is] the single most important shaper of Minnesota's future."[30]

To date the democratic power of higher education is locked up in significant ways. For all the signs of ferment and discontent, the dominant culture of higher education remains highly privatized and self-consciously apolitical. If higher education holds enormous potential power to be a force for democratic change, it is highly unlikely to change itself, from the inside alone.

The fate of civic engagement politics in higher education is inextricably linked to the politics of the larger society and of the broader world.

Chapter 9
Spreading Everyday Politics

We are gradually requiring of the educator that he free the powers of each man and connect him with the rest of life. We are impatient to use the dynamic power residing in the mass of humankind, and demand that the educator free that power.

—Jane Addams

In the face of overwhelming power, it is a human impulse to "retreat back and take care of what you know you can take care of," as the Richmond woman in the Kettering study described in Chapter 1 put it. In the early twenty-first century, the cultural and political force of the market is like a tidal wave rolling across the world. To many the civic identity of consumer seems set in granite. The idea that citizens might be producers and co-creators of the world sounds far fetched.

More, if the forces undermining strong conceptions and practices of citizenship are enormous, technocratic trends, hollowing out the political and civic dimensions of mediating institutions, operate at the micro-level of everyday life in families, schools, religious institutions, sports groups, and many other settings. Technical ways of thinking are the air we breathe. In 1962, Bernard Crick described this pattern as the "social doctrine of Technology." It "holds that all the important problems facing human civilization are technical, and that therefore they are all soluble on the basis of existing knowledge or readily attainable knowledge." The politics of technology, Crick argued, is an anti-politics. Moreover, its view of education is sharply limited. The technocrat will "try to reduce all education to technique and training, and its object will be to produce social-engineers to transform society into something radically more efficient and effective."[1]

Yet from another vantage, countertrends are everywhere. The same in-depth examinations of citizens' attitudes and aspirations that show a widespread sense of powerlessness, such as the Kettering study and Susan Faludi's book on male subcultures, also reveal large discontents about consumerism. If it goes against the grain of dominant professional cultures to "think politically," there are multiplying challenges to conventional wisdom. Technocratic approaches bear similarity to Soviet communism in the 1980s—a dead ideology that people continue to live out, but few any more believe.

The stance of the detached, objective academic has come under withering criticism in recent years through the retrieval of the insight that knowledge is always socially constructed, "not merely through an objectively situated context such as a research project but also through the historical and social situations in which individuals find themselves," as William Tierney recently put it. In Tierney's phrase, knowledge is always "a social product with political roots." Knowledge production is "a dynamic process that helps define and is defined by the worlds in which it is situated."[2]

Similarly, in professional education there are signs of change. In a 2002 address to the nation's public affairs schools, Barbara Nelson, dean of the UCLA School of Public Policy and Social Research, described the trends that displaced politics in public affairs education over the twentieth century. But she argued that in complex institutional environments where conceptions and practices of "the public interest" can never be taken as a given—indeed, must always be negotiated among divergent interests—these trends make for increasingly dysfunctional professional practice and have to be changed. Nelson pointed out that students come into public affairs with a burning passion to make a difference, to create a more just world, "but they have little knowledge of how to get things done," because they lack political skills. The twenty-first-century public affairs curriculum needs "to educate students to work successfully at the seams of institutions, sectors, and jurisdictions as well as within them." To Nelson, this means teaching politics. "Perhaps the greatest lack in our curricula has been attention to politics in the Aristotelian sense of the public mediation of conflicts with public consequences."[3]

In public health, the new systems approach to prevention science (or "syndemics"), now integrated into the Centers for Disease Control and Prevention's (CDC) strategic plan for the public health professions, may foster far ranging change in this field over the next few years. The syndemics approach uses an explicit public work model, based on recognition of the central importance of "community strength" to disease prevention and health promotion. "When [health] problems spread in a weak community, problem-fighting efforts tend to be taken over by small groups of professionals who specialized in these problems," write CDC evaluators Bobby Milstein and Jack Homer. This dynamic, in their view, is "a divided process that ends up reinforcing the community's weakness." In contrast, "when problems spread in a strong community, the response tends to be more multifaceted and elicit greater contributions from ordinary citizens in the form of 'public work.'" Public work, in their view, is "a united process that reinforces the community's strength."[4]

This range of examples suggests the varied organizing needed to a generate a realistic vision of democracy beyond commercial civilization, or an understanding of citizenship beyond protest and voluntarism. Such organizing also challenges citizens' stance of being outside democracy's problems. "Throw the bums out" has been the citizen mood for some years. But simple anger at politicians lets the rest of us of the hook. As a pundit once put it, we get the political leaders we deserve. Today, if most citizens claim a role in public life, it is as outsiders or critics. Until we reinvent the role of productive citizen and the politics to express it, public like is unlikely to improve.

If we are to renew democracy through everyday politics, five things are needed. This first is conceptual: we need an understanding of the commons as something created and sustained by human beings, not simply given. The other four are practical. We need to develop public policy frameworks for productive citizen-government partnerships in problem solving. We need sustained culture-changing organizing in mediating institutions, including the addition of everyday politics to political parties, issue groups, and other structures now dominated by experts. We need to understand popular culture itself as a crucial strategic site of democratic organizing. And we need to develop learning partnerships that spread everyday politics on a global scale.

The Commons

The first element is conceptual: we need to see democracy and its products, the multiple forms of public wealth, as goods we are all responsible for creating and sustaining. This means seeing ourselves, citizens, as democracy's co-creators. This is simple in rhetoric but difficult in practice. The idea that democracy is simply a cornucopia of benefit packages is entrenched. Liberals see democracy largely as a means to disperse resources and rights more equally. Communitarians stress inculcating civic values. But both see politics as state-centered and distributive. And both neglect a robust conception of the commons, where it comes from, and how it is sustained.

All societies have some form of commons or commonwealth, a public scaffolding of physical, cultural, and institutional goods upon which all rely. In modern societies, these include the physical infrastructure like dams, waterways, roads, bridges, internet connections, and other communications systems. The commonwealth also includes lasting cultural, educational, and political institutions. These include the institutions of representative government, vividly captured in the British House of Commons.

Exactly what the commonwealth includes is always debated, but that it exists has rarely been questioned until our time, when some have challenged the existence of any public things.[5] Their view goes against the argument of market economics' own founder, Adam Smith, who argued, "The last duty of the commonwealth is that of erecting and maintaining those public institutions and those public works which, though they may be in the highest degree advantageous to a great society, are, however, of such a nature that the profit could never repay the expense to any individual or small number."[6]

The American commonwealth differed from its European counterparts. It was neither handed down from antiquity nor defined by authoritative religion, neither a gift bestowed by an aristocracy, as in France, nor the product of a benevolent and paternalistic state, as in Prussia. In practice, it was largely the work of citizens. But in recent decades, the commons, however defined, has been eroding.

In an article that defined the intellectual discourse on the topic for a generation, "The Tragedy of the Commons," Garrett Hardin argued that the commons is a "free resource," open to all that inevitably erodes as increasing numbers of people take advantage of it. Hardin's analysis depends on an individualist consumer model:

As a rational being, each herdman seeks to maximize his gain . . . he asks, "what is the utility to me of adding one more animal to my herd?" [Thus] each man is locked into a system that compels him to increase his herd without limit in a world that is limited. Ruin is the destination toward which all men rush, each pursuing his own best interest in a society that believes in the freedom of the commons.[7]

As Peter Levine has observed, Hardin's paradigm has "led most theorists to believe that we must either divide any un-owned resource among private property-holders or else ask the government to manage it."[8]

As government ownership and management have come under assault around the world, one consequence has been a theoretical attack on all forms of property without private title. The pseudo-populist arguments of Hernando de Soto take this approach. De Soto lauds American capitalism as an unparalleled, unalloyed success, the height of human civilization. Its triumphs can be emulated by the world's impoverished nations if they give private titles to all property. His writings, such as *The Mystery of Capital: Why Capitalism Triumphs in the West and Fails Everywhere Else*, have gained an enormous audience in third world policy and political circles.[9]

Both communitarians and participatory democrats have criticized Hardin's explicit and de Soto's implicit individualist, rational choice view of the commons. From a communitarian perspective, the problem with Hardin's view is that in medieval villages "freedom of the commons," as well as individual well-being, was defined in largely communal terms. The commons were *collective resources*, not simply free goods. Their use entailed responsibilities as well as rights. The commons were in the interests of whole communities. Indeed, there is evidence that commons often developed *because* population pressures required more careful tending of resources.[10]

From a participatory democratic perspective, the key issue is patterns of governance. In her pioneering work, Elinor Ostrom examines this question—what she terms "the search for rules to improve the efficiency, sustainability, and equity of outcomes"—in common pool settings. She looked at cases of forest management, irrigation, inshore fishery, and the Internet. In each case, she agrees with Hardin that the problem is "excluding free riders," those who use a commons resource with no regard for its sustainability. Ostrom finds that decentralized governance with higher popular participation has key advantages in terms of efficiency, sustainability, and equity. These include incorporation of local knowledge; greater involvement of those who are trustworthy and respect principles of reciprocity; feedback on subtle changes in the resource; better adapted rules; lower enforcement costs; and redundancy, which decreases the likelihood of a system wide failure. Decentralized systems also have disadvantages, such as the uneven involvement by local users; the possibilities for "local tyrannies" and discrimination; lack of innovation and access to scientific knowledge; and inability to cope with large common pool resources. Ostrom and others argue persuasively for a mix of decentralized and general governance, what she calls "polycentric governance systems . . . where citizens are able to organize not just one but multiple governing authorities at different scales." Such mixed systems may be messy, but in studies of local economies, "messy polycentric systems significantly outperformed metropolitan areas served by a limited number of large-scale, unified governments."[11]

A public work perspective adds to communitarian and participatory democratic critiques of the individualistic view of the commons. It highlights decision-making about the commons (as well as the creation of structures for such decision making) as a public, evolving work. And it emphasizes the identity changes, learning, connections across lines of difference, and the sense of ownership that develop through commons-building labors by groups of people. Perhaps most dramatically in a political culture that takes public wealth for granted even as it privatizes such wealth, public work draws attention to the *creation* of the public world, the what as well as the how of politics.

A splendid study of the New Deal Civilian Conservation Corps (CCC) by Melissa Bass illustrates these dynamics. Bass argues that FDR designed the program to, in his words, "kill two birds with one stone"—to "conserv[e] not only our natural resources, but our human resources." The CCC explicitly embodied the dual purposes of contributing to the nation's commonwealth through conservation and helping and developing unemployed young men in the process. As Bass puts it, by doing useful work, "CCC enrollees were understood to be doing the work of citizens. To a large extent, this was how they *became* citizens." Further, enrollees' civic development, in addition to their conservation work, contributed to society. As one administrator said, "the enrollees' growth" will prove to be a permanent result of incalculable value to the Nation." He saw the benefits as long term: "Who can estimate the unendingly different effects on our country's destiny of the passing into its citizenship of a million young men?"[12]

The CCC employed more than three million young men in conservation efforts between 1933 and 1942. They planted more than 2.3 billion trees, erected 3,470 fire towers, constructed 97,000 miles of roads, logged 4,135,500 days in fighting fires, and reclaimed 20 million acres of land from soil erosion. Over time, CCC participants realized they were helping to create a national treasure and felt a deep connection to the commons they had helped create. As one observer put it, "The CCC enrollees feel a part-ownership as citizens in the forest that they have seen improve through the labor of their hands. These youths are interested because the woods, streams, and lakes are theirs in a new way. They have toiled in them, protected them, improved them, replenished them."[13]

The legacy of parks, forests, and other conservation projects from the New Deal are a powerful example of commons created by citizens' public work. A contemporary example is a new effort to ground internet technologies in local commons created and sustained by citizens and civic associations. The new "information commons" idea has spawned a fledgling movement, building on examples in St. Paul, Madison, Wisconsin, Ann Arbor, Michigan, College Park, Maryland, and elsewhere.

The movement claims the heritage of what political philosopher Peter Levine has called "associational commons," or commons managed and sustained by groups of citizens. The commons in this sense is not synonymous with democracy—the medieval commons, after all, were most often formally owned and governed by the king. But instances when citizens joined together for civic action to protect and sustain the commons furnished a vital schooling in democratic skills and sensibilities, whatever the formal structures of government and or patterns of formal ownership. In American history, commons created and sustained by local communities and civic groups aimed not only at the benefit of their own members but also at contributing to the larger world, have been central to the vitality of democracy itself. As Alexis de Tocqueville observed, America's democracy was indelibly linked to citizens' work in creating public goods. "The American makes associations to give entertainments, to found seminaries, to diffuse books, to build inns, to construct churches, to send missionaries to the antipodes." The creation of newspapers, schools, libraries, settlements, business centers, union halls, community festivals, bands and sports teams, as well as local political parties all were associational commons, in which people participated, around which they gathered, and through which they developed a collective public signature for the larger world.[14]

In Levine's argument, an associational, community-based, public work approach has several advantages over anarchist notions of the Internet as a commons that no one owns. These include the potential political clout, civic learning, and stakeholding that a sense of ownership through shared work can bring. Such an approach also draws specific attention to how public goods come into existence. From the anarchist perspective, the internet simply appeared as the result of millions of anonymous users. A public work lens illuminates the complex, detailed labors on the part of government and higher education, researchers, entrepreneurs, and designers responsible for the creation of this commons.[15]

Citizen Government Partnerships

During the New Deal, the reciprocity between participants and the larger public was tied to citizen-government cooperation. For example, in the Civilian Conservation Corps, Melissa Bass concludes that there was "a strong belief in collaboration, that together participants and the government could make progress in addressing the nation's severe challenges." As CCC enrollee Allen Cook explained, the CCC "was not only a chance to help support my family, but to do something bigger—to help on to success this part of the President's daring new plan to down Old Man Depression."[16]

A conception of partnership between citizens and government to address public tasks is the second key element in a politics that renews public life. But it goes against the grain of conventional political rhetoric. Today, political and other leaders seem to understand the relationship between cocreation and increased stakeholding and feelings of ownership in almost every realm *except politics and public life*. Businesses offer employees multiple ways to feel involved—from quality circles that tap their interests and ideas to stock ownership options. As Lawrence Sommers quipped, people never wash their rented car. The new trend in philanthropy is to connect donors directly to projects in which they have an interest. In pedagogical theory, if still unusual in practice, ideas of learning communities and students as co-creators are gaining currency over instruction. Even in as highly expert-dominated a domain as health care, watchwords now include alternative medicine and patients as co-producers of their health.[17]

Public work reframes an article of faith in citizen organizing, that government agencies should stay out of the business of organizing citizens. A focus on the public outcomes of work illuminates citizen-government partnerships in which government workers "put the civil back in civil service," as Jerome Delli Priscoli of the Army Corps of Engineers put it about their successful public participation efforts.[18]

At the Center for Democracy and Citizenship, we saw the potential for dramatic change in the identity and practices of civil servants and others in government especially through work in the early 1990s with cooperative extension, the nationwide system of county agents (agriculture, 4-H, home economics, and others) coordinated by land grant universities. A project directed by Peg Michels and Carol Shields found that extension workers who began practicing everyday politics, or what we then called "citizen politics," often experienced a dramatic liberation of talents.

In Anniston, Alabama, for instance, the county extension agent had been the guy to call about the sick tree in the yard or the woman to contact about the local 4-H club. Barbara Mobley, a cooperative extension county agent for twenty-nine years, changed to an everyday politics approach. Instead of providing information and services, she helped people organize their own problem solving groups. It meant "letting go of previous methods we used in prescribing a 'fix' for a community problem," Mobley explained. "We shared the ownership, and redefined our role to be a catalyst." As a result people began using extension resources in a new ways. An area-wide health council brought together public health nurses, low income mothers, and teenagers to tackle problems like teen pregnancy. A group called the Women's Empowerment Network provided training in political skills and public speaking for low income women. Cooperative extension also organized public meetings of community residents and military personnel to develop a strategic plan for decommissioning chemical weapons. "On an issue like this, the military typically will say, 'don't get upset. We have a plan. If anything happens we'll let you know," observed Bill Salzer, an Auburn professor who is an expert in community conflicts. "This is ripe for panic. But extension brought all the sides together." In the process citizens developed skills; they learned about the complexity of the problems; and they generated new resources for implementing sustainable solutions.[19]

In the Environmental Protection Agency, the Departments of Housing and Urban Development and Education, and elsewhere, as well as in local government, we discovered many other examples of civil servants developing considerable skill in organizing citizens in sustained partnerships to address tough, long-term problems. To do this, they have to learn to act politically, negotiating diverse interests, framing issues broadly, developing civic capacities. In actual practice, government agencies at every level have begun to involve citizens more directly in co-production of public goods and services. Carmen Sirianni and Lew Friedland describe these in their book, *Civic Innovation in America.* Building on ideas and practices of public participation that began with the "maximum feasible participation" principle of the 1960s and expanded during the Carter administration, federal agencies during the Clinton years experimented with a wide variety of citizen involvement strategies. These strategies often resulted from decades of civic learning about what makes for reciprocal and productive partnerships between citizens and communities and government workers, on issues ranging from environmental sustainability to housing and crime prevention.[20]

In the New Citizenship, a nonpartisan project coordinated by the Center for Democracy and Citizenship with the White House Domestic Policy Council from 1993 to 1995, we developed a number of policy frameworks in areas including health, community development, and the environment. President Clinton drew on these in his 1995 State of the Union address.[21] In 2000, we developed the new information commons framework in response to a request from Bill Galston and other Gore presidential campaign advisors for examples of citizen-government public work partnerships. It was elaborated in a Wingspread Conference, distributed upon request to both Gore and McCain campaigns, and further refined at a conference organized by the University of Maryland in 2001.

The dominant language of politics today largely fails to recognize these innovations. Yet local examples of such partnerships have proliferated.[22] Here and there, agency heads and political leaders talk about citizen involvement in coproduction and partnership in problem solving. Local political leaders who are honest about the capacities of government often talk this way. As Sharon Sayles Belton, former mayor of Minneapolis, has put it, citizen-government partnerships are common sense, even if they go against the penchant of many leaders to over-promise. "If they have a capacity-building component, partnerships between government and citizens and communities save money, produce better outcomes, and increase citizen ownership in politics."[23]

Whether formal partnerships, as in government initiated environmental work, or citizen-designed efforts, such as those of broad based organizing, citizens' everyday politics not does not *replace* representative government. Rather, it *enhances* the performance of politicians who are broad and long range in their thinking. It creates a ballast without which the representative system of politics becomes increasingly ideological and strident. Thus, everyday politics recasts the debate between participatory and representative democracy by demonstrating the useful interactions of both. Richard Wood's study of citizen organizing indicates that though there are inevitable tensions between strong citizen groups and political leaders, both sides can benefit.[24]

Any politics that hopes to repair people's ties with government will have to emphasize citizen-government partnerships. This politics returns, in the simplest terms, to the conception that government is not only *for* the people—the main position of technocratic liberalism—but *of* the people and *by* the people as well. To effect such a change on the government side will require elected public officials as well as government workers seeing themselves again as part of Addams's "common lot," putting the civil back in civil service, as Delli Priscoli put it. If change is needed on the government side, there is also necessary change on the side of the general citizenry and civic institutions.

Mediating Institutions

We used to target "the enemy"—whether government or business or "the system." But over the last generation, the 'enemy' has become ourselves. We have to move from an outside and victim stance—because we're now part of the systems we used to hate. We are now the professional infrastructure of the service economy: government workers, teachers, social workers, lobbyists, advocates. The challenge of change in our time is changing ourselves, and our institutions. (Tony Massengale)[25]

The Center for Democracy and Citizenship began by building on insights like that of Tony Massengale, a Black Power student leader in the early 1970s. To create democratic change within service and educational institutions and to reinvigorate a public politics requires movement beyond a victim stance, or a simplistic division of the world into good and evil, or a marginal role for the citizen as volunteer. We build on the traditions of mediating institutions.

Mediating institutions, settings in which people have significant ownership and space for experiment and self-organization, connect people's everyday lives to larger public arenas and have an overtly political and productive quality. They once existed in abundance—local political parties and trade unions, ethnic organizations, settlement houses, neighborhood schools, colleges, and universities, and many other institutions once were involved in far more than service delivery or ideological advocacy. In 1998, when I conducted interviews with Twin Cities business leaders as part of the University of Minnesota's early civic engagement efforts, I was struck by the sense of loss in men who described the days when organizations associated with the Independent Republican Party undertook nonpartisan community betterment projects.

At the Humphrey Institute in the late 1980s, we made a conceptual distinction between mediating institutions and mediating structures. Mediating structures, as used by conservatives like Peter Berger, are conceived as a *buffer* against the colonizing force of the state and the "winds of modernity." Mediating institutions are *connectors*, through which people act with power in the larger world.

Mediating institutions of many kinds once had a more public and political quality. They were settings where people learned political skills of dealing with different sorts of people—negotiation, bargaining, political discussion, the messy ambiguity of much of public life. They were also settings through which people felt some power in public affairs. Women's suffrage organizations, for instance, did not only fight for the rights of formal citizenship through enfranchisement of women voters. They also sought to teach an understanding of politics as "civic housekeeping" on a range of problems. Thus, the *Woman Citizen's Library*, a 12-volume collection of practical and theoretical material on "the larger citizenship," written by leading suffragists such as Jane Addams and Cary Chapman Catt, declared in 1913 that "the State is as real as the people who compose it. The duties of citizenship are as definite as the duties of housekeeping. Only as these self-evident facts are fully appreciated will women be able to share in those many and splendid reforms which we can see must come in our social life." The volumes included topics that range from the mechanics of political parties to questions of "the larger citizenship" like "the liquor traffic," "child labor," "equal pay for equal work," "schools," and "safeguarding the woman immigrant." Such a view of citizenship inspired lasting organizations such as the League of Women Voters, successor to the American Women's Suffrage Association. Similarly, the YMCA in 1940 had an explicit mission of "educating young men for democracy," which meant sponsorship of a variety of public projects in communities.

None of this should be romanticized. These organizations often had strong personal and parochial elements. Middle class suffrage organizations often had racist and nativist features. They justified women's voting, in part, by arguing that it would reduce the influence of undesirable foreigners and blacks. Ethnic political bosses created organizations that sometimes resembled feudal strongholds. Neighborhoods like Chicago's Bridgeport, the Irish enclave that produced Richard Daley and two previous mayors, was a parochial small town within the city, as quick to threaten an errant black as the Howard Beaches of recent years.

For all their limitations, however, institutions like these also created an everyday scaffolding for productive understandings of politics as about much more than elections or ideology. Under the umbrella of urban machines, for instance, immigrants became involved in a range of civic initiatives, from building churches, synagogues, native language newspapers, and ethnic organizations to the trade unions drives of the 1930s. All these could be considered a form of everyday politics that helped widen people's particular identities to include a larger understanding of their stake and role in the nation. Boundaries between formal institutions like the local school and the union were not nearly as distinct, even rigid, as they were to become.

As we have worked in a variety of such settings—dozens of schools, a Catholic college, cooperative extension, a settlement house, a nursing home, a historically black hospital, community education, arts programs, and others—we came to understand the centrality of the public dimensions of work to changing the contemporary pattern. The civic erosion of these institutions was tied to the loss of public qualities in work.

Like earlier populist movements, the themes of an everyday politics will have various electoral expressions, appearing not only in one political party or program for change. But if we are to renew democracy, connecting nonpartisan everyday politics to political parties, issue groups and other parts of the formal system is essential.

Another dimension is also key to developing a culture changing politics: understanding cultural work, in broad terms, as a vital site of democratic organizing and a meeting ground for diverse political views.

Democratic Culture

For all the ways the times we live in seem to deny the humanities, they also offer tremendous opportunities for putting the humanities to work. Many people are searching for meaning behind scientific progress and economic prosperity. Many feel a hunger for something beyond materialism and consumerism. In this atmosphere, the humanities have something to offer that humanity is eager to receive. (Esther McIntosh)[26]

Historically, democratic politics in America meant not simply challenging politicians and bureaucrats. It also involved a self-conscious organizing and educational process, the making of a democratic political culture. This culture-making process is even more central in our time, when marketplace dynamics have restructured people's basic civic identities, shifting people's very self-conceptions from producers to consumers. Work within the key culture-shaping institutions such as higher education is one strategic priority, if we are to revive a robust conception of productive citizenship. The modern communications industries, for instance, are also of central importance.

Lary May's book on the movies, *The Big Tomorrow: Hollywood and the Politics of the American Way*, holds insights about the potential for organizing in this vein.[27] May treats movies like the World War II classic *Casa-*

blanca and recounts changes in the craft of movie-making, like John Ford's transfer of techniques from modern art "that suggested that the world was less a transparent set of truths than a work of art made by human effort." May also details the physical spaces of the movies. For instance, movie theaters in the 1930s broke the palatial mold of 1920s. Following in the tradition of "populist" architects like John Root, the theaters of the 1930s were smaller, more egalitarian in design, and grounded in local and civic values. Murals on the walls conveyed regional themes of the Southwest, or New England, or the skills and trades that built New York City. In Duluth, they displayed immigrant dockworkers building ships to sail down the Great Lakes. In Minneapolis, they showed German, French, and English explorers encountering native peoples. Theaters often served civic functions as well, as sites for high school graduation ceremonies, political meetings, and amateur talent shows.

A larger dynamic was also at work. May explores the role of the movies in helping to shape a resurgent American populism in the 1930s and '40s. Movies challenged the culture of individualism and consumerism that had dominated the 1920s, and revived the ideal of a producers' republic, a democracy based on the work of diverse peoples. The shift was pioneered by Will Rogers, part Cherokee Indian (fond of claiming the legacy of Washington and Jefferson, he also declared, "my ancestors didn't come over on the Mayflower, they met the boat!"). Rogers's immense popularity as a popular wit and actor allowed him to dictate the plots of his shows. "Though the twenty-four Rogers films differed in setting and emphasis, they served to realign the basis of cultural authority in the community," writes May. "The main characters initially affirm the values of the corporate order, of static gender and racial roles, and of separation of the classes." Yet as the plot lines unfold, "these norms lead to disaster, the characters shed loyalty to the wealthy to reconstruct public life and Americanism itself. They align with the lower class to create a civic arena that begins to include women, minorities and youth . . . and to create a more inclusive public life." Rogers's movies not only reflected popular values; they helped shape people's outlook and civic identities.

Rogers' themes were taken up by stars like Humphrey Bogart, Henry Fonda, Joan Crawford, Bette Davis, Paul Robeson, and Charlie Chaplin and by directors like Frank Capra, Orson Wells, and John Ford. May argues that these artists' movies were essential in creating a "public" from a "crowd." "The audience had become less of a passive 'crowd' than a 'public' that made their own choices," May describes. People found in them a medium for understanding the larger significance of what they were doing as they took part in civic action that crossed class and ethnic and racial lines, ranging from labor organizing to organizing rural cooperatives. "By incorporating into the self the desires of outsiders . . . the new citizen carried into the civic sphere the capacity to cooperative with outsiders to reinvent oneself and society," May writes. These themes were reinforced by the roles that actors and directors took up as supporters of New Deal reforms.

Today, it would be a mistake to underestimate the political challenges of organizing in such contexts. In general, communications industries and organizations have cultures far different from the *New York Times*, which has supported the higher education civic engagement movement. Rather than welcoming diversity, they cater to and further segment specialized tastes and markets. They also narrow the range of viewpoints. Political as well as economic developments in the early twenty-first century furthered this process. In 2003, the Federal Communications Commission ruled that the giant media conglomerates—Viacom (CBS, UPN), Disney (ABC), the Murdock industries (Fox News), and EG (NBS)—could acquire ownership of all the independent stations. A massive outcry led to rapid legislation repealing the FCC ruling, with conservatives and liberals joining in a rare display of populist unity. Conservative columnist William Safire argued that if the FCC ruling remained in place, it threatened "to turn what used to be called public airways into private fiefs." Ever greater media consolidation, following years of growing concentration, could, in Safire's view, "undermine diversity of opinion and, in its antifederalist homogenization of our varied culture, sweep aside local interests and community standards of taste."[28]

Yet there are signs of the reemergence of public cultural organizing in many arenas. These include local cultural work, reviving the traditions of involving the audience in the making of art. They also include efforts to affect public culture.

For instance, a national public humanities coalition, Imagining America, emerged from the White House Millennium Council in 1999 and now involves leading colleges and universities, including the University of Michigan (its inititating institution), Yale, Columbia, the University of Minneosta, and many others. Imagining America, working closely with community arts programs and the federations of state humanities and arts councils, has an explicit goal of building a broad movement for cultural democracy tied to the civic engagement efforts to change the cultures of higher education. It mission is "to bring academic humanists back into public life through reciprocal partnerships with communities." Imagining America, according to Julie Ellison, its director, "is a strategic advocate and citizens' lobby" for artists and humanists aiming to build a national movement in support of ambitious public scholarship." It also "offers an example for other disciplines to emulate as they reclaim their public soul and public muscle."[29]

Cultural work can be a bridge across partisan political divides. Ellison describes her learning a "both/and" politics on the Michigan Humanities Council. "I became much more strategic," she says. "When I go to Washington to lobby for the National Endowment for the Humanities, it was more effective if I was with Sharon Wise, my colleague on the Michigan Humanities Council board." Wise was on the Republican National Committee. Learning to work with Republicans was a challenge. "For academics, 'Republicans are the other.'" But narrow partisanship just didn't make sense in cultural work. "We need to get over it. The ability to say, we disagree on these points, but I can work with you on this other one makes a huge difference."

The challenges and promise of democratic, everyday politics are also worldwide.

Everyday Politics Worldwide

A citizen-centered politics is emerging and re-emerging around the world, a growing movement as citizens, communities, educators, and government officials with a partnership orientation seek to deal with increasingly complex problems that government cannot solve alone. Its growth and development is often a dramatic contrast to the deterioration of organizations and political discourse associated with representative democracy such as political parties. An American approach to dangers and problems that makes common cause with democratic forces across the world also represents a crucial alternative to politics based on manipulation of fear or other elite versions of America's action in the world, as Benjamin Barber has forcefully argued in *Fear's Empire: War, Terrorism, and Democracy.* People around the world continue to identify with America's democratic energy, despite disagreements with the war in Iraq.[30]

Citizen or everyday politics is especially important in contexts where highly moralized and partisan approaches on the one side or narrowly technical approaches to problems on the other are proving increasingly dysfunctional. These involve dynamics where power is not zero-sum (as in re-source-scarce environments) but often revolves around knowledge, a nonfinite power source and one that can be increased through collaboration and sharing exchanges. The complex, interconnected nature of the world's problems and the need for effective and skillful citizen involvement in addressing them was dramatized by the CIA report, "Global Trends 2015," released months before 9/11, at year's end, 2000. The report shows a world spiraling out of control. "International affairs are increasingly determined by large and powerful organizations rather than governments," it read, including alliances between international crime groups, their money coming from "narcotics trafficking; aliens smuggling; trafficking in women and children; smuggling toxic materials, hazardous wastes, illicit arms, military technologies, and other contraband; financial fraud; and racketeering." Such cartels hold potential to "corrupt leaders of unstable, economically fragile or failing states, insinuate themselves into troubled banks and businesses, and co-operate with insurgent political movements to control substantial geographic areas."

The report cited many threats—biological and chemical weapons, the spread of nuclear weapons, population growth, AIDS, famine, sectarian warfare, and three billion people expected to live in areas of short water supply. In the face of these dangers, it concludes, "governments will have less and less control over flows of information, technology, diseases, migrants, arms, and financial transactions whether licit or illicit."[31]

The CIA's spotlight on the need for citizen initiatives in a global context of complex, interconnected problems has been coupled with examples of such initiatives elsewhere. As David Bornstein observed in the *New York Times* in 1999, citizen movements and initiatives have been growing at remarkable rates, with large impacts—the defeat of apartheid, the fall of communism, the overthrow of right wing dictators in Chile and the Phillipines, the establishment of an international criminal court, and the raising of village income, and educational and health levels for millions of peasants by the Bangladesh Rural Advancement Committee. Such efforts show signs of a cumulative process of social learning. William Drayton, president of Ashoka, which seeks to catalyze citizen effort, argues that a movement culture is emerging: "A critical mass of institutions, people, and ideas [that] feed on one another and strengthen one another."[32]

These civic efforts have had strong ethical dimensions, but they have also demonstrated political savvy, practical orientations, and the capacity to enlist people from widely different points of the political spectrum—an organizing capacity much more developed than current anti-globalization protests.[33]

In the early twenty-first century, many civic initiatives have moved from opposition to dictatorial political regimes to the tasks of development and the construction of democracies. As such, the capacity to bring together people with different partisan and moral beliefs to solve pressing problems such as poverty, AIDS, unemployment, housing, water, and other problems is crucial. As Simanga Kumalo, a theologian at the University of Natal, put it at the 2003 South African Christian Leadership Assembly, "The movements against colonialism produced a great generation of liberation leaders. What we need now is a new generation of development leaders.[34]

Over the past two years, as the Center for Democracy and Citizenship has worked with the Institute for Democracy in South Africa (IDASA), we have discovered many rough equivalents to "public work" and deliberative practices in African traditions. In Sesotho, the term *letsema* means cooperative village work on common projects; in isiZulu, *ilimo* is a close equivalent. In Xhosa, *dibanisani* means "let's work together for a better future," while in Afrikaans, *saamspan* means "let's get to work." In Kenya, *harambee*—initially meaning "let's put aside big differences to work on the larger task"—came to be a central idea in the liberation movement. In Swahili, along the East African coast, the phrase *kidole kimoja hakivunji chawa* —literally, one finger cannot kill the lice—is used to convey the importance of cooperative work on a project.

Nelson Mandela described civic practices he observed as a boy in the meetings held at "the Great Place" of Mqhekezweni. "Everyone who wanted to speak did so. It was democracy in its purest form," said Mandela. "There may have been a hierarchy of importance among the speakers, but everyone was heard, chief and subject, warrior and medicine man, shopkeeper and farmer, landowner and laborer." The most striking feature of the Great Place was its inclusive and diverse quality. "People spoke without interruption and the meetings lasted for many hours. The foundation of self-government was that all men were free to voice their opinions and equal in their value as citizens."[35]

It is be a mistake to romanticize these traditions, freighted as they were with contradictions. For instance, women were not allowed to speak at the Great Place of Mqhekezweni in Xhosa culture. Yet it is also equally in error to construct a unilinear arrow of progress which ignores the deliberative and cooperative work practices that once lent vitality to public life in communities, or to slight the prophetic resources to be found in African cultural traditions. Popular traditions of deliberation and cooperative work in South Africa and other developing nations may well furnish resources for revitalization of democracy around the world. There are many voices in South Africa arguing that western notions of success and politics are inadequate. Thus, Mvume Dandala, bishop of the Methodist church, is an outspoken advocate of what he calls "look[ing] afresh at the gospel with African eyes." In Dandala's view, "the collective weight of the church [is] imprisoned in the Western paradigm." Africa, he argues, "has a profound understanding of life that can never be met and satisfied by the individualistic emphasis" of such a paradigm. Idasa has explicitly dedicated itself to claiming and promoting African understandings of democracy, informed by themes and conceptions of democracy, such as levels of popular participation, that are neglected by the other large, international democracy promoting organizations from Europe and the United States. At the University of Natal in Durban, the African integration initiative directed by Mammo Muchie seeks to generate a new panAfrican intellectual movement across the continent in which ordinary citizens take central roles.[36]

In South Africa challenges to technocratic approaches have parallels with the organizing tradition which nourishes everyday politics in the United States. For instance, Xolela Mangcu, founder and director of the Biko Foundation, named for the Black Consciousness leader Steve Biko, argues that the Black Consciousness movement of the 1970s bears resemblance to the "organizing tradition" identified by Charles Payne in the civil rights movement. Black Consciousness organizers created a process of community organizing and empowerment, beginning in 1970 with the Black Community Programme (BCP) that emerged out of the South African Council of Churches and the Christian Institute. The BCP "built schools, day-care centers, and clinics throughout the country," Mangcu describes. "It established home-based industries and cooperatives in remote rural settings and townships, and published community newspapers and journals such as the *Black Voice, Black Review, Black Perspective,* and *Creativity in Development.*" It also generated what was called the "Black Renaissance" in South Africa, a cultural political expression with parallels to the Harlem Renaissance, whose products were as much public leadership development as they were about culture.

The Biko Foundation seeks to spread these lessons and this approach, "attentive to the development of human values, capabilities, and social networks," into contemporary, post-apartheid South Africa. Mangcu calls for an alternative to both "right wing and left wing modernism," or public policies dominated by technocratic elites.[37] In this vein Omano Edigheji, a social theorist at the University of the Witwatersrand, adds marketplace thinking to Bernard Crick's list of politics' enemies. Marketplace thinking, he argues, results in "the individualisation and monetisation of life." Edigheji similarly emphasizes "a different kind of politics" to counter the "false god of the market."[38]

Idasa's citizen leadership training program explicitly teaches nonpartisan, everyday politics and organizing skills to community activists from townships and rural communities. The idea that politics is not only "party politics" comes as a surprise, but it is seen by people as a potent and exciting resource for making change. "Politics is our everyday life whether we like it or not. It shapes the future of everyone," said one participant from Winterfeldt, a township outside Pretoria. "I will be more responsible in my community. I will no longer sit around and complain about how government does nothing," said another. "I was so ignorant about politics," said a third. "Now I eat, talk and sleep politics. I see the importance of it."[39]

Idasa's practice of a deprofessionalized, constructive politics has parallels elsewhere in the developing world. For instance, a similar view of politics as about democratic empowerment, horizontal relations among citizens, and the negotiation among diverse interests, groups, cultures, and perspectives, animates the highly effective education reform effort Hakielimu (quality education), in Tanzania. Hakielimu organizes across government, civil society, community, and other borders to involve citizens in school reform and governance structures in Tanzania, while it also affects national policy. An explicit attention to nonpartisan politics that empowers citizens is also taught in the faith based organizing networks developing among low income church communities in Johannesburg, Cape Town, Port Elizabeth, Durban, and elsewhere.

There is, we have discovered, a great deal to be learned from exchange of theory and practice across both societies. In both, there are growing concerns about increasing distrust that citizens express toward government and deepening alienation toward political parties across the spectrum. In both, there is some urgency to renewing an understanding of politics as productive, not simply distributive—a renewal that can only take place with the spread of everyday politics.

Public Life in the Information Age

Describing our society as an information society grows particularly from the work of theorists like Raymond Aron and Daniel Bell, who drew attention to the increasing power of knowledge creation in its own right. Richard Florida has recently argued that knowledge workers, or what he calls "the creative class," account for 30 percent of the workforce. Places where such workers are concentrated are the nation's main centers of economic growth.[40]

Energy generated by steam and electricity transformed preindustrial societies into industrial societies. Money replaced raw materials as the main strategic resource. Today, data-transmission systems and the theoretical knowledge required to organize information drive innovation, comprise strategic resources and power, shape the world economy, and alter human relationships. "The industrial era was characterized by the influence of humankind over things, including Nature as well as the artifacts of Man," wrote Harlan Cleveland, an astute analyst of knowledge-as-a-resource. "The information era features a sudden increase in humanity's power to think, and therefore to organize." Such a process, in turn, puts those who do the conceptual organizing in a particularly powerful position. Bell assumed meritocracy, seeing a "knowledge elite" of scientists, economists, engineers, and professionals of all sorts progressively replacing the traditional governing groups of managers, captalists, and business executives.[41]

One need not subscribe to extravagant arguments that we are entering a qualitatively new world—arguments that slight the growing concentration of multinational corporate power—to note the profound changes that the growing centrality of knowledge and its use are bringing about in patterns of power and politics. We are at the end of what might be called the meritocratic era which defined citizenship in weak and attenuated ways in significant part because of the centralization of knowledge, reflected in and produced by institutions of higher education. In the twentieth century Americans handed over to experts and technicians the power to make key decisions about our basic public goods.

Today knowledge itself has become more and more central both to patterns of domination and to democratic action. Power is gathered not only in corporate boardrooms; it is as close as the doctor's office or the social agency waiting room or the childrearing advice manual. In our educated, service society, most middle class and professional people can be both the "power elite" and the "powerless," depending on the system or institution.[42]

As knowledge power grows in importance, the struggle around its accessibility and use becomes more and more central to democracy. The success of contemporary citizen politics in a variety of contexts depends upon the ability to discover key information, often against the efforts of powerful interests to restrict access. From the housewife worried about local school dropout rates to the rancher fighting to preserve the open range, from community activists organizing around toxic waste to small businesspeople trying to increase resources for local entrepreneurial start-up projects, people need information to act. They need organizational and communication skills. Studies of successful grassroots leaders show that they have considerable talents at gaining access to information, and the organizing skills to facilitate action.[43]

Patterns of knowledge power present a further problem, harder for citizen activists to overcome. Large-scale organizations not only centralize information; they also strip it of meaning, mirroring the excessive specialization in academic life and professions. Housing data are rarely related to crime statistics or health care availability. Issues are separated from the larger context. Longitudinal knowledge disappears.

Knowledge must be guided by wisdom—by broader frameworks, concepts, and values that integrate information and the knowledge of how to use it, that contextualize, prioritize, and guide action. It goes against the grain of the times to think in broad and integrative ways about civic practice or to operate at multiple levels of community institutions and life, professional systems, and larger culture-making structures.

An information society has its dangers, but it also offers opportunities. Knowledge, unlike capital or land, is not used up if it is shared; in many cases, it increases in value. While large institutions try mightily to keep secrets, they are fighting a losing battle. One of the distinctive features of the "knowledge revolution" is that information is harder and harder to hoard (community organizing lore abounds with stories of the "inside sympathizer" who leaked critical information against a bank or developer or chemical company). Further, efforts to hoard information typically backfire, leading to inertia and stagnation—a lesson learned by Soviet Bloc officials, by tobacco company executives, and by intelligence officials after 9/11.

Information lends itself to sharing transactions, rather than the exchange transactions of the marketplace. And if it is unusual to think about framing values and concepts in our age of excessive specialization, skillful efforts to do so produce considerable power. Anne Fadiman's book, *The Spirit Catches You and You Fall Down*, about a disastrous encounter between American medical practice and Hmong culture, simultaneously contains striking examples of alternative democratic practice that increased the power and effectiveness of professionals who paid attention and showed respect. Doctors like Dwight Conquergood successfully introduced public health practices in Thai refugee camps by drawing on Hmong cultural symbols and by showing connections between western medicine and traditional practices.[44]

Teaching and Learning Everyday Politics

Given the obstacles—from old fashioned ones like plutocrats, bureaucrats, and the occasional tyrant, to subtle but pervasive ones like a technocratic culture that derogates the talents and intelligence of the vast majority of the world's people—it would be naïve to imagine that the work of democratization will be easy or simple. How a new wave of democracy, building on but different than the movements that toppled dictatorial regimes in the late 1980s and early 1990s, will emerge is impossible to predict.

Yet it also is clear that citizen groups and initiatives that engage in teaching everyday politics and the work of renewing the public world are more than isolated oases. Something is stirring in the early twenty-first century, against the grain of dominant trends. Political education and learning are emerging adapted to complex and technological societies. Such education and its politics develop people's power to shape this world. Everyday politics breaks down the walls that keep us isolated and powerless. Finally, teaching, learning, and practicing such politics recall an experience of freedom suggested by Jane Addams more than 100 years ago, of growing relevance in our time: freeing the powers of citizens for public work.

Chapter 10
Freedom

The great problem to be solved by the American people is this, whether or not there is strength enough in democracy, virtue enough in our civilization, and power enough in our religion to have mercy and deal justly with four millions of people lately translated from the old oligarchy of slavery to the new commonwealth of freedom.
—Frances Harper, 1875

In South Africa in the early years of the twenty-first century, against the background of continuing poverty, high unemployment, the AIDS epidemic, and other social ills, left wing critics attack the African National Congress-led government for not solving the problems. One vignette, from a piece of satire often heard, tells of a group of unemployed people interacting with their legislator. "'What shall I tell them back in parliament?' the legislator asked. The unemployed people thought for a moment. Then, a mother of four, wearing a small green hat, spoke, 'Tell them that we fought for freedom. All we got was democracy.'"[1]

Others rejoin, "Who chooses?" As Claude Ake put it, "even if it were true that democracy is competitive with development, the primary issue is not whether it is more important to eat well than to vote, but who decides which is more important."[2]

The freedom versus democracy debate in South Africa has some parallel with clashing proponents of "freedom" or "justice" in the United States, but, interestingly, the partisan roles of freedom champion are reversed. Justice proponents are on the left, as they are in South Africa, but they use virtually no freedom rhetoric. Rather, they argue simply for government action to remedy problems such as poverty, racism, lack of health care, and economic inequalities. Champions of freedom are on the right, calling for freedom from the intrusive state. In both South Africa and the United States, another question arises: "What does freedom mean?"

Social critics in South Africa beyond the orthodox left wing have long challenged efforts simply to equate freedom with material abundance. In his 1971 article, "The Relevance of Contemporary Radical Thought," Rick Turner argued that "the 'Old Left' criticised capitalism largely on the grounds that it leads to an unfair distribution of wealth and an inefficient use of productive resources. [Yet] on the whole it accepted the capitalist human model of fulfillment through the consumption and possession of material goods." Turner and others in his tradition agreed that ending enormous economic equalities and overcoming poverty are essential, but argued that the liberation of society must include more than material abundance and economic justice; liberation includes changes in values, institutions, and social relationships as well.[3]

In the United States, as well as in South Africa, freedom is an idea with fiercely contested meanings, a history richly documented by Eric Foner in *The Story of American Freedom*. Freedom has meant freedom from want (one of FDR's Four Freedoms), freedom from joblessness, free speech, free assembly, and other meanings associated with progressive politics. Freedom has also meant other things as well and, as Foner shows, the balance of meanings has shifted toward a conservative claim on the word in recent decades. Freedom conveys the right to do what one likes with one's property, the right to bear arms, the right to worship as one chooses. Overall, an integrative theme, freedom means the right to be free of government actions that are seen as coercive or intrusive. These include a range of measures, from school bussing and environmental regulation, to prohibitions on religious practices in schools or red tape on small business.[4] All these, constitutive elements of the conservative populism described in Chapter 2, can be seen in certain respects as defensive reactions against the technicization of modern society. Indeed, the call for freedom from intrusive government has become the rallying cry of America's red, Republican-oriented regions. There is some irony in this pattern since, as David Brooks, a Republican columnist for the *New York Times*, points out, government actually grew considerably during the administration of George W. Bush, even discounting for the Iraqi war. Yet whatever the ironies, the theme of freedom remains a centerpiece of the administration, internationally as well as domestically. "We have important work today," wrote Condoleezza Rice, national security advisor for the Bush administration, in the special issue of *Newsweek* bridging 2003 and 2004. "We must abandon the quest for new multipolarity and instead work for a balance of power that favors freedom, that defends freedom against its enemies and supports those seeking to build freedom in their own societies."[5]

The African-American freedom movement—always more a "freedom" movement in its popular resonance than a "rights" movement—provides a different angle of vision on freedom than conventional partisan perspectives of left or right. Freedom meant escape from the degradations and brutalities of slavery and racial oppression. It entailed the capacity to name oneself, to define African-American identities free of the imposed categories of white society. It suggested the ability to participate fully in a public life, a capacity both material and psychological. "Forty acres and a mule," the demand of freed slaves and their allies, also posited material self-sufficiency as the requirement for the independence needed to take one's place in the democracy as a free, self-directed citizen.

Freedom also conveyed the idea of productive citizens who build the commonwealth. The commonwealth of freedom illuminates not only who *decides* but also who *creates*. It rests on the conviction that ordinary people need to be the authors of their own development, not in need of rescue by elites of any variety.

The commonwealth of freedom thus brings together developmental notions of freedom and productive understandings of democracy. It calls for a society to live up to its public values, beyond oppression and injustice, a challenge vivid in Frances Harper's comment. It also conveys the idea of democracy as a work in progress, a journey not a destination as the first black federal judge, William Hastie, defined it. Langston Hughes's great poem "Freedom's Plow" brilliantly combined the two elements. Struggle against injustice was integrated with the vision of America as an ongoing work created by the people, whose labors generate civic authority as well as ownership. Other democratic movements have produced similar views of freedom. Frances Willard, leader of the Women's Christian Temperance Union, the largest women's association of the nineteenth century in the United States, believed that "the larger liberty for women" lay in the freedom to develop individually and to contribute to the democracy, or commonwealth. Such perspectives fed Jane Addams's understanding of the catalytic practice of educators, as "freeing the powers" of each person.[6]

The vision of a commonwealth of freedom highlights dimensions of public work I have often observed over the last sixteen years. In the twenty-first century, I believe that the two sides of freedom, what the philosopher Isaiah Berlin called the negative and positive aspects of liberty, can be phrased as freedom from oppression and freedom for public creation. And they are inextricably intertwined in the commonwealth.

Young people in Public Achievement teams, for instance, often say their experiences in working and fighting for their projects also help them "remove masks" and "try out new roles" and "give us freedom to be ourselves." Professionals who learned to work collaboratively with other citizens, on tap not on top, discarding the notion that they have can single-handedly fix the problem or provide the answers, say the work liberates their expertise. Parents in suburbs who work through Putting Family First to counter frenetic scheduling and consumer pressures talk about the freedom that comes from regaining control over family life. New immigrants are the driving force behind the annual Freedom Festival at the Jane Addams School for Democracy. The Freedom Festival is a way to celebrate their freedom from repressive regimes and also their contributions to the American democracy.

As such examples suggest, everyday politics generates an experience of freedom that counters the trends toward an increasingly technical, rationalized, elite dominated civilization. These trends have long been assumed to be virtually ineluctable in social theories such as Max Weber's "Iron Cage" of bureaucratic rationality, Michel Foucault's disciplinary discourses and practices, or James C. Scott's high modernism tied to state power, among others.[7] By contrast, everyday politics breaks the tyranny of technique that locks people into expert-defined roles and tightly circumscribed identities.

Everyday politics also prefigures the future in the present. The work of democracy, from the vantage of everyday politics, has abundant room for diverse ideologies, histories, and interests, in the U.S. and elsewhere. "Our whole philosophy is that everyone needs to be included in the work of democracy," says Paul Graham, Executive Director of the Institute for Democracy in South Africa (Idasa). "You can't exclude this group or that group because you think they're bad. You can't legislate them away. The people who are excluded will come back to act like the social problem you expect them to be."[8] The commonwealth does not require conversion, nor does it divide the world into believers and unbelievers. If it lacks the pleasures of unwavering conviction to be found in absolute certainties, it also offers the distinctive rewards of seeing a public world grow in cumulative, everyday fashion in settings where diverse people make public contributions. It vests ownership and pride in a vision of a democratic way of life taking shape in the here and now.

The concept of commonwealth as well as the term once radiated across

American politics. Commonwealth ideals created a civic, populist vision of democracy as a way of life, not simply a set of formal institutions or private relationships. This vision had broad appeal across the political spectrum.

In various formulations (e.g., "cooperative commonwealth," "maternal commonwealth"), the commonwealth was the idiom of choice for radicals and reformers, labor organizers, small farmers, suffragists and feminists, and those who struggled against racial bigotry and oppression. It challenged America in a prophetic voice to live up to its ideals, as Harper's poem illustrates.

Yet the commonwealth was not the sole province of activists or radicals. Theodore Roosevelt provides an illustration. Roosevelt, president from 1901 through 1908, is regularly invoked as a heroic figure in the American pantheon. He now ranks in the polls as one of the genuinely "great" presidents, behind Washington, Lincoln, and FDR. He is also described as a role model by American politicians such as John McCain and George Pataki. Roosevelt "detested bullies" abroad, as Louis Auchincloss has put it. He sought domestically to tame the power of those he called "malefactors of great wealth." Yet it is rarely noted that the commonwealth animated his politics. Thus, in his famous "New Nationalism" speech of 1908, Roosevelt challenged "the sinister influence or control of special interests," which he identified with older threats. "Exactly as the special interests of cotton and slavery threatened our political integrity before the Civil War," he said,

So now the great special business interests too often control and corrupt the men and methods of government for their own profit. . . . The true friend of property, the true conservative, is he who insists that property shall be the servant and not the master of the commonwealth.

Roosevelt's remedy was democracy. "The citizens of the United States must effectively control the mighty commercial forces which they have themselves called into being."[9]

The concept of commonwealth was associated with other public ideas, like "the common good" and "government by the people," not special interests. These phrases surfaced in the 2000 election in attenuated fashion, severed from the civic labor and the popular power needed to create and sustain a robust sense of commonwealth.

As a concept in the American political tradition, commonwealth had three main meanings. It meant government of and by the people. It emphasized the social nature of property. It entailed the productive agency of the people. These meanings were contested, used differently by different groups, but intertwined they created an enduring legacy, a vision which was both gritty, down to earth and familiar, and also luminous in its appeal.

In the first instance, commonwealth was virtually synonymous with republican or popular government for the nation's founders, and thus also closely associated with the ideals of liberty and self-directed rule. Insurgent colonists saw themselves in the footsteps of earlier English who had battled the crown. The Parliamentary act of 1649 ending the monarchy declared "the People of England . . . shall henceforward be Governed as a Commonwealth and Free State." As Edmund Pendleton put it, commonwealth meant "a state belonging to the whole people rather than the crown." Four states (Massachusetts, Pennsylvania, Virginia, and Kentucky) took up John Adams's urging to be official commonwealths. Every state was once called, more informally, a "commonwealth."[10]

What was distinctive in America—as contrasted with the British use of the term, "commonwealth," as well as classical references—was the idea that citizens were its architects. "We the people . . . do establish the constitution," as the Preamble puts it. Or in the words of Thomas Paine describing America, "A constitution is not the act of a government but of a people constituting a government." This way of thinking about government as the people's creation fed Abraham Lincoln's famous formulation at Gettysburg in 1863, "government of the people, by the people, for the people."[11]

Commonwealth also conveyed the social or public nature of property, individual and collective. Theories about the social nature of property drew on both religious and civic values. In the biblical Jubilee tradition, for instance, God instructed the Jewish people that every forty-ninth year private lands should be returned to the common tribal pool, so that no large private accumulations could develop, good news should be declared to the poor, and liberty should be given to the captives. "Your land must not be sold on a permanent basis, because you do not own it; it belongs to God, and you are like foreigners who have been allowed to make use of it" (Leviticus 25: 23). Such a tradition, the "Year of the Lord," continued as a major thread in Isaiah and in the New Testament, especially the Gospel of Luke. Jesus claimed this prophetic legacy in his depiction of his mission at Nazareth. Reading from the scroll of Isaiah, Jesus said,

The spirit of the Lord is upon me
because he has anointed me;
he has sent me to announce good news to the poor,

to proclaim release for prisoners
and recovery of sight for the blind;
to let the broken victims go free,
to proclaim the year of the Lord's favour. (Luke 4: 18)[12]

Thomas Aquinas, the Catholic theologian, drew on this conceptual legacy in stressing the social dimensions of property. Aquinas argued that individuals may own property, but they do not have the exclusive right to use it as they wish. Property entails the concept of a social obligation—an emphasis at the heart of the subsequent Catholic social doctrine.[13]

In secular terms, emphasis on the public nature of property drew from village traditions of collective moral obligations, from practices of "the commons" such as pasture lands, streams, and rivers in which whole communities had rights of use, and from goods of general benefit like community centers, wells, roads, and bridges. For many immigrants, America represented a chance to recreate commons that had been destroyed or privatized by elites in European societies.

During the Revolution, ideas of commons and the public dimensions of property served as rallying cries for popular protest. Thus, in the midst of an economic crisis in Philadelphia in 1779, artisans challenged Robert Morris, a wealthy merchant, for shipping grain outside the city. In the view of the scarcity of bread, they argued that Morris's property rights to use his ship were checked by the social origins of the property and the needs of the community. "We hold that [the shipyard workers] and the state in general have a right in the service of the vessel," they argued, "because it constitutes a considerable part of the advantage [the workers] hoped to derive from their labors."[14]

Lemuel Shaw, chief justice of the Massachusetts Supreme Court from 1830 to 1860, used this conceptual tradition as the justification for government control over unbridled business interests, especially those with large public impacts such as railroads and taverns. "The commonwealth idea precluded the laissez-faire state whose function was simply to keep peace and order," as Shaw's biographer, Leonard Levy, put it. In Shaw's words, "all property . . . is . . . held subject to those general regulations which are necessary to the common good and general welfare." Shaw put together commonwealth notions of government and property. "All power resides originally in the whole people as a social community," he wrote. "All political power is derived from them [and] is designed to be exercised for the general good, and limited to the accomplishments of that object."[15]

Shaw's reference to "social community" is important. As people created or sustained public things, they also forged a deeper sense of community by developing its public side. The third meaning of commonwealth entailed this creative activity of public creation itself, cooperative labors by citizens on common tasks and projects of mutual benefit. This idea fed back into the first two by investing popular authority and ownership in goods created through public work and by legitimizing government action, the instrument of the citizenry, to protect the commonwealth. Thus Theodore Roosevelt argued in his New Nationalism speech that, because citizens had "called into being" the commercial forces, they had a controlling interest.

This tradition of cooperative work on common projects long predated the Revolution and, as I argued in Chapter 9, it can be found widely, in different forms, in traditional societies around the world. After the revolution, as the United States took shape the commonwealth public work approach continued in myriad interactions between citizens, doing work that was formal and paid, as well as unpaid, what today would be called "voluntarism," but was earlier called work, government, and economic enterprises. The idea of a commonwealth created by the labors of citizens brought together what now is theorized as the three sectors of government, business, and civil society. Historians Oscar and Mary Handlin described the associations with the word commonwealth in Massachusetts colonial history,

For the farmers and seamen, for the fishermen, artisans and new merchants, commonwealth repeated the lessons they knew from the organization of churches and towns, and it embodied the wisdom of a people many decades in the wilderness . . . the value of common action. The Revolution was, at once, evidence of their power when united, and the repository of hopes for which . . . they had endured hardships and sacrifices.[16]

Citizen efforts that recall and employ this legacy—democracy as a way of life, and freedom as a liberation of talents, as well as the basic requirements of survival—have sometimes prevailed against tremendous obstacles. In the process, they have demonstrated multiple forms of power in an information age. A story from the 1960s of a community battling for its survival in Seattle, led by Terry Pettus, a long time activist and journalist, illustrates.

Commonwealth Organizing

Terry Pettus moved to Seattle in the 1920s. Over the next two decades he was a leading figure in a number of popular organizations and movements, from labor organizing to fights for public utilities and old age pensions. Pettus was deeply shaped by the populist politics of the New Deal. In the mid-1930s, he helped to organize the Washington Commonwealth Federation, a political group with roots in labor unions, farming communities, and neighborhood organizations.[17] By the 1940s, the Commonwealth Federation held a majority of seats in the state legislature.

Pettus and his wife Berta lived in a freewheeling houseboat community on Lake Union, near downtown. Boatyard workers, sailors, students, poor people, and bohemians mingled with retired radicals from the Industrial Workers of the World. Along the shore, speakeasies and brothels were scattered through small shacks and apartments. City officials had always looked askance at the community, and in 1962 moved to dismantle it to make room for development projects, including high-rise lakefront apartments. The key complaint against the houseboaters was the sewage they dumped in the lake, though the boaters' sewage was a minuscule one half of one percent of the total.

Few thought that the iconoclastic individualists of Lake Union could be organized, but Pettus knew they could. "People will fight for their existence, if not for abstractions," he explained. He and others formed the Floating Homes Association to solidify the community. Most important, they redefined the issue, from survival of the houseboats to the meaning of "progress" and the future of the region. "We knew we could never win if the issue was simply the survival of the house boats," said Pettus. He drew on the commonwealth legacy that had shaped his politics for decades. Pettus and his neighbors created a broad vision of Lake Union as the commonwealth of the people of Seattle, "a gift to us from the Ice Age," as he put it.

To dramatize the theme, they turned the complaint against the houseboaters for pollution on its head. "I knew we could never win by debating percentages, or claiming 'less responsibility' for pollution than others," said Pettus. Houseboaters, to the consternation of city officials, demanded that they be permitted to pay for sewer lines to their boats. The association held workshops on how to weld pipes and how to hook up sewer lines. They gained new allies, like the city's Health Department.

They also organized on multiple levels. Pettus and others worked with journalists to place articles on the lake and its history in magazines and newspapers. They worked with teachers to sponsor historic tours of the lake. They held festivals, in concert with neighborhoods. They launched an aggressive speaking campaign across the city. They solicited support from faculty and students in urban planning and other departments at the University of Washington. Throughout, their message connected the lake and its history with work. It had always been a "working lake," Pettus argued. They also tied the message to the vision of a lake with multiple uses: recreation, commerce, residence, and scenes of beauty and culture. It was in this context that the fate of the house boats took on enormous symbolic significance, as emblematic of a choice between unreflected consumer progress—the apogee of a commercial republic—and the commonwealth.

The organizing effort had dramatic impact because it tapped deep unease about the environment—it was a precursor to the national environmental movement—and the nature of progress itself. By late 1963, the city was forced to respond in dramatic fashion to the Association's swelling support. It issued a study calling for protection of the lake. The Association was able to block industrial uses, press the city to acquire a large area for a public park, and get the state legislature to pass the strongest shoreline management legislation in the country. Pettus, who had been jailed under the Smith Act as a "subversive" in the 1950s, helped write the legislation.

The Lake Union effort had contagion effects. It was a model for the 1970s fight to save the Pike Place market along the Seattle waterfront. It inspired neighborhood efforts in the 1980s. Establishment figures who had once battled Pettus acknowledged the benefits. "Seattle had a major era of citizen participation," said James Ellis of the prestigious firm of Preston, Torngrimson, Ellis, and Holman, a man sometimes called "the informal leader of the city's elite." As a result, Ellis believed, "there was an incredible flowering in the city."[18]

The limits of the Seattle effort can be traced to its failure to change the technocratic cultures of mediating institutions. By the late 1980s, new developments threatened the shoreline, and much of the once vibrant neighborhood organizing had ebbed. But the deeper lesson of Lake Union houseboaters' effort, whatever its limits, is the interplay between community-level action, generous democratic vision, and information-age savvy. Unlike most citizen activism—but suggesting the wide promise of everyday politics that engages organized knowledge systems—the Floating Homes Association understood multiple sources of power. It made alliances, worked with communications groups, created allies among diverse professionals, and articulated a vision of the commonwealth of freedom that had appeal across the political spectrum. The house boaters impacted the future of the region.

The story of the Floating Homes Association's practice of everyday politics that built the commonwealth, like the African American freedom struggle, holds prophetic resources for transforming understandings of freedom and for democratic renewal in ways appropriate to the twenty-first century. Its vision held in combination elements that modern, twentieth-century politics sundered: conservative politics that values heritage, realpolitik, focused on the world as it is, and visionary politics, concerned with the world as it should be.

By integrating things that the modern world broke apart, everyday politics points beyond the givens of our age and toward a different future. One outcome of the growth of everyday politics will be the reinvigoration of the language of commonwealth.

There are also larger implications and possibilities in this kind of story. Everyday politics, attentive to the complex power relations of the twenty-first century, holds potential to regenerate vision and hope within and across societies. Because it taps the energies and aspirations of diverse people for a better life, it can challenge and overcome the fatalism and frequent despair that has come to be widespread. Fatalism can be seen in the United States. It is a telling commentary that suburban Public Achievement teams frequently focus on issues such as teen suicide and teenage despair. Fatalism is also vivid in settings seemingly a world removed, such as the angry "Arab street," seething with humiliation and hopelessness.

Because it generates hope, another outcome of the spread of everyday politics will be the consciousness that we are not at "the end of history," as those such as Francis Fukuyama would have it.[19] Rather, we are at the threshold of history. We stand at the beginning of a world in which free citizens, across boundaries and borders, learn to act together in consciously political ways to create the future.

Notes

Preface: Developing a Theory and Practice of Everyday Politics

1. This incident was described to me by Doug Miles and several others in BUILD in 1988, as a way to describe their philosophy of public relationship-building.

2. For an excellent discussion of the technical approach and the fashion in which it has infused professions and public affairs—an approach that assumes there is "one best way" to solve human problems—see Robert Kanigel, *The One Best Way: Frederick Winslow Taylor and the Enigma of Efficiency* (New York: Viking, 1997).

3. As Aristotle had put it in the second book of *The Politics*: "The nature of the *polis* is to be a plurality. A *polis* is not made up only of so many men but of different kinds of men; for similars do not constitute a *polis*. It is not like a military alliance." *Aristotle: The Politics and the Constitution of Athens*, ed. Stephen Everson (Cambridge: Cambridge University Press, 1996), 31.

4. See the web site on revitalizing public spaces, full of examples, stories, and practice based wisdom accumulated over a quarter century, www.pps.org.

5. Richard L. Wood, *Faith in Action: Religion, Race, and Democratic Organizing in America* (Chicago: University of Chicago Press, 2002) and Carmen Sirianni and Lewis Friedland, *Civic Innovation in America: Community Empowerment, Public Policy, and the Movement for Civic Renewal* (Berkeley: University of California Press, 2001).

6. See Harry C. Boyte, *CommonWealth: A Return to Citizen Politics* (New York: Free Press, 1989).

7. The ideas of political concepts generally and politics specifically have roots in the ancient Greek experience. As Christian Meier describes in his book, *The Greek Discovery of Politics*, the emergence of political ideas was part and parcel of a transformation of Greek society itself that occurred in the fifth and sixth centuries B.C. and led to recognition of the concept of politics and its importance.

Greeks articulated a wide-ranging and remarkable language of public life. Against the background of an ancient world where radical inequalities of political power were seen as immutable and concepts such as democracy, equality, freedom, or power itself had never emerged, there was, Meier argues, an exhilarating quality in the transformations for those directly involved—an exhilaration linked to the new ability to name experiences. For the first time, ordinary (male) citizens came to develop a way of describing the idea that they could be masters of their fate.

Christian Meier, *The Greek Discovery of Politics* (Cambridge, Mass: Harvard University Press, 1990).

Feminist and other scholars have also pointed out the sharp ironies and inequities built into the Greek construction of public life. See, for instance, Jean Bethke Elshtain, *Public Man, Private Woman: Women in Social and Political Thought* (Princeton, N.J.: Princeton University Press, 1981), and Helen P. Foley, ed., *Reflections on Women in Antiquity* (New York: Gordon and Breach, 1981).

The development of the idea of politics occurred over centuries. But in the later decades of the fifth century B.C., a clear shift in identity took place among the ordinary people of Athens. Even the poorest male Athenians came to see politics, or the public sphere, as a vital part of their lives. Family, economics, and leisure pursuits—though perhaps not "work," as conventional theory has had it—became seen as *different* from public life, an arena especially characterized by freedom and public power. The Assembly, the body in which the citizenry as a whole met, deliberated, and took action, came to be seen and experienced as a qualitatively different setting. Aeschylus's great play, *The Eumenides*, performed for an audience of 15,000 in 458 B.C., conveyed these revolutionary transformations in consciousness. The political became the constituting feature of Athenian identity.

It is worth noting that work, conventionally opposed in political theory to politics, was not necessarily seen in such a fashion by ordinary Greek citizens themselves. Victor Hanson has persuasively argued that work, in particular the emergence of a new practice of family farming, individual small farms, worked by fiercely independent and ingenious farmers, generated the ethos and practice of public life—a perspective sharply at odds with the dominant theoretical tradition that sees work and politics opposed. In Hanson's terms, "The rise of independent farmers who owned and worked without encumbrance their small plots at the end of the Greek Dark Ages (1100–800 B.C.) was an entirely new phenomenon in history. . . . The material prosperity that created the network of Greek city-states resulted from small-scale, intensive working of the soil, a complete rethinking of the way Greeks produced food and owned land, and the emergence of a . . . person for whom work was not merely a means of subsistence or profit but an ennobling way of life, a crucible of moral excellence in which pragmatism, moderation, and a search for proportion were the fundamental values." Victor Davis Hanson, *The Other Greeks: The Family Farm and the Agrarian Roots of Western Civilization* (New York: Free Press, 1995), 3.

For the Greeks, naming civic experiences as "politics" allowed them to claim and understand in new ways what it was they experienced. The naming process also shaped new identities for people as citizens. "Up to now [people] had been first and foremost nobles, farmers or artisans, or retainers, townsmen, or villagers," writes Meier, in his account of how the Greeks discovered politics. "Their role as citizens, which involved certain political and military rights and duties, had been negligible." As a result of the changes, the citizen role acquired a tremendous vitality. It was "taken so seriously that one can actually speak of a change in the structure of social affiliations. . . . The citizens were expected to act as citizens, that is 'politically' (in the Greek sense of the word), and this expectation was now given institutional form." Meier, *Discovery*, 146.

One thing that emerges from reflection on the Greek experience is the craft of political concept-making itself. The making of powerful political ideas was like the creation of a map. It opened up new ways of thinking, new identities, and new directions. Subsequent theorists who have explored the nature and function of political ideas in public life have advanced a number of other insights.

First, intellectual historians have proposed that while the explicit articulation of political concepts often comes after the experience itself, the process of naming and using such ideas allows engagement by those far beyond the original conceptual pioneers. Thus, in the Greek case, the emergence of political ideas such as politics, democracy, freedom, power, equality, and citizen meant that over time the practices associated with these concepts were spread, tested, discussed, debated, and developed across the world.

Furthermore, growing especially from the pragmatic tradition of theorizing about the function and nature of knowledge, theorists have stressed the constructed, open-ended nature of our conceptual world. As Terence Ball, James Farr, and Russell L. Hanson argued in their important work, *Political Innovation and Conceptual Change*, from this vantage human beings are not reporters or objective observers of some fixed and external reality. Rather, we are all creators of the world of ideas in which we live and work. This world, in turn, shapes our sense of possibility and our range of action. Terence Ball, James Farr, and Russell L. Hanson, *Political Innovation and Conceptual Change* (Cambridge: Cambridge University Press, 1989).

Yet the notion that a broad range of people, people who are not recognized as intellectuals, might be involved in the creation of such ideas—or even much interested in how political ideas are created—goes against the grain of the overwhelming predominance of academic theorizing. With a few exceptions—John Dewey stands out, and is treated at length in *Everyday Politics*—philosophers have generally held that creating and even thinking about "great ideas" is largely the activity of a class of intellectuals who stand apart from common life. As Peter Berger and Thomas Luckmann put it in their classic work, *The Social Construction of Reality*, "only a very limited group of people in any society engages in theorizing, in the business of 'ideas,' and the construction of *Weltanschauungen*. . . . Only a few are concerned with the theoretical interpretation of the world, but everybody lives in a world of some sort." *The Social Construction of Reality* (New York: Doubleday, 1966), 15. Similarly, Isaiah Berlin, the great cosmopolitan British philosopher, expressed conventional intellectual wisdom in his *Concepts and Categories*. "Men cannot live without seeking to describe and explain the universe to themselves," Berlin argued. "The models they use in doing this must deeply affect their lives." Yet, in his view, "Ordinary men regard [the work of thinking] about these models with contempt, or awe, or suspicion, according to their temperaments." *Concepts and Categories: Philosophical Essays* (New York: Penguin, 1981), 4, 10.

The assumptions about publicness and by implication politics embedded in such treatments of idea-making are useful to analyze. Theorists such as Berger, Luckmann, and Berlin clearly hold that ideas are public in their impact and their usage alike. The work of idea-making is not, however, seen in their view as a public process. Recently, there are signs of dissent with this perspective.

Viewing public concepts as political in their construction opens up possibilities for thinking about the work of their creation as itself a public activity, engaged in by publics. In Jim Farr's view, for instance, concepts partly constitute politics and political practices, while they are also pragmatically constituted by political practice. Cornel West captures well the democratic implications of an approach that sees theorizing as a popular activity. "What was the prerogative of philosophers, i.e., rational deliberation, is now that of the . . . citizenry in action." The philosophical method in *Everyday Politics* has much in kinship with Cornel West. Especially, it seeks to convey what he calls the "Niebuhrian strenuous mood, never giving up on new possibilities for human agency—both individual and collective—in the present, yet situating them in light of Du Bois' social structural analyses that focus on working-class, black, and female insurgency." *The American Evasion of Philosophy: A Genealogy of Pragmatism* (Madison: University of Wisconsin Press, 1989), 228. The difference is that I believe West, like other left critics of Habermas and deliberative theory, neglects the pragmatic and constructive tasks of politics with his almost singular focus on its distributive and social justice aspects.

8. Outside evaluations have been done by Gregory Markus from the University of Michigan, Michael Baizerman and Robert Hildreth from the University of Minnesota, Rainbow Research, a Minneapolis-based evaluation group, and the Kauffman Foundation, which did a two-year evaluation of the youth civic engagement sponsored by the CDC. Carmen Sirianni did a historical account and theoretical mapping of the CDC's theoretical approach, as part of his book on civic change with Lew Friedland, *Civic Innovation in America: Community Empowerment, Public Policy, and the Movement for Civic Renewal* (Berkeley: University of California Press, 2001), chapter 6. This book also draws on his outstanding efforts as research director for the New Citizenship.

9. For instance, we at the CDC have often felt too busy in projects with partners to interact sufficiently with each other!

10. James Farr, a theorist of political concepts and a senior associate from the outset of our efforts, first suggested the term public work for one of our semi-annual institutes in 1992. Nan Kari, also a senior associate from the beginning, played a formative role in developing public work theory and practice, drawing on her own deep sense of the loss of what she calls "the luminous philosophy of work" that once animated her profession, occupational therapy.

Chapter 1. The Stirrings of a New Politics

Epigraph from Daniel Elazar, quoted in "The Language of the Commonwealth," proceedings of a seminar Boyte moderated in 1997 at the beginning of work at the Humphrey Institute. It included Helen Ayala, Larry Batson, Robert Bellah, Yvonne Cheek, Harlan Cleveland, Earl Craig, Rich Dethmers, E. J. Dionne, Sara Evans, John Gardner, Daniel Kemmis, Jane Mansbridge, David Mathews, Peg Michels, Bernard Murchland, Barbara Nelson, Pat Scully, Alan Stoskops, Ellen Tenity, and Eddie Williams.

1. Moynihan quoted in Michael Novak, "Rediscovering Culture," *Journal of Democracy* 12, 2 (2001): 170.

2. Joan Didion, *Political Fictions* (New York: Knopf, 2001), 28.

3. Andrew Ferguson, quoted in Didion, *Fictions*, 279.

4. Didion, *Fictions*, 253–54; Alan Stimpson quoted, 279.

5. "Bush Outlines His Goals," *New York Times*, August 4, 2000, A20.

6. George W. Bush, "The American Spirit: Meeting the Challenge of September 11," *Life*, September 2002, 4.

7. Moynihan, in Novak, "Rediscovering," 170.

8. Jefferson's full quote is important, not only for its populist faith in the citizenry but also for its realism, pointing toward the importance of political education as well as political action: "I know of no safe repository of the ultimate powers of the society but the people themselves; and if we think them not enlightened enough to exercise control with a wholesome discretion, the remedy is not to take it from them, but to inform their discretion by education." Thomas Jefferson, *The Works of Thomas Jefferson*, ed. Paul Leichester Ford (New York: Knickerbocker Press, 1903), 278.

9. David Mathews has been a creative theorist of productive, citizen-centered politics. See for instance David Mathews, *Politics for People: Finding a Responsible Public Voice* Urbana: University of Illinois Press, 1994/99). On the work traditions of American democracy, see Robert Wiebe, *Self-Rule: A Cultural History of American Democracy* (Chicago: University of Chicago Press, 1995), and Harry C. Boyte and Nan Kari, *Building America: The Democratic Promise of Public Work* (Philadelphia: Temple University Press, 1996).

10. E. J. Dionne, Jr., and Kayla Meltzer Drogosz, "The Promise of National Service," in Dionne, Drogosz, and Robert E. Litan, eds., *United We Serve: National Service and the Future of Citizenship* (Washington, D.C.: Brookings Institution Press, 2003), 8; they use the definition from Boyte and Kari, *Building America*, 16.

11. Johnson quoted in Harold Cruse, *The Crisis of the Negro Intellectual* (New York: Quill, 1984), 34.

12. Mark Ritson, "The Reversal of Production and Consumption at the Minnesota State Fair," *CURA Reporter* 30, 3 (2000): 1–4.

13. Susan Faludi, quoted in Harry C. Boyte, "Reconstructing Democracy, response to critics," in the Symposium on Commonwealth, Civil Society, and Democratic Renewal, *PEGS Journal: The Good Society* 9, 2 (1999): 33. See also Susan Faludi, *Stiffed: The Betrayal of the American Male* (New York: William Morris, 1999).

14. Richard C. Harwood, "The Nation's Looking Glass," *Kettering Review* (Spring 2000): 15–16.

15. Harwood, "The Nation's Looking Glass," 7–8.

16. Nader, quoted in Harry C. Boyte, "Nader's Trial Lawyer Populism," New Democrats On-Line (September 8, 2000): 1. www.ppionline.org/ppi_ci.cfm?contentid = 2231&knlgAreaID = 127&subsecid = 17 0.

17. Al Gore, New York University speech, July 20, 2003, accessed at www .Alternet.org August 7, 2003.

18. Convention speech, quoted in "Bush Outlines His Goals."

19. Bush quoted in Michael Schudson, "How People Learn to be Civic," in Dionne, Drogosz, and Litan, *United We Serve,* 270.

20. Amitai Etzioni, *The Spirit of Community: Rights, Responsibilities, and the Communitarian Agenda* (New York: Crown Publishers, 1993).

21. On Bush as a communitarian, see Dana Milbank, "Catchword for Bush Ideology: 'Communitarianism' Finds Favor," *Washington Post,* February 1, 2001.

22. Jean B. Elshtain, David Blankenhorn, and the Council on Civil Society, eds., *A Call to Civil Society: Why Democracy Needs Moral Truths* (New York: Institute for American Values, 1998), 3, 5.

23. *Declaration on Education and Civil Society,* www.aacc.nche.edu/Content/ NavigationMenu / ResourceCenter / Projects_Partnerships / Current / Community Building1/Partnering_Initiative.htm. Accessed April 1, 2003.

24. William A. Galston, "Political Knowledge, Political Engagement, and Civic Education," *Annual Review of Political Science* 4 (2001): 217–34.

25. Dan Conrad, "Learner Outcomes for Community Service," *The Generator* (September 1989): 1–2.

26. For an etymology of service, see *New World Dictionary of the American Language* (New York: William Collins, 1972).

27. Schudson, "How People Learn to Be Civic," 270.

28. Seyla Benhabib, *The Claims of Culture: Equality and Diversity in the Global Era* Princeton, N.J.: Princeton University Press, 2002), 57, 60; Rogers M. Smith, *Civic Ideals: Conflicting Visions of Citizenship in U.S. History* (New Haven, Conn.: Yale University Press, 1999), 30, 36; Harold Lasswell, *Politics: Who Gets What, When, How* (New York: McGraw-Hill, 1936). Theda Skocpol, Marshall Ganz, and Ziad Munson make a similar critique of recent communitarian writings in "A Nation of Organizers: The Institutional Origins of Civic Voluntarism in the United States," *American Political Science Review* 94, 3 (2000): 527–46.

29. National Commission on Civic Renewal, *A Nation of Spectators: How Civic Disengagement Weakens America and What We Can Do About It* (College Park, Md.: Institute for Philosophy and Public Policy, 1998), 8–9. The Commission, directed by William Galston, co-chaired by William Bennett and former Senator Sam Nunn, and including many of the nation's leading intellectuals in its advisory groups, after two years of detailed research into America's civic practices detected "stirrings of a new movement of citizens acting together," through which people are taking public action on problems and tasks, a movement "largely unnoticed, unappreciated, and unsupported" by official policies. The Commission's diagnosis of "the problem" in the nation's civic life had a richer and more political approach than most others, which have tended to highlight the purported moral failings of citizens and ignore questions of power, politics, and even democracy. The Commission focused on widespread feelings of powerlessness and loss of citizen authority. "Too many of us lack confidence in our capacity to make basic moral and civic judgements, to join . . . to do the work of community, to make a difference . . . rarely have we felt so powerless." *A Nation of Spectators,* 9.

30. Harry Boyte and Nan Kari interview with Elizabeth Kautz, Burnsville, Minnesota, April 22, 1995.

31. The Centers for Disease Control emphasis on public work is described in Chapter 9.

32. For instance, Elaine Pagels, in *The Gnostic Gospels* (New York: Vintage, 1979) and subsequent works, has found a wide audience for her arguments that the Hammadi texts show a Christianity of early centuries that is far more appreciative of women's roles, more pluralist in its conceptions of spirituality, and less focused on doctrines such as the virgin birth or even Christ's divinity. See also the *Time* cover story, "The Lost Gospels," December 22, 2003.

33. Dean Mohs, "Celebrating and Encouraging Community Involvement of Older Minnesotans: A Snapshot of Current Minnesota Baby Boomers and Older Adults," Minnesota Board of Aging, April 2000, 6, 3.

34. John Lukacs, *Outgrowing Democracy: A History of the United States in the Twentieth Century* (New York: New York University Press, 1984), 123.

Chapter 2. Populisms

Epigraphs from John M. Jordan, *Machine Age Ideology: Social Engineering and American Liberalism, 1911–1939* (Chapel Hill: University of North Carolina Press, 1984), 1; and *Business Week*, front page editorial, October 12, 1974.

1. For the text of the Moyers speech, see www.comondreams.org/views03/0610–11.htm

2. Adam Cohen, "What Would Jesus Do? Sock It to Alabama's Corporate Landowners," *New York Times*, June 10, 2003.

3. See, for instance, Lawrence Goodwyn, *The Populist Moment: A Short History of the Agrarian Revolt in America* (Cambridge: Oxford University Press, 1978); and Lary May, *The Big Tomorrow: Hollywood and the Politics of the American Way* (Chicago: University of Chicago Press, 2000). These arguments are also developed in Harry C. Boyte, *Community Is Possible: Repairing America's Roots* (New York: HarperCollins, 1984) and *CommonWealth: A Return to Citizen Politics* (New York: Free Press, 1989). See also Harry C. Boyte and Nan Kari, *Building America: The Democratic Promise of Public Work* (Philadelphia: Temple University Press, 1986). My treatments and co-authored treatments build on Rowland Bertoff's analysis of the middle peasant and artisan backgrounds of immigrants who brought with them everyday democratic practices of decision-making and collaborative work around questions such as care for common lands and village upkeep, regardless of the formal political regime.

Frederick Harris and a new group of young black historians have described the more complex and political relationship of blacks to America's civic traditions. As Harris put it, "Black mainstream institutions—churches, social clubs, Masonic orders, community organizations, schools—have traditionally nurtured norms that both legitimized the civic order and subtly and at times overtly serve as sources of opposition to white supremacist practice and discourse." Frederick Harris, "Will the Circle Be Unbroken? The Erosion and Transformation of African American Civic Life," report for the National Commission on Civic Renewal (College Park,

Md.: Institute for Philosophy and Public Policy, 1999), 21; see also the web page on black populism, http://kalamumagazine.com/black_populism_intro.htm.

4. Saul Alinsky makes this point about democracy in *Reveille for Radicals* (New York: Random House, 1946), but elsewhere identifies his "only ideology" as populist.

5. Michael Kazin, *The Populist Persuasion: An American History* (New York: Basic Books, 1995).

6. Lisabeth Cohen, *Making a New Deal: Industrial Workers in Chicago, 1919–1939* (Chicago: University of Chicago Press, 1992).

7. This critique of the New Populism is partly adapted from Harry Boyte and Nan Kari, "The Limits of the New Populism," unpublished manuscript, as well as "Tale of Two Playgrounds," a paper delivered at the American Political Science Association, San Francisco, September 1, 2001. For other treatments of the New Populism, see Boyte, *CommonWealth* and Carmen Sirianni and Lew Friedland, *Civic Innovation in America* (Berkeley: University of California Press, 2001).

8. Paul Krugman, "Toward One-Party Rule," *New York Times,* June 27, 2003; and Krugman, "For Richer," *New York Times Magazine,* October 20, 2002, 2, 6.

9. The threat of the new corporate politics was my motivation for a series of articles in the mid-1970s as well as my first book project, which became *The Backyard Revolution: Understanding the Citizen Movement* (Philadelphia: Temple University Press, 1980). The notes in that book elaborate the brief argument in the text with detailed accounts of the growth of new forms of business organization and culture-shaping efforts through corporate advertising. As I undertook the book, I also came to understand that a different, more culturally rooted politics was beginning to take hold in a new generation of citizen groups, based mainly in mainline religious congregations.

10. This was a major emphasis for instance in the shortlived but splendid magazine, *democracy,* edited by Sheldon Wolin from 1980 to 1982. See, for instance, Harry C. Boyte, "Populism and the Left," *democracy* 1, 2 (April 1981): 53–66.

11. Byron Dorgan, quoted in Boyte and Kari, "The New Populism," 5.

12. For a discussion of the Camp David meeting and many of its dynamics—though not this point by Hillary Clinton—see Benjamin Barber, *The Truth of Power: Intellectual Affairs in the Clinton Era* (New York: Norton, 2001).

13. Chris Williams, quoted in Harry C. Boyte, Heather Booth, and Steve Max, *Citizen Action and the New American Populism* (Philadelphia: Temple University Press, 1986), 76. In *Citizen Action and the New American Populism,* we surveyed the literature through 1985. For one treatment, see John Herbers, "Canvassers Hope to Reach 15 Million on Energy Costs," *New York Times,* March 27, 1983.

14. Marx, quoted in *Citizen Action,* 72, 78.

15. John Judis, "The Pressure Elite," *American Prospect* 9 (1992).

16. On Gorz's influence on the New Populism, see Boyte, *The Backyard Revolution.*

17. Ralph Nader quoted from Sam How Verhovek, "An Unrepentant Nader unveils a new Grass-Roots Project," *New York Times,* August 6, 2001.

18. Telephone interview with Dana Fisher, August 15, 2001, Minneapolis to New York.

19. Interview with Kathy Magnuson, Minneapolis, February 14, 2002.

20. The Humphrey drug store is a window into the vitality of everyday politics that once was widespread. Humphrey continues to convey this energy and vitality in his further description of the citizen efforts that emerged from his father's drug store, "When most of the town wanted to sell the municipally owned power plant to a private utility, Dad was against it . . . he fought the idea tooth and nail. I was twelve years old, and he would take me to the evening meetings of the council, install me in a chair by a corner window, and then do battle, hour after hour." Hubert H. Humphrey, *The Education of a Public Man: My Life and Politics* (Minneapolis: University of Minnesota Press, 1991), 8–10.

21. Arlie Hochschild, "Let Them Eat War," www.Alternet.org , October 2, 2003.

22. Jane Addams, "On Political Reform," in *Democracy and Social Ethics* (New York: Macmillan, 1902), 270.

23. Addams, *Democracy,* 256

24. Daniel Rodgers, *Atlantic Crossings: The Rise of Social Politics, 1900–1945* (Princeton, N.J.: Princeton University Press), 108.

25. Lippman quoted from John Jordan, *Machine-Age Ideology: Social Engineering and American Liberalism, 1911–1939* (Chapel Hill: University of North Carolina Press, 1994), 75.

26. Editorial and other anonymous writers quoted in Jordan, *Ideology,* 76, 77, 78.

27. In Jordan, *Ideology,* 81–82.

28. In Jordan, *Ideology,* 79.

29. Dewey, "School as Social Centre," *Elementary School Teacher* 3 (1902): 86.

30. See, for instance, Burton Bledstein, *The Culture of Professionalism: The Middle Class and the Development of Higher Education in America* (New York: Norton, 1976); Robert Wiebe, *The Search for Order, 1870–1920* (New York: Hill and Wang, 1967); Michael B. Katz, *In the Shadow of the Poorhouse: A Social History of Welfare in America* (New York: Basic Books, 1986).

31. Guidance counselors quoted in Christopher Lasch, *Haven in a Heartless World: The Family Besieged* (New York: Basic Books, 1977), 18. On domestic science, see Laura Shapiro, *Perfection Salad: Women and Cooking at the Turn of the Century* (New York: Farrar, Straus & Giroux, 1987), 91–95.

32. Gunnar Myrdal quoted in Howard Zinn, "Middle Class America Refurbished," in Allen Davis and Harold Woodman, eds., *Conflict and Consensus in American History* (Lexington, Mass.: D.C. Heath, 1972), 306.

33. Arnold Toynbee quoted in John Kenneth Galbraith, *New Industrial State* (New York: Signet Books, 1967), 109; Gunnar Myrdal, quoted in Jeffrey Galper, *The Politics of Social Services* (Englewood Cliffs, N.J.: Prentice-Hall, 1975), 113.

34. Alan Ehrenhalt, *The United States of Ambition* (New York: Times Books, 1991); Rick Knobe quote, 73.

35. Richard Darman quoted in Boyte, *Commonwealth,* 26. Reagan quoted from William Schambra, *The Quest for Community and the Quest for a New Public Philosophy* (Washington, D.C.: American Enterprise Institute, 1983), 30. See also Hedrick Smith, "Reagan's Populist Coalition," *New York Times,* March 16, 1980. For

intellectual wellsprings of conservative populism, see Robert A. Nisbet, *The Quest for Community* (New York: Harper, 1954); Peter Berger, *Facing Up to Modernity: Excursions in Society, Politics, and Religion* (New York: Basic Books, 1977); and Peter Berger and Richard John Neuhaus, *To Empower People: The Role of Mediating Institutions in Public Policy* (Washington, D.C.: American Enterprise Institute, 1977).

36. David Brooks, "The Presidency Wars," *New York Times*, September 30, 2003, A29.

37. Charles Payne, *I've Got the Light of Freedom: The Organizing Tradition and the Mississippi Freedom Struggle* (Berkeley: University of California Press, 1996).

Chapter 3. The Growth of Everyday Politics

Epigraph from Saul Alinsky, *Reveille for Radicals* (New York: Random House, 1946), 13–14.

1. Carmen Sirianni and Lew Friedland, *Civic Innovation in America; Community Empowerment, Public Policy, and the Movement for Civic Renewal* (Berkeley: University of California Press, 2001); William J. Doherty, and J. M. Beaton, "Family Therapists, Community, and Civic Renewal," *Family Process* 39 (2000): 149–61; Julie Ellison, "Foreseeable Futures: The New Politics of Public Scholarship and Cultural Knowledge," speech to the University of Minnesota, May 7, 2003; Thomas A. Lyson, "Moving Toward Civic Agriculture," *Choices* 3 (2002): 42–45.

2. Bernard Crick, *In Defense of Politics* (London: Continuum, 1962). Crick, drawing on Aristotle, stresses the irreducible *plurality* of politics as negotiation of diverse and particular interests. See also Arlene Saxonhouse's treatment of Aristotle in *Fear of Diversity: The Birth of Political Science in Ancient Greek Thought* (Chicago: University of Chicago Press, 1992). Giovanni Sartori, in his history of the word, "What Is Politics," *Political Theory* 1, 1 (1973): 1–36, details the horizontal relationships of equal citizens at the heart of the language of politics and associated ideas. Not until the nineteenth century did "politics" acquire its associations of "verticality," or relations to the state. See also Harry C. Boyte, "A Different Kind of Politics: John Dewey and the Meaning of Citizenship in the Twenty-First Century," Dewey Lecture at the University of Michigan, November 1, 2002, at www.cpn.org/crm/contemporary/different.html. For a history of theorizing politics at the Humphrey Institute, see also Harry C. Boyte, "A Conceptual History of Public Work,"in Harry C. Boyte Boyte, Nan Kari, Jim Lewis, Nan Skelton, et al., *Creating the Commonwealth* (Dayton, Oh.: Kettering Foundation, 1999).

3. Richard Wood, *Faith in Action: Religion, Race, and Democratic Organizing in America* (Chicago: University of Chicago Press, 2002), 211. There are now four major networks of citizen organizations, based in religious congregations of different faiths and also including unions, local schools, and other groups. These involve more than two million families. They have often had large impact on local economic and social life in some of the nation's poorest communities, and, especially in California and Texas, won significant victories on statewide policy questions. Parallel civic innovations, moreover, can be seen in other arenas such as environ-

mental activism, as Carmen Sirianna and Lew Friedland document. For accounts of lessons from citizen politics that we built upon in the early Humphrey work, see Harry C. Boyte, *CommonWealth: A Return to Citizen Politics* (New York: Free Press, 1989). For other accounts, see Mark Warren, *Dry Bones Rattling: Community-Building to Revitalize American Democracy* (Princeton, N.J.: Princeton University Press, 2001); Sirianni and Friedland, *Civic Innovation in America.*

4. Mike Gecan, *Going Public* (Boston: Beacon Press, 2002), 5, ix.

5. Wood, *Faith in Action*; Warren, *Dry Bones Rattling*; Paul Osterman, *Gathering Power: The Future of Progressive Politics in America* (Boston: Beacon Press, 2003); Dennis Shirley, *Valley Interfaith and School Reform: Organizing for Power in South Texas* (Austin: University of Texas Press, 2002).

6. IAF handout, quote from Thucydides, *The Peloponnesian War*, 1, 6.

7. First-hand observations, IAF 10-Day Training Session, Baltimore, November 1987.

8. "Essay," *Time*, March 2, 1980; Charles E. Silberman, *Crisis in Black and White* (New York: Vintage, 1964), 318.

9. Silberman, *Crisis*, 314–15.

10. Telephone interview with Ed Chambers, from Minneapolis to Franklyn Square, N.Y., May 2, 1988.

11. "Sordid raiment" quote from "Citizen Participation" speech, 5, in author's possession. On Alinsky's theory of power and his view of clergy members' avoidance of the concept, see Dan Dodson, "The Church, Power, and Saul Alinsky," *Religion in Life* (Spring 1967): 2.

12. See Green, *World*, 28 -31.

13. Vorse quoted in Green, *World*, 163.

14. John S. McGrath and James J. Delmont, *Floyd Bjornsterne Olson: Minnesota's Greatest Liberal Governor, a Memorial Volume* (Minneapolis: McGrath and Delmont, 1939), 249.

15. Nelson quoted in Robert Fisher, *Let the People Decide: A History of Neighborhood Organizing in America* (Boston: Twayne, 1986) 38. See also David Brody, "The Emergence of Mass Production Unionism," in John Braeman, Robert H. Bremner, and Everett Walters, eds., *Change and Continuity in Twentieth-Century America* (Columbus: Ohio State University Press, 1964), 221–64; on radical uses of democratic themes, Irving Howe and Lewis Coser, *The American Communist Party: A Critical History* (New York: Praeger, 1962). Jefferson quoted in Fisher, *Let the People Decide*, 36.Terry Pettus, interview, Seattle, March 14, 1983.

16. The founding statement of the BYNC is quoted in Robert A. Slayton, *Back of the Yards: The Making of a Local Democracy* (Chicago: University of Chicago Press, 1986), 203; Slayton describes the organizing work of BYNC in detail. See also Fisher, *People*, 54–56.

17. Saul David Alinsky," *Reveille for Radicals* (New York: Random House, 1946), 76, 79.

18. Simone Weil, *The Need for Roots* (New York: Harper and Row, 1971). For a fine treatment of Weil's political theory, see Mary G. Dietz, *Between the Human and the Divine: The Political Thought of Simone Weil* (Totowa, N.J.: Rowman and Littlefield, 1988).

19. Alfred Schutz, *Collected Papers*, vol. 1, ed. Maurice Natanson (The Hague: Martinus Nijhoff, 1962), 53; Peter L. Berger and Thomas Luckmann, *The Social Construction of Reality: A Treatise in the Sociology of Knowledge* (London: Penguin, 1967), 37, 43, 44, 45, 48.

20. Richard J. Bernstein, *The Restructuring of Social and Political Theory* (New York: Harcourt Brace, 1976), 168. For a discussion of the conservative consequences, see, for instance, Harry C. Boyte, *The Backyard Revolution: Understanding the New Citizen Movement* (Philadelphia: Temple University Press, 1980).

21. Alinsky, *Reveille*, 76.

22. This history is drawn from interview with Ed Chambers, May 2, 1988.

23. For a candid description of some of the problems in ACORN, written by one of ACORN's chief theoreticians, see Gary Delgado, *Organizing the Movement: The Roots and Growth of ACORN* (Philadelphia: Temple University Press, 1986); see also Boyte, *The Backyard Revolution*, for a detailed description of the differences in organizing methods.

24. For summaries of this strategy, see John McKnight and John Kretzmann, "Toward a Post-Alinsky Agenda," *Social Policy* (Winter 1984): 15–18; Harry C. Boyte, *Community Is Possible: Repairing America's Roots* (New York: Harper and Row, 1984); and Fisher, *Let the People Decide.*

25. Quote from "The Professional Radical: Conversations with Saul Alinsky," from *Harper's*, June, July 1965, 9; interview with Father John Egan, South Bend, Ind., August 2, 1980.

26. Saul Alinsky, "Is There Life After Birth?" Speech to the Centennial Meeting of the Episcopal Theological School, Cambridge, Mass., June 7, 1967 (Chicago: IAF reprint), 12–13.

27. See Fisher, *Let the People Decide*, for a detailed discussion of the issue of BYNC's shifting racial stance.

28. Interview with Wade Goodwyn on Chambers's "relational" quality, November 8, 1987, Baltimore; Charles Payne, *I've Got the Light of Freedom: The Organizing Tradition and the Mississippi Freedom Struggle* (Berkeley: University of California Press, 1996).

29. Interview with Christine Stephens, San Antonio, July 4, 1983. Also drawn from interviews with Ernesto Cortes, July 4, 1983, and Beatrice Cortes, July 8, 1983, both in San Antonio. Cortes was the first to describe COPS as like a "university of public life." See also Peter Skerry, "Neighborhood COPS," *New Republic*, February 6, 1984, 23.

30. Telephone interview with Gerald Taylor, Minneapolis to Durham, April 26, 2002.

31. Quotes from *IAF 50 Years: Organizing for Change* (New York: IAF, 1990), 8, 15. An exchange with Ed Chambers, the successor of Alinsky as head of the IAF training institute, illustrated their epistemology. Chambers, describing the importance that IAF organizing has come to place on people's disentangling of "public" and "private" realms, remarked that people lose the "public" side of "mediating institutions," associations between the individual and the state or large-scale systems. "They think of things like churches simply as private, so they make all sorts of inappropriate demands," he argued. I replied that the very concept of mediating

institutions (seeing them as private) maintains a narrow view of public life. Chambers went off on another track: "I haven't read Berger in years. The only thing I know is that this thing is very close to the truth." He continued, "I've seen the response to this now in hundreds of meetings across the country over ten years now. It strikes home. People come up, sometimes with tears in their eyes, priests, women religious, lay leaders, saying 'I wish I'd known this years ago.'" Interview with Ed Chambers, Baltimore, November 6, 1987.

The exchange illustrated IAF's feedback process. What it calls universals of organizing are always contextualized, provisional, and aimed at the particular problems they encounter in their work. As Ernie Cortes, a key figure in their network, pointed out, the IAF methodology bears some resemblance to the critical method of Karl Popper, a philosopher of science who argued for a view of truth not as positive assertion but as theories formulated out of practice and aimed at problem-solving that had not yet been refuted. See for instance, Popper's selections in Theodor Adorno et al., *The Positivist Dispute in German Sociology* trans. Glyn Adey and David Frisby (London: Heinemann, 1976).

32. Gecan, *Going Public*, 35.

33. Gecan, *Going Public*, 171.

34. Osterman, *Gathering Power*, 82–83.

Chapter 4. Citizenship as Public Work

Epigraphs from "Work," *New World Dictionary*; and Plublius quoted in Michael Kazin, The Populist Persuasion: An American History (New York: Basic Books, 1995), 9.

1. This sketch of the concept follows Marvin B. Becker, *The Emergence of Civil Society in the Eighteenth Century* (Bloomington: Indiana University Press, 1994); Ferguson quoted xii; Smith xiii.

2. Hegel, quoted in Becker, *Emergence of Civil Society*, 122, 123.

3. Karl Marx, *The German Ideology* (New York: International Publishers, 1981), 84.

4. This treatment of Rick Turner's important work is taken from Tony Fluxman and Peter Vale, "Re-reading Rick Turner in the New South Africa," *International Relations* 18, 2 (2004). Fluxman and Turner, seeking to retrieve a participatory politics for a political environment in which they rightly argue that alternatives to marketplace politics have radically eroded, have a thorough treatment of the insights in the tradition of critical theory. Manuscript in author's possession.

5. Michael Harrington, *The Twilight of Capitalism* (New York: Simon and Schuster, 1976), 291; Ralph Miliband, *Marxism and Politics* (Oxford: Oxford University Press, 1977), 44; Stanley Aronowitz, "The Working Class: A Break with the Past," in Colin Greer, ed., *Divided Society: The Ethnic Experience in America* (New York: Basic Books, 1974), 312–13. From a parallel South African vantage, the strategies of Turner, Sartre, and other modern critical theorists are well described in Fluxman and Vale, "Re-reading Rick Turner." This analysis of the left wing stance of outside

critic and the theories of social change involved was outlined in Harry C. Boyte, "Populism and the Left," *democracy* 1, 2 (April 1981): 53–66, and developed in *CommonWealth: A Return to Citizen Politics* (New York: Free Press, 1989), especially chapter 3.

6. E. P. Thompson, *The Making of the English Working Class*, 2nd ed. (New York: Vintage, 1966).

7. I saw the power of the prophetic imagination first hand as a young field secretary for the Southern Christian Leadership Conference. It was Martin Luther King's genius to draw on and radically rework core American and southern symbols, traditions, and themes—"freedom," "democracy," "citizenship" and others—to frame the goals and meaning of the movement itself. Sara Evans and I made this point about the prophetic imagination in contrast to the stance of left wing critic in Harry C. Boyte and Sara M. Evans, "Democratic Politics and a Critique of the Left," *Tikkun* (Summer 1987). For a parallel treatment also contrasting the prophetic stance with the stance of outside critic, see Michael Walzer, *Interpretation and Social Criticism* (Cambridge, Mass.: Harvard University Press, 1987).

8. Sara M. Evans and Harry C. Boyte, *Free Spaces: The Sources of Democratic Change in America* (New York: Harper and Row, 1986; Chicago: Chicago University Press, 1992); Lawrence Goodwyn, *The Populist Moment* (Cambridge: Oxford University Press, 1980); Frederick Harris, "Will the Circle Be Unbroken? The Erosion and Transformation of African American Civic Life," Report for the National Commission on Civic Renewal (College Park, Md.: Institute for Philosophy and Public Policy, 1999).

9. For a magisterial treatment of the ways in which high modernism, infused with egalitarian ideals, wedded to state power and weak civil society have had devastating effects around the world, see James C. Scott, *Seeing like a State: How Certain Schemes to Improve the Human Condition Have Failed* (New Haven, Conn.: Yale University Press, 1998). The way this has played itself out "after the revolution" forms a complex story. For an argument that movement intellectuals often feared the democratic movements of which they were a part, see Lawrence Goodwyn, *Breaking the Barrier: The Rise of Solidarity* (Cambridge: Oxford University Press), 338–90.

10. For an example of conservative arguments, see Peter Berger and Richard John Neuhaus, *To Empower People: The Role of Mediating Structures in Public Policy* (Washington, D.C.: AEI, 1977).

11. For a discussion of the reliance of even ardent early twentieth-century participatory democrats on scientific epistemology, see William Sullivan, *Reconstructing Public Philosophy* (Berkeley: University of California, 1985). See also Cornel West, *The American Evasion of Philosophy: A Genealogy of Pragmatism* (Madison: University of Wisconsin Press, 1989). For treatments of the implicit condescension of experts toward amateurs and traditional communities in liberal, as well as socialist ideologies, see Boyte, "Populism and the Left" and Boyte and Nan Kari, *Building America: The Democratic Promise of Public Work* (Philadelphia: Temple University Press, 1986).

12. Jürgen Habermas, "Historical Materialism and the Development of Nor-

mative Structures," in *Communication and the Evolution of Society* (Boston: Beacon Press, 1979), 97.

13. Immanuel Kant quoted in Raul Tyson, *Odysseus and the Cyclops* (Dayton, Oh.: Kettering Foundation, 1988), 1.

14. Jürgen Habermas, *Transformation of the Public Sphere* (Cambridge, Mass.: MIT Press, 1989).

15. Cornel West, quoted in Sheldon Hackney, "Toward a National Conversation," *Responsive Community* (Spring 1994): 36.

16. For instance, *A Call to Civil Society: Why Democracy Needs Moral Truths* (New York: Institute for American Values, 1998); E. J. Dionne, *Why Civil Society? Why Now?* (Washington, D.C.: Brookings Institution Press, 1998).

17. Jean L. Cohen and Andrew Arato, *Civil Society and Political Theory* (Cambridge, Mass.: MIT Press, 1992), ix.

18. Jürgen Habermas, *Knowledge and Human Interests* (Boston: Beacon Press, 1971), 58.

19. Habermas, *Knowledge*, 58.

20. Langston Hughes, *Collected Poems of Langston Hughes* (New York: Vintage, 1995), 267.

21. Frances Willard, *Woman and Temperance: The Work and Workers of the Women's Christian Temperance Union* (1883; New York: Arno Press, 1972).

22. *Wall Street Journal* citation from "Voluntarism" entry in *Oxford English Dictionary*.

23. Melinda Chateauwert in *Marching Together: Women of the Brotherhood of Sleeping Car Porters* (Urbana: University of Illinois Press, 1997).

24. Cynthia Estlund, "Working Together: The Workplace, Civil Society, and the Law," *Georgetown Law Journal* 89, 1 (2000): pp. 1–96. Estlund's argument, in its critique of the civil society map, is like my own in "Off the Playground of Civil Society," a lecture delivered at Duke on October 23, 1998; see also the symposium on Commonwealth, Civil Society, and Democratic Renewal in *Pegs Journal: The Good Society* 9, 2 (1999): 1–23.

25. Estlund, "Working Together," 25.

26. Estlund, "Working Together," 65.

27. See, for instance, Nancy Fraser, "Rethinking the Public Sphere," Mary P. Ryan, "Gender and Public Access," and Geoff Eley, "Nations, Publics, and Political Cultures," in Craig Calhoun, ed., *Habermas and the Public Sphere* (Cambridge, Mass.: MIT Press, 1992), 99–108, 259–88, 289–339.

28. Habermas, *Transformation*, 52.

29. For elaborations of the theory of relational, interactive power sketched here, see Sara M. Evans and Harry C. Boyte, "Introduction," in *Free Spaces* (University of Chicago edition), and Boyte, *CommonWealth*, especially chapter 8, "The Larger Lessons of Community Initiative."

30. Benjamin Barber, *A Place for How: How to Make Society Civil and Citizenship Strong* (New York: Hill and Wang, 1998), 132. The following treatment of Arendt is adapted from Boyte and Kari, *Building America*, and Harry C. Boyte, "Civic Populism," *Perspectives on Politics* (2003).

31. Hannah Arendt, *The Human Condition* (Chicago: University of Chicago Press, 1958), 160–61.

32. Arendt, *Condition*, 19.

33. Arendt, *Condition*, 57, 19.

34. This argument is developed in detail in Boyte and Kari, *Building America,* especially chapters 2 and 3.

35. Ohio Trustees quoted in Edward Danforth Eddy, *Colleges for our Land and Time: The Land Grant Idea in American Education* (New York: Harper and Row, 1956). The following account of land grant schools builds directly on the work of Scott Peters, now on the faculty at Cornell, formerly a graduate student at the Humphrey Institute and with the CDC. In 1993, Peters asked for references on the civic traditions of land grant universities. I told him I knew of no such histories, and he would have to go to work to create them. Peters turned out to be an assiduous researcher. He discovered a rich and largely unknown land grant democratic civic history

36. Liberty Hyde Bailey, *New York State Rural Problems* (Albany: Lyon, 1913), 11–12, 133, 29–30.

Chapter 5. Citizen Education as a Craft, Not a Program

Epigraphs from Pope Leo XIII, Rerum Novarum, 1891, and Matt Anderson quoted in Harry C. Boyte, "Civic Education as a Craft, not a Program," in Sheilah Mann and John J. Patrick, eds., *Education for Civic Engagement in Democracy: Service Learning and other Promising Practices* (Washington: APSA and EPIC Clearinghouse, 2001), 61.

1. William Galston, "Political Knowledge, Political Engagement, and Civic Education," *American Review of Political Science* 4 (2001): 219.

2. Galston, "Political Knowledge," 219; figures from web site of National Alliance for Civic Education, www.puaf.umd.edu/NACE.

3. Michael X. Delli Carpini and Scott Keeter, *What Americans Know About Politics and Why It Matters* (New Haven., Conn: Yale University Press, 1996); Galston, "Political Knowledge"; www.puaf.umd.edu/NACE.

4. On income correlations with political knowledge, see Carpini and Keeter, *Why It Matters*; yearbook quote on NACE web site. National Commission on the High School Senior Years, "Raising Our Sights: No High School Senior Left Behind," Washington, D.C., October 4, 2001.

5. Richard Battistoni, *Civic Engagement Across the Curriculum* (Providence, R.I.: Campus Compact, 2001).

6. David Easton, *A Systems Analysis of Political Life* (New York: John Wiley, 1965); Harold Laswell, *Politics: Who Gets What, When, How* (New York: Prentice-Hall, 1935). In a useful forthcoming article, Constance A. Flanagan describes the growing evidence that young people's active voice and productive roles in everyday life contexts makes a large difference in their successful socialization in politics and civic life. Flanagan's argument, however, would be stronger if she had a more pro-

ductive, less professionalized and state centered view of politics; she gets her definition from David Easton. Constance A. Flanagan, "Volunteerism, Leadership, Political Socialization, and Civic Engagement," in Richard M. Lerner and Lawrence Steinberg, eds., *Handbook of Adolescent Psychology* (Hoboken, N.J.: John Wiley 2002).

7. See Harry C. Boyte and Nan Kari, *Building America: The Democratic Promise of Public Work* (Philadelphia: Temple University Press, 1996); Harry C. Boyte and Nan Skelton, "The Legacy of Public Work: Educating for Citizenship," *Educational Leadership* 54, 5 (1997): 12–17; Harry C. Boyte and James Farr, "The Work of Citizenship and the Problem of Service-Learning," in Richard M. Battiston and William E. Hudson, eds., *Experiencing Citizenship: Concepts and Models for Service-Learning in Political Science* (Washington, D.C.: AAHE, 1999): 35–48; Jim Lewis, "Public Achievement at St. Bernard's School, in Harry C. Boyte, ed., *Creating the Commonwealth: Public Politics and the Philosophy of Public Work* (Dayton, Oh.: Kettering, 1999), 12–23; Robert Hildreth, "Theorizing Citizenship and Evaluating Public Achievement," *PS: Political Science and Politics* 33, 3 (2000): 627–34; Boyte, "Civic Education as a Craft, Not a Program"; and Harry C. Boyte, "A Tale of Two Playgrounds," paper delivered at the American Political Science Association, September 1, 2001, now on the CDC web site, www.publicwork.org/research/ See also the Public Achievement web site, organized by Elaine Eschenbacher, www.publicachievement.org.

8. See the Mankato PA site http://krypton.mankato.msus.edu/%7Ejak3/pa/welcome.html

9. Taylor Branch, *Pillar of Fire: America in the King Years, 1963–65* (New York: Simon and Schuster, 1998), 77.

10. Frederick Harris, "Will the Circle Be Unbroken? The Erosion and Transformation of African American Civic Life," *Report from the Institute for Philosophy and Public Policy*, 1998, 20–26; Rev. Johnny Ray Youngblood quoted from "Democratic Promise," 2000 PBS documentary on Saul Alinsky.

11. Sara M. Evans and Harry C. Boyte, *Free Spaces: The Sources of Democratic Change in America* (New York: Harper and Row, 1986); Harry C. Boyte, *Common-Wealth: Return to Citizen Politics* (New York: Free Press, 1989).

12. See www.publicachievement.org; and especially the Southwestern Minnesota Mankato site for an extensive set of tools.

13. Circe Torruelas, account on the world wide PA List Serve, July 15, 2002.

14. Robert Hildreth, "Theorizing Citizenship," on CDC web site, www.publicwork.org, research/working papers); quoted from p. 4.

15. Ross Roholt, Robert Hildreth, and Michael Baizerman, "Year Four Evaluation of Public Achievement, 2002–3: Examining Young People's Experience of Public Achievement," June, 2003, 3, 13, 5, 6; Hildreth quotes, 5; see www.publicwork.org

16. Roholt, Hildreth, Baizerman, "Year Four Evaluation," 7, 8.

17. Chou Yang, quoted in Harry C. Boyte, "Citizen Education as a Craft," 61.

18. Michael Kuhne, "Public Achievement Teaching Circle: Introducing the Core Concepts of Public Achievement," discussion guide for faculty at MCTC, February 2003, 3.

19. Student quotes from Michael Kuhne, *Listening to the Students' Voices: An*

Early Document in the Ongoing Assessment of the Relationship between Public Achievement and the Urban Teacher Program (Minneapolis: MCTC, 2001), 5, 6, 18.

20. Joe O'Shea, quoted in Boyte, "Civic Education as a Craft," 67.

21. Roholt, Hildreth, Baizerman, "Year Four Evaluation," 14.

Chapter 6. The Jane Addams School for Democracy

Epigraphs from Jane Addams, quoted in D'Ann Urbaniak Lesch, "Settlement House Tradition Alive and Well in St. Paul," October, 2000, 1, paper in author's possession. Koua Yang Her, quoted in Nan Skelton with Nick Longo and Jennifer O'Donoghue, "Jane Addams School for Democracy," in Harry C. Boyte, ed., *Creating the Commonwealth* (Dayton, Oh.: Kettering Foundation, 1999), 24.

1. Account of the Freedom Festival from See Moua, "The 5th Annual Freedom Festival," *JAS Express*, July 2003, 1, 2; and from an interview with Derek Johnson, an organizer with the JAS, Minneapolis, September 15, 2003. Comparisons with early twentieth century from Harry C. Boyte, *Community Is Possible: Repairing America's Roots* (New York: Harper and Row, 1984), chapter 2, "Those Were the Days."

2. Dudley Cocke, Director of Roadside Theater at Appalshop, Kentucky, at the Imagining America conference, November 4, 2002, Ann Arbor, Michigan.

3. From evaluation interviews by Mike Baizerman, 2000.

4. Interviews by Baizerman.

5. Mary Harrison, Mary Harrison, Bina Nikrin, Jeffrey Stanton, Stacy Walshire, Kelly Wolfe, Shannon Joern, in "Group Paper: Reflections on the Jane Addams School for Democracy," PA 5012, May 12, 2003.

6. Notes from D'Ann Lesch, Post Session wrap up, in author's possession.

7. Jane Addams, *On Education* (New Brunswick, N.J.: Transaction Publishers, 1994), 98–99.

8. Gioia Diliberto, *A Useful Woman: The Early Life of Jane Addams* (New York: Scribner, 1999), quoted in Harry C. Boyte, "The Struggle Against Positivism," *Academe* (August 2000), on the web at http://www.aaup.org/publications/Academe/2000/00ja/JA00Boyt.htm, reprinted in *Campus Compact Reader*, special issue (Summer 2003).

9. Diliberto, quoted in Boyte, "The Struggle Against Positivism."

10. Himmelfarb, quoted in Boyte, "Professions as a Public Craft," working paper for the 2000 Wingspread conference on the New Information Commons, January 8, 2000, 6.

11. Simone Weil, *Oppression and Liberty* (Amherst: University of Massachusetts Press, 1973), 83, 106, 101.

12. Jane Addams, quoted in Boyte, "The Struggle Against Positivism."

13. Canon Barnett "Report to the Bush Foundation," Year 3, June 30, 2003, 1.

14. Myles Horton, *The Long Haul: An Autobiography* (New York: Doubleday, 1990), 101; Robinson quoted 103.

15. Kathleen Winters in Skelton et al, "Jane Addams School," 30–31.

16. Nan Skelton, quoted in "Creating a Culture of Learning: The West Side Neighborhood Learning Community," *University of Minnesota Research Review* (Spring 2002): 7. See also Boyte et al., *Creating the Commonwealth*.

17. Harvard Family Research Project FINE interviews, on JAS, on web at FINE Forum e-Newsletter, Fall 2002, http://ww.gse.harvard.edu/hfrp/projects/fine/fineforum/forum5.

18. This account here is taken from Skelton et al., "Jane Addams School," 28–29, 32.

19. Benitez quoted in Skelton et al., "Jane Addams School," 28.

20. Moua quoted in Skelton et. al., "Jane Addams School," 32.

21. Skelton et al., "Jane Addams School," 32.

22. Nikrin, in "Group Paper," 4.

23. The table builds on the contrast between "service" and "organizing" presented by Sister Judy Donovan of the Texas Industrial Areas Foundation at the Kellogg Forum held at Rye River in Minnesota, June 3, 2002. For a useful discussion of the close parallels between teaching, on the one hand, and organizing, on the other, see Phillip H. Sandro, "An Organizing Approach to Teaching," *Higher Education Exchange 2002*: 37–48.

24. Mai Neng Moua quoted in Harry C. Boyte and Jennifer O'Donoghue, "The Jane Addams School for Democracy," *Blueprint: Ideas for a New Century* (Spring 1999): 63; Meghen Kelley quoted in Skelton et al., "Jane Addams School," 32.

25. Homeland mission quoted in Jeff Bauer, "Homeland Project: The Story of Five Hmong Girls and Their Journey Home," master's paper, Humphrey Institute, June 2003, 14–15.

26. Account from Bauer, "Homeland Project," 5, 11–12 and also interview with Jeff Bauer, Minneapolis, June 27, 2003.

27. Judy Ly quoted from Tom Webb, "Citizenship Put to Test," *St. Paul Pioneer Press*, June 19, 2001; Yang Yang from Elaine Eschenbacher, "Public Achievement Group Gets National Recognition for Video," *Creating the Commonwealth* newsletter, Summer 2000, 1.

28. Stories of Washington trip and meetings with Wellstone from Webb, "Citizenship Put to Test."

29. Interview with Nick Longo, phone from Minneapolis to Providence, R.I., October 4, 2003.

30. Terri Wilson quoted in Skelton et al, "Jane Addams School," 33.

31. Interview with Nan Kari, Minneapolis, October 3, 2003.

Chapter 7. Professions as Public Work

Epigraph taken from interview with Nan Kari, Minneapolis, June 22, 2001.

1. James Farr, "The Secret History of Social Capital," paper presented in the Department of Political Science, University of Minnesota, April, 2002, 36.

2. Lewis S. Feuer, "Dewey and Back-to-the-People Movement," *Journal of the History of Ideas* 20 (1959): 546.

3. Quoted in Feuer, "Dewey," 546.

4. This portrait is drawn from George Dykhuizen, "John Dewey: The Vermont Years," *Journal of the History of Ideas* 20 (1959): 515–44.

5. These accounts of Michigan, including the Dewey quotes, are from Feuer, "Dewey," 550–53.

6. John Dewey, "The Obligation to Knowledge of God," *Monthly Bulletin Student Christian Association* 6 (University of Michigan, November 1884): 24. I am indebted to the work of Ira Harkavy and Lee Benson, in numerous essays, for deepening my understanding of the democratic and communal content of Dewey's writings.

7. Dewey, Introduction, *The Living Thoughts of Thomas Jefferson* (New York: Longman, Green, 1940), 20, 22.

8. Excerpt from *Quest for Certainty* reprinted in the collection, *The Philosophy of John Dewey*, ed. John McDermott (Chicago: University of Chicago Press, 1981), 357, 382.

9. *The Philosophy of John Dewey*, McDermott, 351.

10. *The Philosophy of John Dewey*, McDermott, 651, 649–50.

11. John Dewey, "The School as Social Centre," *Elementary School Teacher* 3 (1902): 86.

12. John Dewey, *The Teacher and Society* (New York: Appleton-Century, 1937), 335.

13. Dewey, *The Teacher and Society*, 336, 334.

14. *Philosophy of John Dewey*, McDermott, 457.

15. Interview with Deborah Meier, Boston, November 1, 2001.

16. *Tent of the Presence*, internal IAF document in author's possession. I learned about this document and its importance first from Ed Chambers in an interview June 1, 1988.

17. Interview with Moriba Karamoko, Washington, June 1, 2001.

18. Interview with Nan Kari, Minneapolis, June 22, 2001. The work at St. Catherine is described in Anne Colby, Thomas Ehrlich, Elizabeth Beaumont, and Jason Stephens, *Educating Citizens: Preparing America's Undergraduates for Lives of Moral and Civic Responsibility* (San Francisco: Jossey Bass, 2003).

19. Quoted from interview with Kari, June 22, 2001.

20. The following story of the Lazarus Project is adapted from Harry C. Boyte and Nan Kari, "Citizen Politics: Breaking the Iron Cage," *Dissent* (Spring, 1994): 205–11.

21. William J. Doherty and Jason S. Carroll, "The Citizen Therapist and Family-Centered Community Building: Introduction to a New Section of the Journal," *Family Process* 41,4 (2002): 561, 567.

22. William Doherty, *Soul Searching* (New York: Basic Books, 1995).

23. Interview with William Doherty, Minneapolis, July 22, 2001; quote on expert model from William Doherty web site at http://fsos.che.umn.edu/doherty/profautobio.html.

24. The following account is from an interview with William Doherty, Min-

neapolis, July 22, 2001. For the full interview, see www.publicwork.org/research and also the Doherty web site.

Chapter 8. "Architects of Democracy"

Epigraph from *Renewing the Covenant: Learning, Discovery, and Engagement in a New Age and Different World* (Washington, D.C.: Kellogg Commission on the Future of State and Land-Grant Universities/NASULGC, 2000), 24.

1. Felice Nudelman, Manager of the College Marketing Program for the *Times*, and her colleague Eric Hellstern recounted this study in depth, and Nudelman later sent me the internal summary of the focus groups. In author's possession.

2. Mark Yudof, quoted from minutes of Board of Regents, May 12, 2001, in author's possession.

3. The definition of civic engagement is taken from the first document of the Civic Engagement Task Force, *Preliminary Report to the Provost*, December 15, 2000, available on the University of Minnesota's public engagement web site (www .umn.edu/civic) under reports.

4. Association of American Colleges, Pew Roundtable, Allan Bloom, and Page Smith, quoted in William F. Massy, *Honoring the Trust: Quality and Cost Containment in Higher Education* (Bolton, Mass.: Anker, 2003), 3, 9, 10.

5. These views are described in Harry C. Boyte, *Public Engagement in a Civic Mission* (Washington, D.C.: Council on Public Policy Education, 1999); department chair quoted in Boyte, *Public Engagement*, 6.

6. William Sullivan, *Institutional Identity and Social Responsibility* (Washington, D.C.: Council on Public Policy Education, 2001), 2, 3.

7. Interview with John Saltmarsh, telephone, Minneapolis to Providence, June 15, 2002.

8. Bryan Turner, "Introduction to Second Edition," in Bryan Turner, ed., *The Blackwell Companion to Social Theory* (Oxford: Blackwell, 2000), xviii; Craig Calhoun, "Social Theory and the Public Sphere," in Turner, *Blackwell Companion*, 510.

9. Peter M. Senge, *The Fifth Discipline: The Art & Practice of the Learning Organization* (New York: Doubleday, 1994), frontispiece; on politics, 273.

10. Massy, *Honoring the Trust*, 24.

11. Lee G. Bolman and Terrence E. Deal, *Reframing Organizations: Artistry, Choice, and Leadership*, 2nd ed. (San Francisco: Jossey-Bass, 1997), 14.

12. Bolman and Deal, *Reframing Organizations*, 193.

13. Rom Coles, "Moving Democracy: IAF Social Movements and the Political Arts of Listening, Traveling, and Tabling in a Heterogeneous World," paper for APSA, August 19–September 2, 2002, Boston, 5.

14. Maria Avila, "Transforming the Culture of Academia: An Organizing Based Model of Civic Engagement," draft in author's possession, August 11, 2003.

15. What kept the Federal Writers Project together—and produced a treasure trove of essays and books and other written products depicting of American culture, history, architecture, the natural environment, and everyday life—was the demo-

cratic politics of the New Deal. This politics, rooted in earlier civic and populist traditions, was by and large quite different from the Marxism that often dominated intellectual life. "The project members . . . provided a powerful antithesis to the widespread obsession with proletarian writing that dominated the literary atmosphere of the thirties," wrote Jerre Mangione in his history of the Project, *The Dream and the Deal: The Federal Writers Project, 1935–1943* (Boston: Little, Brown, 1972), 373. As Louis Filler observed, "the Communist-minded writers could only talk about the bad time here and the good time coming, but the Federal writers could write about *their* country, *their* government: its present sorrows, weaknesses, and promise." In Mangione, *The Dream*, 373.

16. *Civic Engagement Task Force Final Report*, 5.

17. Edwin Fogelman, Preliminary Report to the Provost, December 15, 2000, 2.

18. This account is from the Harry Boyte memo to the Institutional Connections Advisory Committee, February 14, 2001.

19. Interview with Julie Ellison, Ann Arbor, November 2, 2002.

20. Interview with Victor Bloomfield, Minneapolis, November 14, 2001.

21. Justice Sandra Day O'Connor, "Excerpts from Justices' Opinions," *New York Times*, June 24, 2003, 26.

22. Mary Vogel, quoted in *Civic Engagement News 7* (2003), 3. At the University, the people dedicated to strong partnerships include administrators, faculty, and staff such as Sandra Gardebring, vice president for external relations; Billie Wahlstrom, associate vice provost for distributed education; Scott Peters, director of the Center on Urban and Regional Affairs; Marti Erickson, director of the Children, Family, and Youth Consortium; Carl Brandt and Laurel Hirt of the Community and Career Learning Center; Joe Massey, chair of the Department of Wood Products and also chair of the Faculty Consultative Committee in 2001–2; Mary Vogel, director of the Sustainable Regional Partnerships; William Doherty, director of the "Families and Democracy" cluster of civic partnerships in the College of Human Ecology; Nan Skelton, co-director of the Jane Addams School for Democracy partnership with new immigrants in St. Paul and the Center for Democracy and Citizenship; Melissa Stone, who led the University's Task Force on Nonprofit Management; Sam Meyers, director of the Wilkins Center on Human Rights and Social Justice; Joe Nathan, director of the Center for School Change; Cathy Jordan and Naomi Scheman, who have worked with Susan Gust, a neighborhood leader in Minneapolis, to translate lessons of collaborative research to other parts of the university. Deans whose colleges have strong community ties, such as Steve Rosenstone, Brian Atwood, Tom Fisher, Shirley Baugher, and David Taylor, among others, also provide leadership. Allies and civic leaders, such as Robert Berglund and Michael O'Keeffe, on the board of regents, Sandra Pappas and Steve Kelley, state senators, Lori Sturdevant, a columnist for the *Star Tribune*, Mark Langseth, director of Minnesota Campus Compact, and Gary Cunningham, director of the African American Men's Project, were allies in Minnesota. National civic leaders such as David Mathews, Bill Galston, Elizabeth Hollander, Julie Ellison, Gerald Taylor, Tom Ehrlich, John Dedrick, Barry Checkoway, Ira Harkavy, Peter Levine, Carmen Siri-

anni, Scott Peters, and Melissa Bass have been part of a national intellectual community.

23. James Madison, quoted in Harry C. Boyte, *CommonWealth: A Return to Citizen Politics* (New York: Free Press, 1999), epigraph, vii.

24. Richard Wood, *Faith in Action: Religion, Race, and Democratic Organizing in America* (Chicago: University of Chicago Press, 2002), 211, 153.

25. Vic Bloomfield and Ed Fogelman gave this account to the group from AASCU and the *New York Times* who came to the University of Minnesota on April 2 to meet with the steering committee of COPE.

26. Julie Ellison, "Foreseeable Futures," Lecture at the University of Minnesota, May 7, 2003, 6, 9.

27. The Mary Parker Follett quote is from her 1924 book, *Creative Experience*, sent in private correspondence from Scott Peters, July 5, 2001.

28. Other similar statements about the democracy role of higher education include Harry C. Boyte and Elizabeth Hollander on behalf of a group of higher education leaders convened by Barry Checkoway, "The Wingspread Declaration: Renewing the Civic Mission of the American Research University" (June 1999), and "The Presidents' Declaration on the Civic Responsibilities of Higher Education," by Tom Ehrlich and Elizabeth Hollander, now signed by more than 800 presidents (July, 1999). The two declarations are available at Campus Compact, www.compact-.org, as well as the University COPE web site, www.umn.edu/civic .

29. *Renewing the Covenant*, 24; Michael McPherson ad, called "Beyond the Campus Wall," *New York Times*, September 29, 2002.

30. *Star Tribune*, June 1, 2002.

Chapter 9. *Spreading Everyday Politics*

Epigraph taken from Jane Addams, *On Education* (New Brunswick, N.J.: Transaction Publishers, 1994), 98–99.

1. Bernard Crick, *In Defense of Politics* (Chicago: University of Chicago Press, 1962, 1992), 96, 98.

2. William Tierney, "The Academic Profession and the Culture of the Faculty: A Perspective on Latin American Universities," in Kenneth Kempner and William Tierney, eds., *The Social Role of Higher Education: Comparative Perspectives* (New York: Garland, 1996), 15, 16.

3. Barbara Nelson, "Education for the Public Interest," speech at NASPAA, October 17, 2002, at http://unpan1.un.org/intradoc/groups/public/documents/aspa/unpan006959.pdf.

4. Jack Homer and Bobby Milstein, "Optimal Decision Making in a Dynamic Model of Community Health," Syndemics Prevention Network, http://www.cdc.-gov/syndemics, 4.

5. There are also multiplying expressions of alarm about the threat to common properties, understood as the broad, multi-faceted public infrastructures and goods on which we all depend. The New America Foundation has initiated a large

project, "Reclaiming the American Commons," which has detailed the threats. As their report by David Bollier, *Public Assets, Private Profits: Reclaiming the American Commons in an Age of Market Enclosure*, puts it: "Many of the resources that Americans own as a people—forests and minerals under public lands, public information and federally financed research, the broadcast airwaves and public institutions and traditions—are increasingly being taken over by private business interests. These appropriations of common assets are siphoning revenues from the public treasury, shifting ownership and control from public to private interests, and eroding democratic processes and shared cultural values" (Washington, D.C.: New America Foundation, 2001), quoted from web, www.NewAmerica.org

6. Quoted from Harry C. Boyte and Nan Kari, "Commonwealth Democracy," *Dissent* (Fall 1997): 56.

7. Garrett Hardin, "The Tragedy of the Commons," *Science* 162 (1968): 1244.

8. Peter Levine, "Building the Electronic Commons," forthcoming in *The Good Society*, copy in author's possession, 4; as Levine observes, there is considerable ferment about the information commons idea. See for instance Lawrence Lessig's influential work, *The Future of Ideas: The Fate of the Commons in a Connected World* (New York: Random House, 2001).

9. De Soto argues that "the cities of the Third World and the former communist countries are teeming with entrepreneurs," whose productive energies are only held back because all properties are "held in defective forms"—not formally, explicitly, publicly turned into privately recognized titles. Unlike the West, he proposes, where "every parcel of land, every building, every piece of equipment or store of inventories is represented in a property document . . . the poor inhabitants of these nations—five-sixths of humanity—do have things but they lack the process to represent their property and create capital." Hernando de Soto, *The Mystery of Capital: Why Capitalism Triumphs in the West and Fails Everywhere Else* (New York: Basic Books, 2000), 5, 6, 7.

10. On the origins of commons, see for instance Warren Ortman Ault, *Open Field Farming in Medieval England* (London: Allen and Unwin, 1992); Robert Dodgshon, "The Interpretation of Subdivided Fields: A Study in Private or Communal Interests," in Trevor Roley, ed., *The Origins of Open-Field Agriculture* (London: Croom Helm, 1981).

11. Elinor Ostrom, "Polycentricity, Complexity, and the Commons," lead article in the Symposium on Community Governance of Common Resources, *A PEGS Journal: The Good Society* 9, 2 (1999): 37, 38, 39, 40.

12. Melissa Bass, from "The Politics and "Civics" of National Service," Ph.D. dissertation in process (Brandeis, Political Science), Chapter 3.

13. For detailed discussion, see Harry C. Boyte and Nan Kari, *Building America: The Democratic Promise of Public Work* (Philadelphia: Temple University Press, 1996), figures on CCC work, 107. The observer is C. H. Blanchard, "I Talk with My CCC Boys," *Phi Delta Kappan* (special edition on Education in the CCC Camps) 19, 9 (1937): 354.

14. This discussion draws from Lew Friedland and Harry Boyte, "The New Information Commons," a working paper produced for the Wingspread Conference on civic uses of technology. On the web at www.publicwork.org; also Peter

Levine, "Building the Electronic Commons," and other Levine articles. Alexis de Tocqueville quoted from Levine, "Civic Renewal and the Commons of Cyberspace," *National Civic Review* 90, 3 (2001): 206.

15. See Harry Boyte and Paul Resnick, "Civic Extension for the Information Age," http://www.si.umich.edu/~presnick/papers/civicextension/, also Peter Levine, 'Civic Renewal and the Commons in Cyberspace," *National Civic Review* 90, 3 (2001): 205–12; Levine "Can the Internet Rescue Democracy? Toward an On-line Commons," in Ronald Hayduk and Kevin Mattson, eds. *Democracy's Moment: Reforming the American Political System for the 21st Century* (Lanham, Md.: Rowman and Littlefield, 2002), 121–37. Gar Alperovitz's writings over many years have also articulated public-work perspectives on multiple forms of public wealth. See, for instance, Gar Alperovitz, Thad Williamson, and David Imbroscio, *Making a Place for Community* (New York: Routledge, 2002); Gar Alperovitz, "Systemic Issues and Sustainability in the New Era," in Jonathan Harris, ed., *Rethinking Sustainability: Power, Knowledge and Institutions* (Ann Arbor: University of Michigan Press, 2000); Gar Alperovitz and Jeff Faux, *Rebuilding America* (New York: Pantheon, 1984).

16. Melissa Bass, "National Service."

17. Lawrence Sommers quote paraphrased from Thomas Friedman, "There Is Hope," *New York Times*, October 27, 2002.

18. Jerome Delli Priscoli remark at the Reinventing Citizenship/New Citizenship meeting in Washington, February 4, 1994.

19. Alabama story from interview with Carol Shields, Minneapolis, June 15, 1995. This also draws from Harry C. Boyte and Nancy N. Kari, "Democracy of the People," in Dwight F. Burlingame, William A. Diaz, Warren F. Ilchman and Associates, eds. *Capacity for Change? The Nonprofit World in the Age of Devolution* (Bloomington: Indiana Center on Philanthropy, 1996), 109–24.

20. Carmen Sirianni and Lewis Friedland, *Civic Innovation in America: Community Empowerment, Public Policy, and the Movement for Civic Renewal* (Berkeley: University of California Press, 2001). See also the case studies and working papers on the Civic Practices Network web site, www.cpn.org.

21. Carmen Sirianni was research director of the New Citizenship. Sirianni and Friedland describe the effort in *Civic Innovation in America.* For an account of the Camp David seminar on the future of democracy in which we presented findings to Clinton and other leaders, see Benjamin Barber, *The Truth of Power* (New York: Norton, 2001).

22. For local government examples, see Harry Boyte and Josh Zepnick, "We Own the Store," at the Pew Mapping Project, www.publicwork.org.

23. Interview with Sharon Sayles Belton, Minneapolis, April 4, 2003. Another example, from Anthony Lewis, "The Feeling of a Coup," *New York Times*, October 31, 2001, suggests agency leaders' understanding of the importance of partnerships. Lewis quotes Michael Dombeck, who resigned as head of the Forest Service with a letter to Ann Veneman, Secretary of Agriculture, urging her not to carry out the proposed abandonment of bans on roads. "Doing so would undermine the most extensive multi-year environmental analysis in history," he wrote, "a process that included over 600 public meetings and generated over 1.6 million comments."

24. On productive relationships, see Richard L. Wood, *Faith in Action: Reli-*

gion, Race, and Democratic Organizing in America (Chicago: University of Chicago Press, 2002), and Michael Gecan, *Going Public* (Boston: Beacon Press, 2002).

25. Tony Massengale, quoted from Boyte field notes, Active Citizenship Southern conference, Tallahassee, Florida, Los Angeles, May 15, 1998.

26. Boyte field notes, Imagining America Conference, Chicago, November 30, 2000.

27. Lary May, *The Big Tomorrow: Hollywood and the Politics of the American Way* (Chicago: University of Chicago Press, 2000), 83, 34, 95, 87.

28. William Safire, "Bush's Four Horsemen," *New York Times,* July 24, 2003.

29. Julie Ellison, "The Public Soul of the Humanities," essay on the CDC web, www.publicwork.org.

30. Benjamin Barber, *Fear's Empire: War, Terrorism, and Democracy* (New York: Norton, 2003).

31. Quoted from "Global Trends 2015," a paper approved for publication by the National Foreign Intelligence Board under the authority of the Director of Central Intelligence (Washington, D.C.: U.S. Government Printing Office, 2000), 15.

32. David Bornstein, "A Force Now in the World, Citizens Flex Social Muscle," *New York Times,* July 10, 1999.

33. For instance, Nelson Mandela's autobiography, *Long Walk to Freedom* (New York: Little, Brown, 1994), is remarkable for its capacities to understand and even respect the leaders in the apartheid government.

34. Kumalo's presentation was in the Civil Society Forum of SACLA, Pretoria, South Africa, July 7, 2003; we subsequently have discussed the need for a "Nehemiah theology," to describe the tasks of development, to complement the more common "Moses" theology of liberation.

35. Mandela, *Long Walk to Freedom,* 21.

36. Bishop Mvume Dandala, "Calling the Church to Repentance," Keynote speech to South African Christian Leadership Assembly, Pretoria, July 7, 2003.

37. 31 Xolela Mangcu, in *Emerging Johannesburg: Perspectives on the Postapartheid City,* Richard Tomlinson, Robert Beauregard, Lindsay Bremner, and Xolela Mangcu, eds., *"Johannesburg in Flight from Itself: Political Culture Shapes Urban Discourse,"* (New York: Routledge, 2003), 284, 290. Mangcu's point about the parallels with the organizing tradition in the American civil rights movement was made in a private conversation and also in his presentation at the "Government and Social Activism Conference," organized by Idasa, Gordon Bay, South Africa, August 11, 2003. Mammo Muchie, director of the Programme on Civil Society and African Integration at the University of Natal in Durban, argues that ordinary people must become central actors in the African Renaissance, a term made popular by South African president Thabo Mbeki. This has economic, social, and cultural aspects. Muchie dissents from both state-centered views of politics or the perspective, fashionable among many international donors, that civil society will itself solve the problems facing emerging democracies. In the view of donors, Muchie argues, "the state has been demoted; civil society along with the market [has] been promoted . . . by an unverified and empirically unsubstantiated attribute of metaphysical benign

goodness." In Muchie's view, NGOs (nongovernmental organizations) can be subject to the same logic of rationalization and professional domination evident in government and politics—"NGOism" he calls the problem. Muchie's African Integration initiative, housed at the important Centre for Civil Society at the University of Natal, is creating a network of public intellectuals across the continent dedicated to public engagement with citizens, civic institutions, and communities for a new "pan Africanism." His approach resonates closely with a nonprofessionalized, productive view of politics and perspectives like Mangcu's and Omano Edigheji's. From *Civic Engagement News* 2003, 14 (December 5, 2003), electronic newsletter of the Public Engagement Task Force at the University of Minnesota.

38. Omano Edigheji, "The Challenges of Globalisation on Cooperative Governance: State-Society Relations in Post-Apartheid South Africa," unpublished paper in author's possession. Peter Vale, a social theorist at the University of the Western Cape, made a compelling case that the African experience of self-affirmation in the course of overcoming the all encompassing colonial legacy position the continent for an African Renaissance, leadership against dominant constructions of power and wealth and human civilization in the global economy. The same could be said of civic theory and practice, a related point.

39. Quotes compiled by Marie-Louise Ström, manager of Idasa's Citizen Leadership Programme, from participant evaluations, distributed at Idasa's management retreat, August 5, 2003.

40. Daniel Bell, *The Coming of Post-Industrial Society: A Venture in Social Forecasting* (New York: Basic Books, 1973). See also Kenneth Boulding, *Meaning of the Twentieth Century: The Great Transition* (New York: Harper and Row, 1964); Richard Florida, *The Rise of the Creative Class: How It's Transforming Work, Leisure, Community, and Everyday Life* (New York: Basic Books, 2002).

41. Harlan Cleveland, *The Knowledge Executive* (New York: Dutton, 1985), 20. For critical perspectives, see Peter N. Stearns, "Is There a Post-Industrial Society?" reprinted in Leigh Estabrook, ed., *Libraries in Post-Industrial Society* (Phoenix: Oryx Books, 1977), 8–18; and Michael Harrington, "Post-Industrial Society and the Welfare State," in Estabrook, *Libraries*, 18–29.

42. On the clientization of the citizenry, see for instance, Barton Bledstein, *The Culture of Professionalism: The Middle Class and the Development of Higher Education in America* (New York: Norton, 1976); Christopher Lasch, *Haven in a Heartless World: The Family Besieged* (New York: Basic Books, 1977); and Joseph Tussman, "Obligation and the Body Politic," in Henry Kariel, ed., *Frontiers of Democratic Theory,* (New York: Random House, 1970), 18–21.

43. For instance, Joan C. Durrance in her book, *Armed for Action: Library Response to Citizen Information Needs* (New York: Neal Schuman, 1984), studied a cross section of citizen activists and found almost all successful leaders were sophisticated consumers and users of information, skilled in knowing where to find out what they needed to know.

44. Anne Fadiman, *The Spirit Catches You and You Fall Down: A Hmong Child, Her American Doctors, and the Collision of Two Cultures* (New York: Farrar, Straus, and Giroux, 1997).

Chapter 10. Freedom

Epigraph from Frances Harper, quoted in Philip Foner, *The Voice of Black America* (New York: Simon and Schuster, 1972), 431.

1. Adapted from Ian Taylor, "South Africa's Transition to Democracy and the 'Change Industry': A Case Study of IDASA," *Politikon* 29, 1 (2002): 31, who got it from Pieter Dirk Uys, South Africa's foremost satirist, in a skit in 1999.

2. Claude Ake quoted in Paul Graham, "Decade of Democracy" concept paper, December 12, 2003, in author's possession, 1.

3. Richard Turner, "The Relevance of Contemporary Radical Thought," in *Directions of Change in South African Politics*, Spro-cas Publications 3 (Johannesburg, 1971), 76. This is well treated in Tony Fluxman and Peter Vale, "Re-Reading Rick Turner in the New South Africa," *International Relations*18, 2 (2004).

4. Eric Foner, *The Story of American Freedom* (New York: Norton, 1998).

5. David Brooks, "Running on Reform," *New York Times*, January 3, 2004. Condoleezza Rice, "You're Safe with Us," *Newsweek Special Edition, Issues 2004* (December 2003–February 2004), 104.

6. Langston Hughes, "Freedom's Plow," in *The Collected Poems of Langston Hughes* (New York: Vintage, 1995), 263–68. Frances Willard quoted in Foner, *The Story of American Freedom*, 110; Jane Addams, *On Education* (New Brunswick, N.J.: Transaction Publishers, 1994), 98–99.

7. We make the argument that democratizing health professions through citizen politics shatters Max Weber's "Iron Cage" in Harry C. Boyte and Nan Kari, "Citizen Politics: Breaking the Iron Cage," *Dissent* (Spring 1994): 205–11. For a splendid discussion of the fashion in which Public Achievement helps young people break free of what Michel Foucault called disciplinary discourses and disciplinary practices of power, built on the qualitative evaluations done by Hildreth and others, see Robert Hildreth, "Theorizing Citizenship and Evaluating Public Achievement," *PS: Political Science and Politics* 33, 3 (2000): 627–34. See James C. Scott, *Seeing like a State: How Certain Schemes to Improve the Human Condition Have Failed* (New Haven, Conn.: Yale University Press, 1998). In my October 23, 1998 lecture at Duke University, "Off the Playground of Civil Society," I acknowledge the force of Scott's argument (as well as perspectives of conservative theorists seeking to resist the technicization of the world), but propose that the public work approach points toward a politics that makes the boundaries between state and society more porous and fluid, while democratizing practices in settings structured by knowledge hierarchies. See the symposium on Commonwealth, Civil Society, and Democratic Renewal in *A Pegs Journal: The Good Society* 9, 2 (1999): 1–23.

8. Interview with Paul Graham and Ivor Jenkins, Pretoria, December 1, 2003.

9. Auchincloss quoted from James Chace, "TR and the Road Not Taken," *New York Review of Books* 50, 12 (July 17, 2003): 35. "Roosevelt's New Nationalism," in *Law, Justice, and the Common Good*, ed. Sidney Hyman (Minnneapolis: Humphrey Institute, 1981), 334–35.

10. Edmund Pendleton quoted in Gordon Wood, *Creation of the American Republic: 1776–87* (Chapel Hill: University of North Carolina Press, 1969), 56.

11. Thomas Paine quoted in Hannah Arendt, *On Revolution* (New York: Penguin, 1963), 145.

12. *Revised English Bible* (Oxford: Oxford University Press, 1989). Some biblical scholars, such as Norman Gottwald, *The Tribes of Yahweh: A Sociology of the Religion of Liberated Israel, 1250–1050 B.C.E.* (New York: Orbis, 1979), argue that the commons tradition in Jewish history derives from a premonarchical struggle in Palestine, pitting a loose egalitarian confederation of anti-imperial groups—hill people, itinerant laborers and artisans—against city-state empires).

13. See "Common Good," *New Catholic Encyclopedia* (Washington, D.C.: Catholic University Press, 1967).

14. For detailed accounts of commons traditions, see Ronald Lee Fleming and Lauri A. Halderman, *On Common Ground: Caring for Shared Land from Town Commons to Urban Park* (Cambridge, Mass.: Harvard University Press, 1982). Rowland Bertoff discusses the social foundations of the popular republican themes, drawing on immigrant traditions, in "Peasants and Artisans, Puritans and Republicans," *Journal of American History* 69, 3 (1982): 579–98. Philadelphia workers quoted from Gary B. Nash, *Race, Class, and Politics: Essays on American Colonial and Revolutionary Society* (Urbana: University of Illinois Press, 1986), 249.

15. Leonard W. Levy, *The Law of the Commonwealth and Chief Justice Shaw* (New York: Oxford University Press, 1957), 306. Shaw quoted from p. 306.

16. Oscar Handlin and Mary Handlin, *Commonwealth: A Study of the Role of Government in the American Economy: Massachusetts, 1774–1861* (Cambridge, Mass.: Harvard University Press, 1969), 30, 16.

17. The quotes from Pettus are taken from interviews in Seattle, March 14, 17, 18, 1983. Other accounts are found in "Subversive?" a documentary by John de Graaf for station KCTS, aired in Seattle, September 5, 1983; see also Harry C. Boyte, *CommonWealth: A Return to Citizen Politics* (New York: Free Press, 1989); and Harry C. Boyte and Nan Kari, *Building America: The Democratic Promise of Public Work* (Philadelphia: Temple University Press, 1996).

18. Ellis quoted from Leonard Silk, "Seattle Looks for Its Future," *New York Times*, April 22, 1983.

19. Francis Fukuyama, *The End of History and the Last Man* (Glencoe, Ill.: Free Press, 1992).

Index

Acknowledgments

Everyday Politics emerges from a long intellectual and practical collaboration. At the CDC itself, Nan Skelton, Dennis Donovan, Elaine Eschenbacher, Jim Lewis, D'Ann Lesch, See Moua, Danielle Peterson, Derek Johnson, Martin Wera, and earlier, Jennifer O'Donoghue, Jeff Bauer, Margaret Post, Nick Longo, Aleida Benitez, Roudy Hildreth, Francis Green, Josh Zepnick, Bridget Erlanson, Zachary Koub, Melissa Bass, Denise Beal, Robert Ceresa, Peg Michels, Carol McGee Johnson, among others, have created a vital culture of learning and theory building over the years.

Since the beginning of the work at the Humphrey Institute and, in some cases, before, I have had the good fortune to have had a dynamic intellectual community of regular critics of my writing, colleagues who are also often collaborators and contributors. Although no one bears responsibility for whatever lapses of argument there may be here, I want to acknowledge my appreciation (in order of appearance in my life) to others who have contributed to these ideas over a long period of time, including Dorothy Cotton, Elizabeth Tornquist, Sara Evans, Deborah Meier, Lawrence Goodwyn, Benjamin Barber, Gerald Taylor, Mary Dietz, Jim Farr, David Thelen, David Mathews, Lary May, William Schambra, Edwin Fogelman, Carmen Sirianni, Scott Peters, John Dedrick, William Doherty, John Saltmarsh, Sallye McKee, and Julie Ellison. Nan Kari, my collaborator on many articles and co-author of *Building America: The Democratic Promise of Public Work*, has played an especially central role in developing the practice and theory of public work.

At the University of Minnesota, J. Brian Atwood, our dean at the Humphrey Institute, is a continuing source of helpful criticism and support, and my colleagues among the faculty, fellows and staff over the years have made the Humphrey Institute a stimulating intellectual environment in which to do our work. In central administration, Robert Bruininks, Robert Jones, Victor Bloomfield, Craig Swan, and Sue Engelmann, among others have formed a lively community in both intellectual and practical terms on culture change and public engagement. The article that Bruininks coordinated on the public promise of the land grant tradition for a forthcoming Campus Compact book on civic engagement in higher education helps to inform Chapter 8.

Public Achievement colleagues have contributed to this vital political education and engagement initiative, increasingly no longer for young people alone. These include, as a very partial list, Elizabeth Budd, Karisse Whyte, Jerry Kitzi, Sister Carol Ann Peterson, Lynn Leonard, Mishkat Az-Zubair, Sue Dorrel, Shelly Robertson, Bob Bush, and Nettie Doyle with Missouri and Kansas Public Achievement; Joe O'Shea, Bobbi Aguero Lipeles, Cynthia Ellwood, Danny Goldberg, and Dan Grego with Milwaukee Public Achievement; David Lisman and Frank Coyne with Denver Public Achievement; Serdar Degirmencioglu with Turkey Public Achievement; Taraq el-Bakri and Suzanne Hammad with Palestine Public Achievement; Ehud Peleg and Orly Alon with Israel Public Achievement; and Paul Smythe with Northern Ireland Public Achievement. Minnesota is the foundation for Public Achievement, and many have contributed to theory building as well as practice. A partial listing includes Dennis Donovan, Jim Scheibel, Carol McGee Johnson, Jim Farr, Jennifer Cassidy, Leon Oman, Robert Hildreth, Father Mike Anderson, Sue Hendricks, Jeff Maurer, Lt. Colonel Howard Johnson, Juan Jackson, Michael Kuhne, Joe Kunkel, and Carolyn Evans, among many others.

In higher education, Elizabeth Hollander, Barry Checkoway, Ira Harkavy, Tom Ehrlich, David Scobey, Michael Schudson, Rick Battistoni, Michael Delli Carpini, David Cooper, Judith Ramaley, George Mchaffy, among others have been allies and colleagues in the fledgling democracy movement. In the national political scene, William Galston, E.J. Dionne, Richard Louv, Will Marshall, David Cohen, Gar Alperovitz, Steve Elkin, Linda Williams, and Peter Levine, keen observers, albeit from different vantages, have all contributed insights and challenges over the years.

Respondents and organizers of the seminars and lectures at North Carolina, Duke, and Wisconsin, and Michigan—Craig Calhoun, Rom Coles, Lew Friedland, Barry Checkoway, Lorraine Gutierrez, David Scobey, Greg Markus, Sylvia Hurtado, Julie Ellison, and Alma Blount—provided important feedback in several key lectures.

Carmen Sirianni and David Scobey both pushed for clarity in the original design of this book. I hope the effort has in some fashion accomplished what they urged.

For the book itself, Larry Goodwyn, Gerald Taylor, Omano Edigheji, Paul Graham, Xolela Mangcu, Bobby Milstein, Nan Kari, Bill Doherty,

Peter Levine, John Saltmarsh, Maria Avila, John Dedrick, and Margaret Post gave valuable feedback on sections of the manuscript. Nick Longo furnished resources for a final revision of the Jane Addams School chapter. At the CDC, Nan Skelton and Dennis Donovan both gave extensive feedback, while Derek Johnson and D'Ann Lesch were helpful critics. I count on continuing conversations with Elaine Eschenbacher on these ideas. The last chapter emerges from exchanges with Peter Vale about a participatory democratic politics for our age.

Robert Lockhart at the University of Pennsylvania Press has been an extraordinary editor, the best I have had in a book project. Lockhart sorted through a mountain of essays to help craft a coherent proposal in the first instance. He pushed to make the proposed collection into a book, instead, in the second. And he made a key suggestion as the book unfolded, that Chapter Two treat both conservative and progressive forms of populism. Working on this helped illuminate for me the history of power and politics over the last generation.

Melissa Bass did extremely careful editing of the manuscript, for which I am very grateful.

Finally, I want to thank Marie-Louise Ström for the many ways she is a presence in this work. Marie is my partner in populist politics as well as in my life. She is also a wonderful intellectual companion and a fierce critic of fuzzy thinking. *Everyday Politics* is written out of a sense of hope born in no small measure from our partnership. She helps me to believe that for all the turbulence and terrors of our times, it is also a period of unfolding democratic possibilities.

Printed in the United States
27616LVS00002B/81

9 780812 238143